HOW TO DRAW
EVERYTHING IN 3D

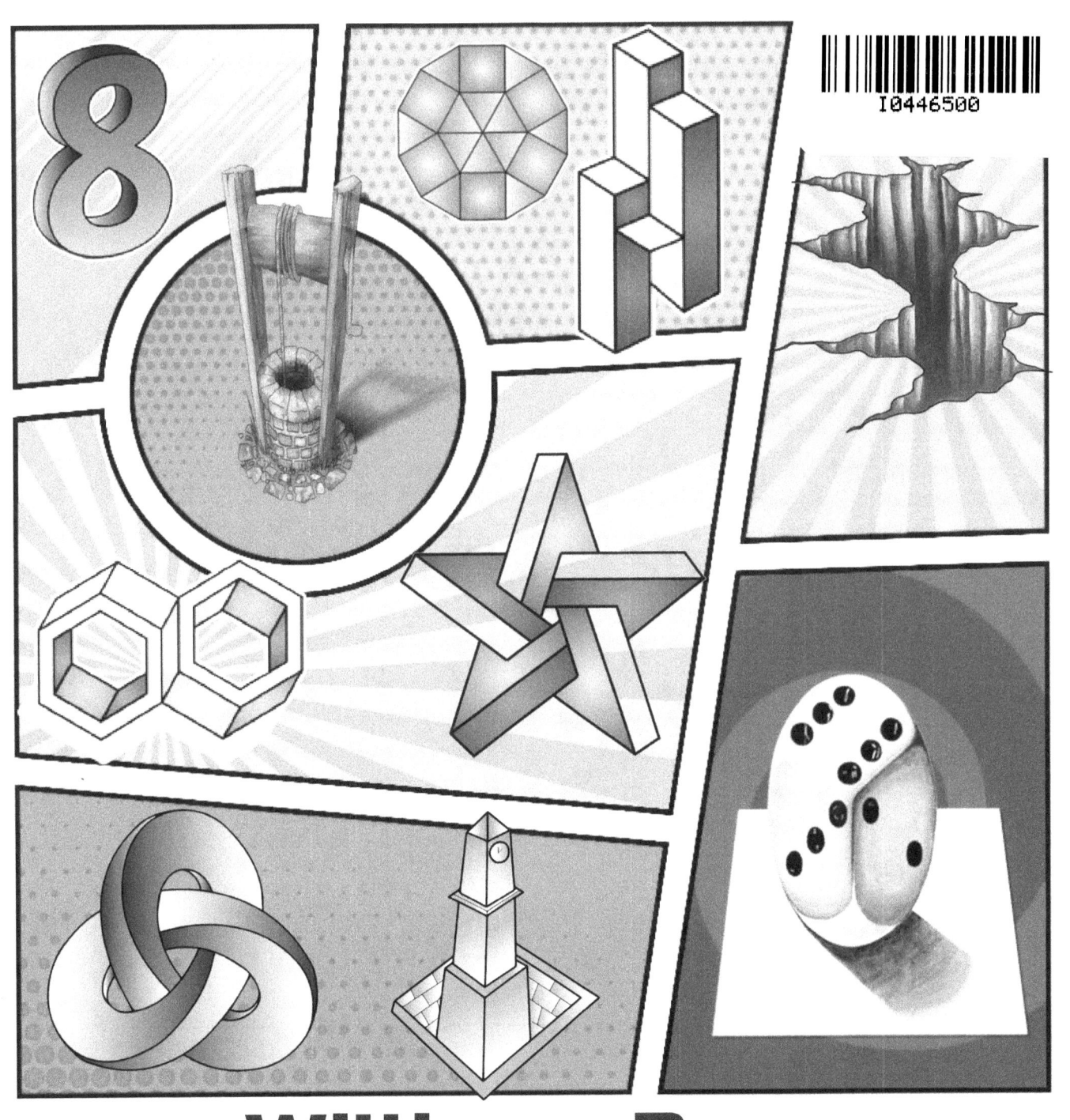

Williams Press

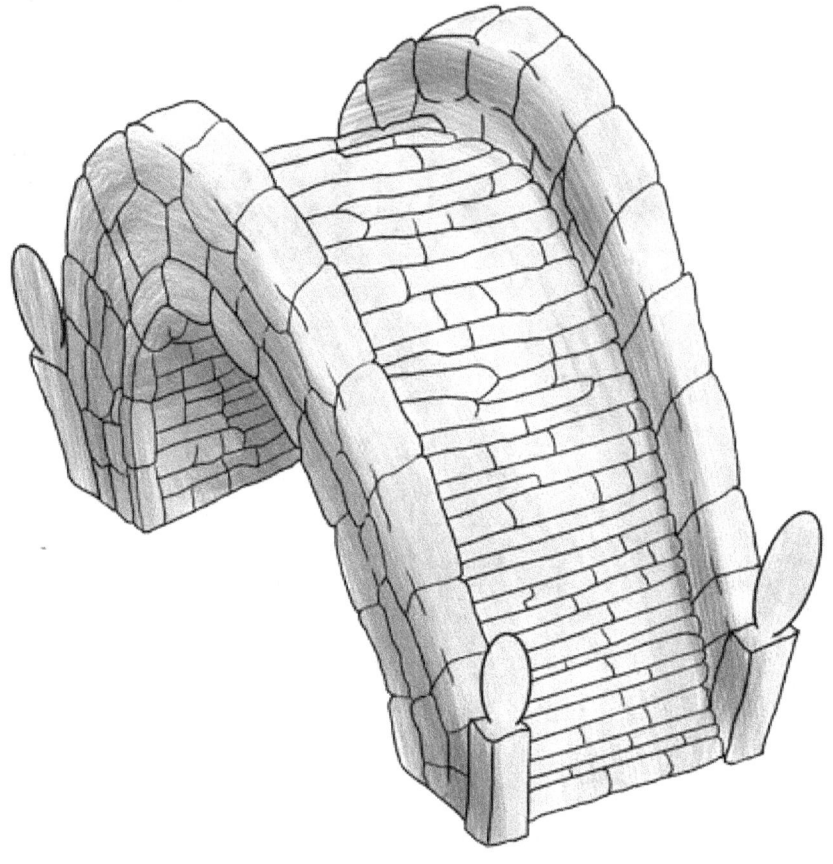

THIS BOOK BELONGS TO

....

....

EVERYTHING IN 3D

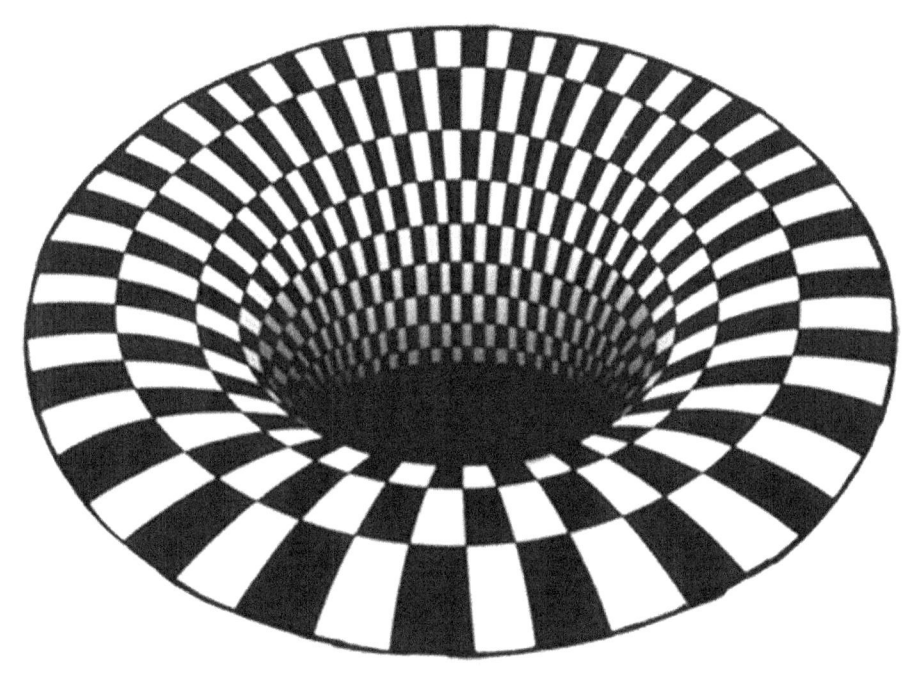

How to use this book,
All you need to get started is a piece of
paper, a pencil and an eraser, but feel
free to use any tool you want, to draw
the characters

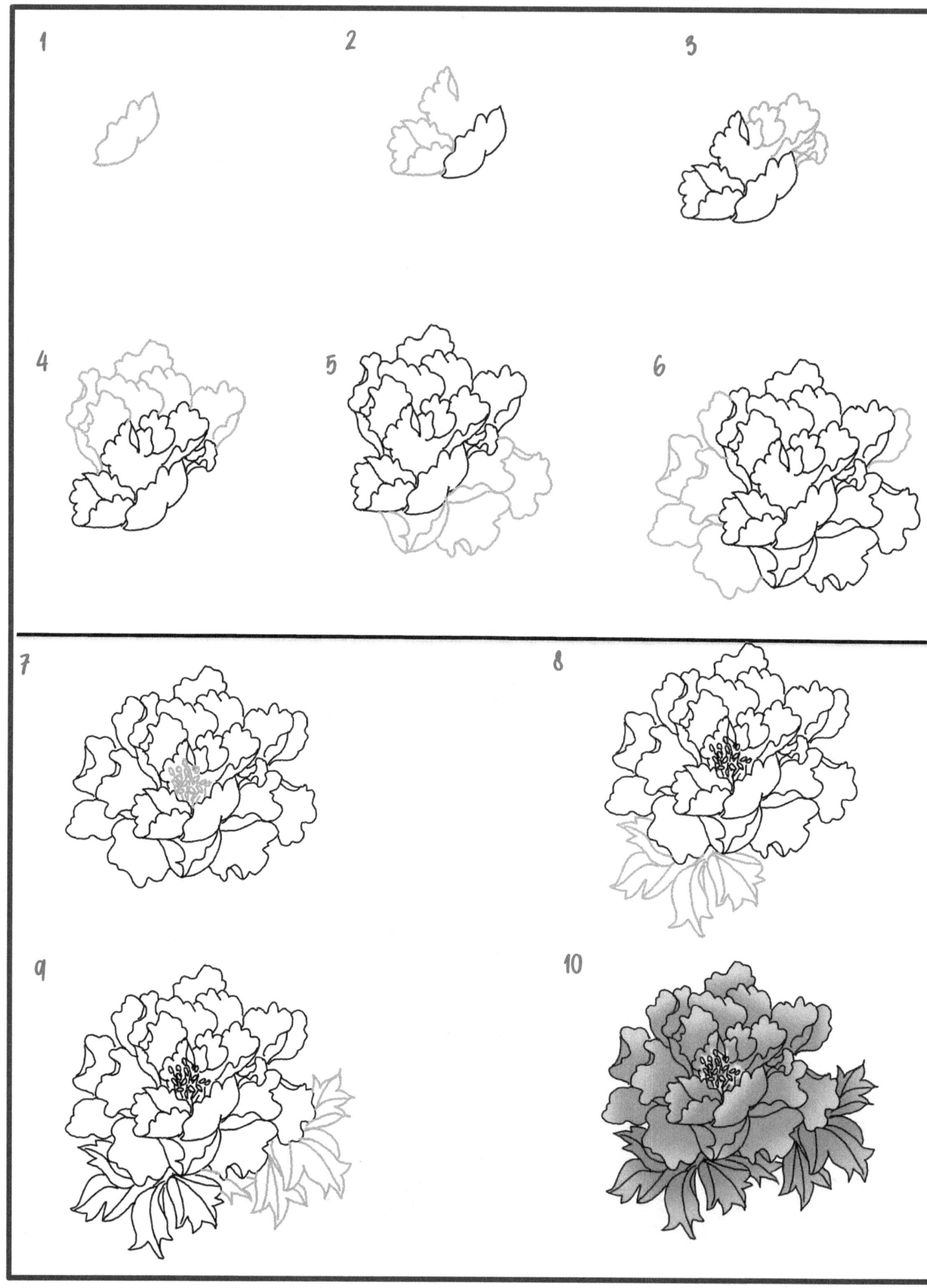

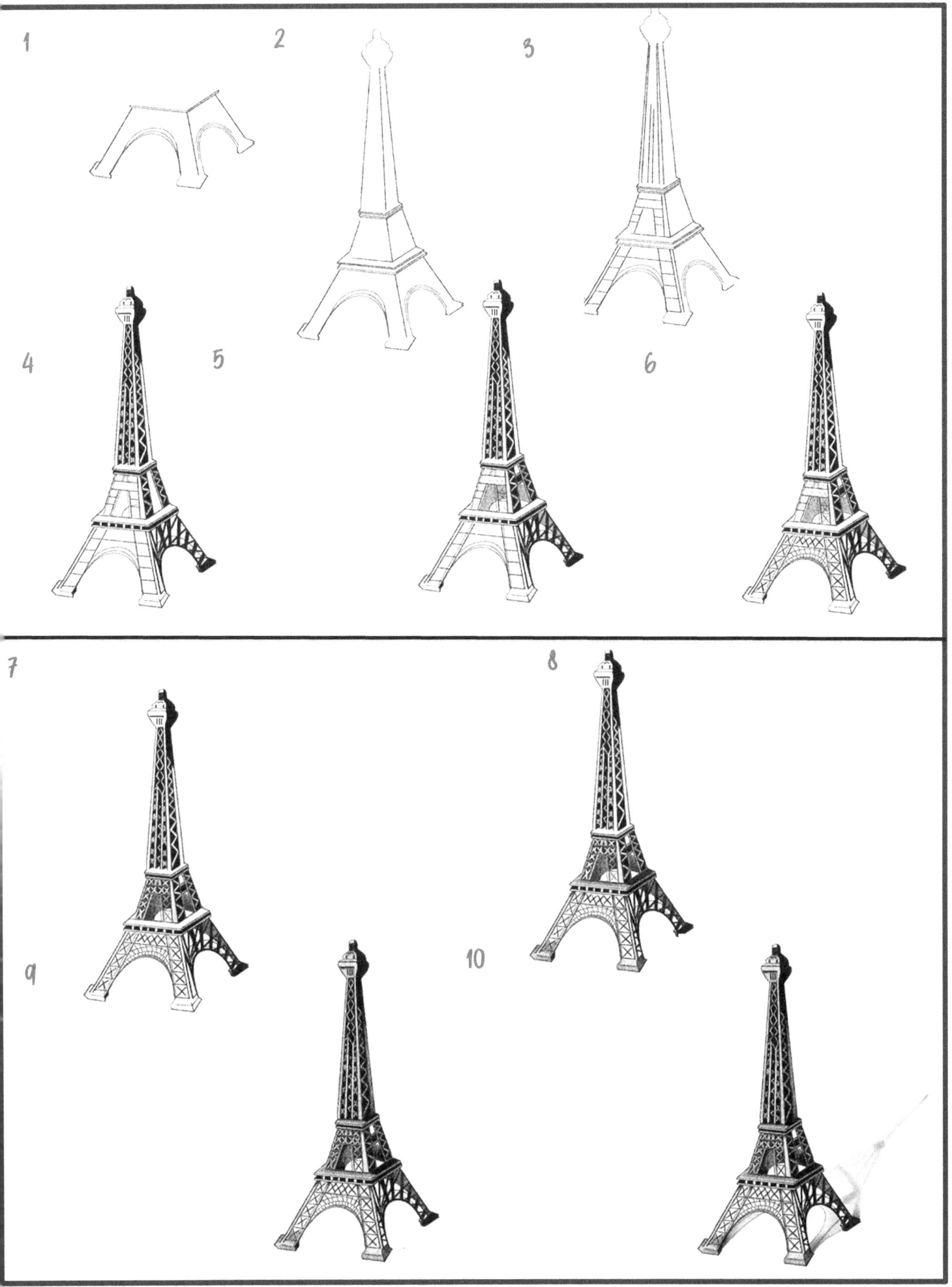

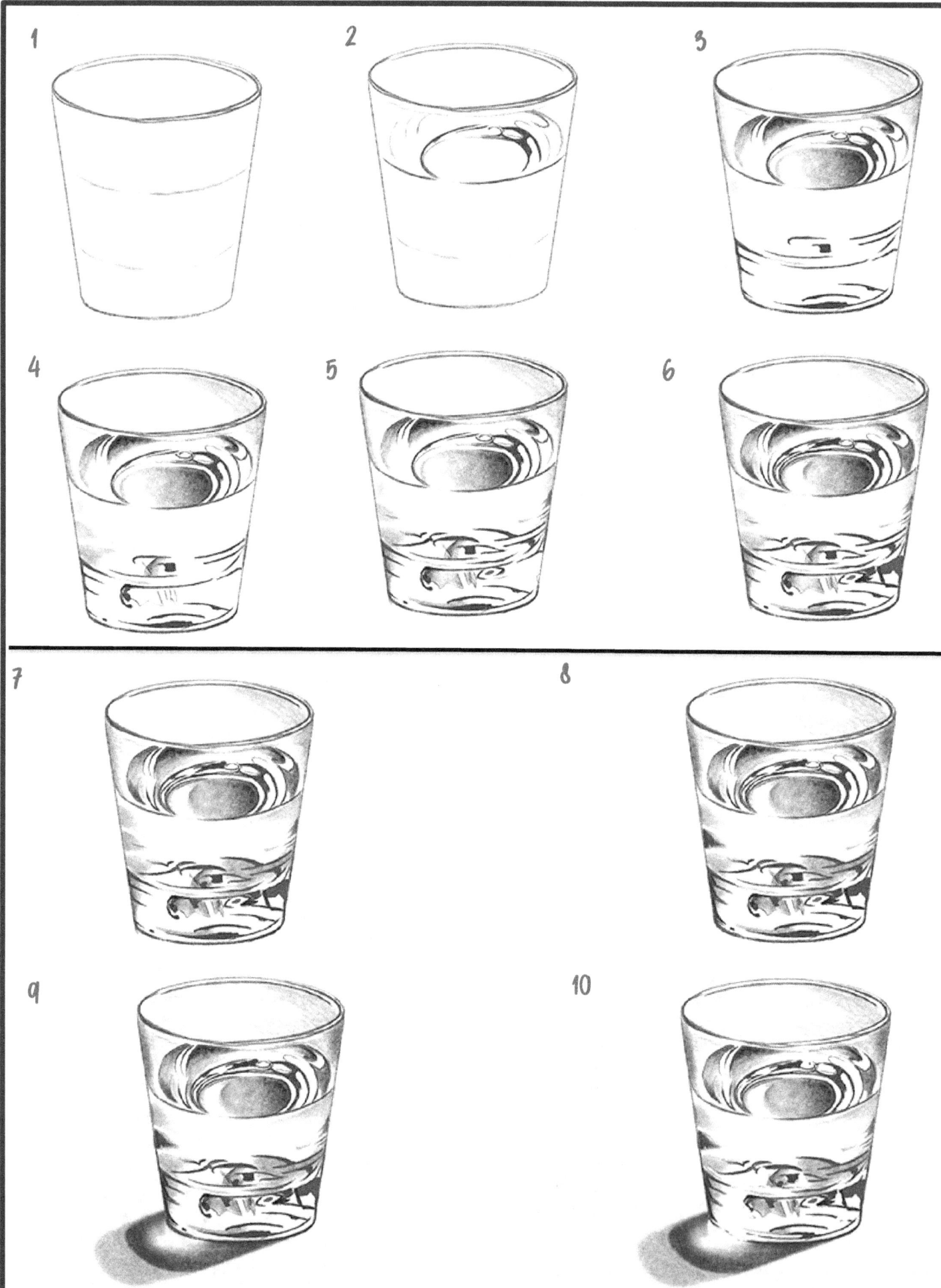

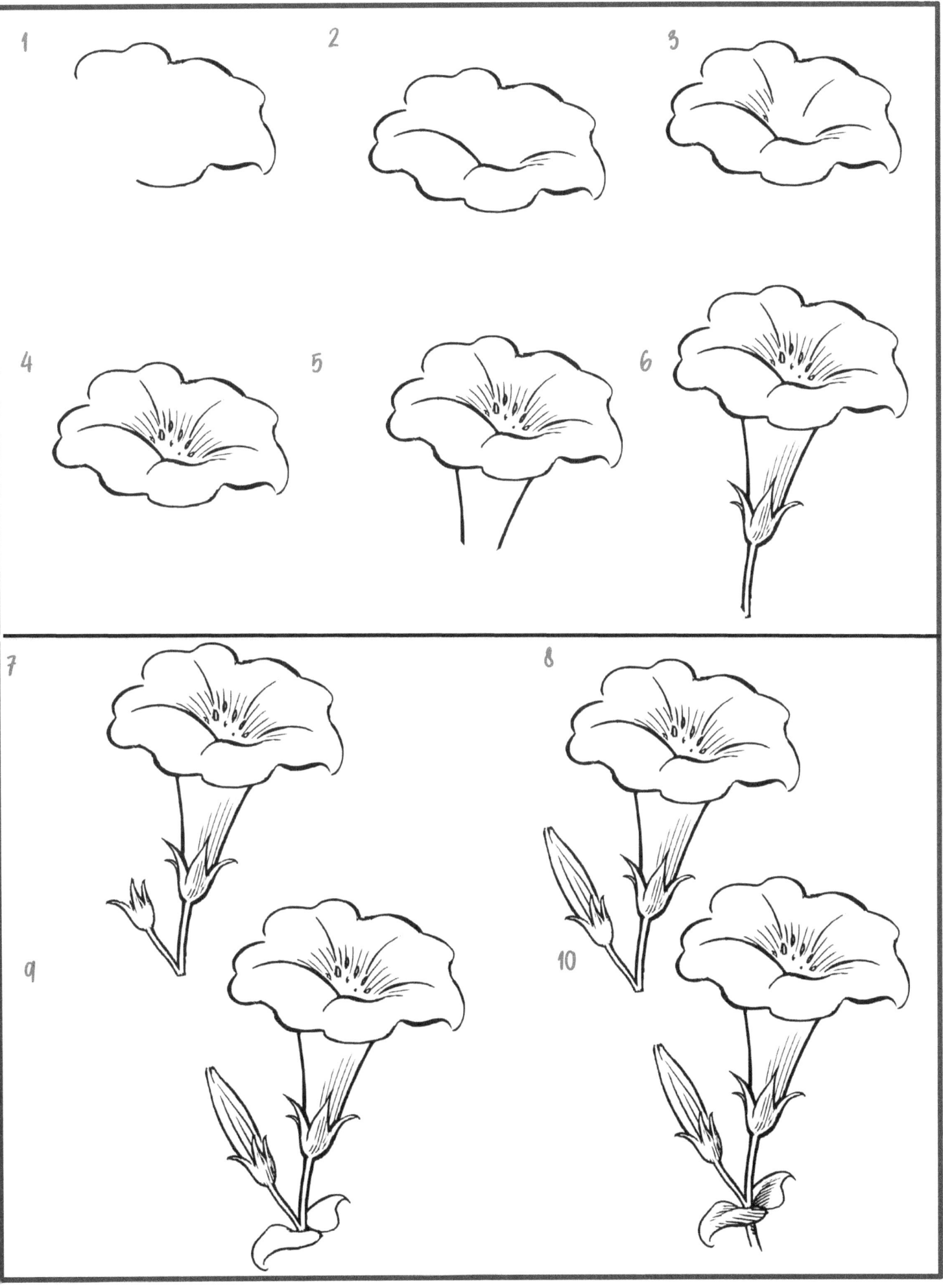

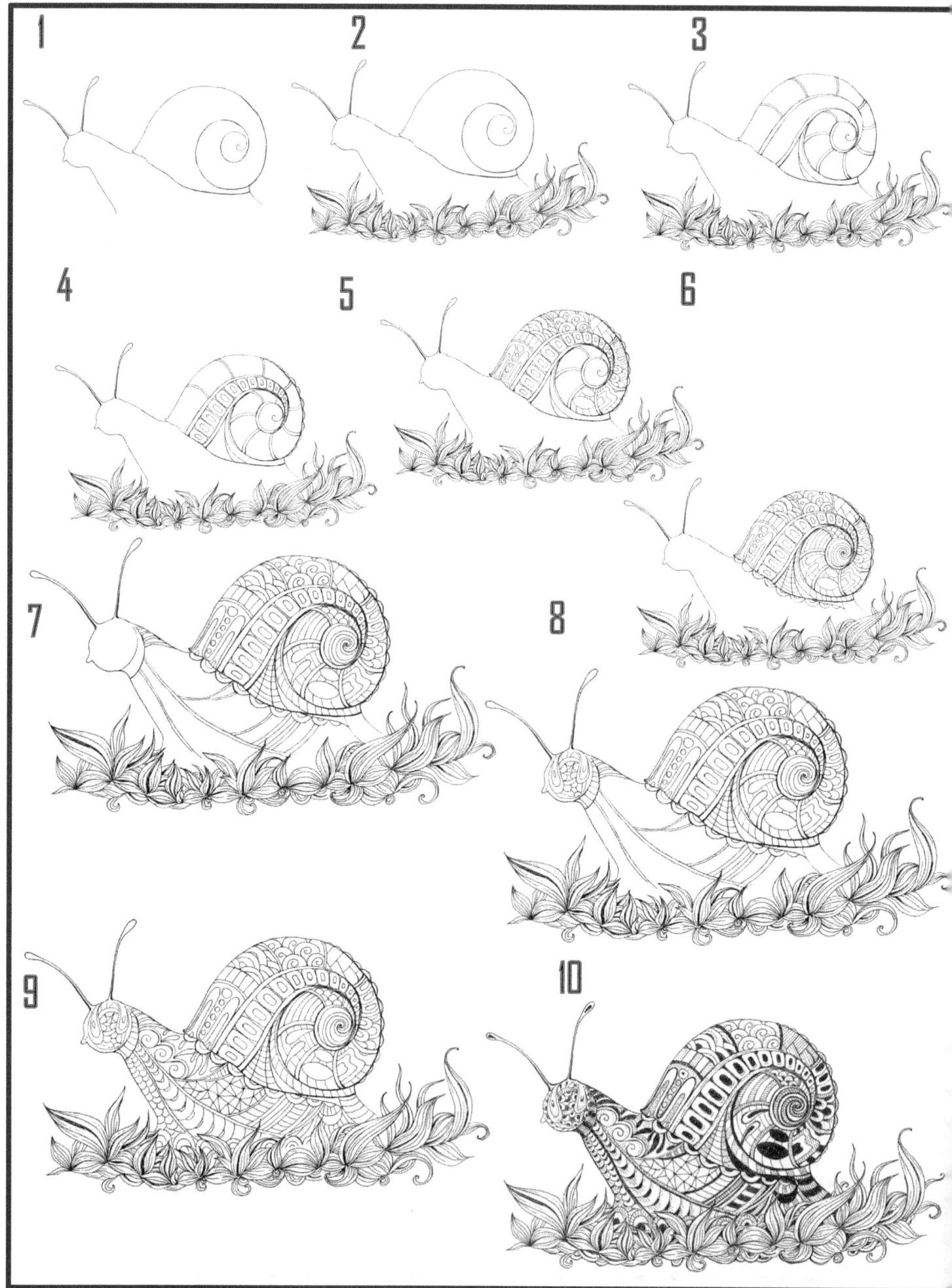

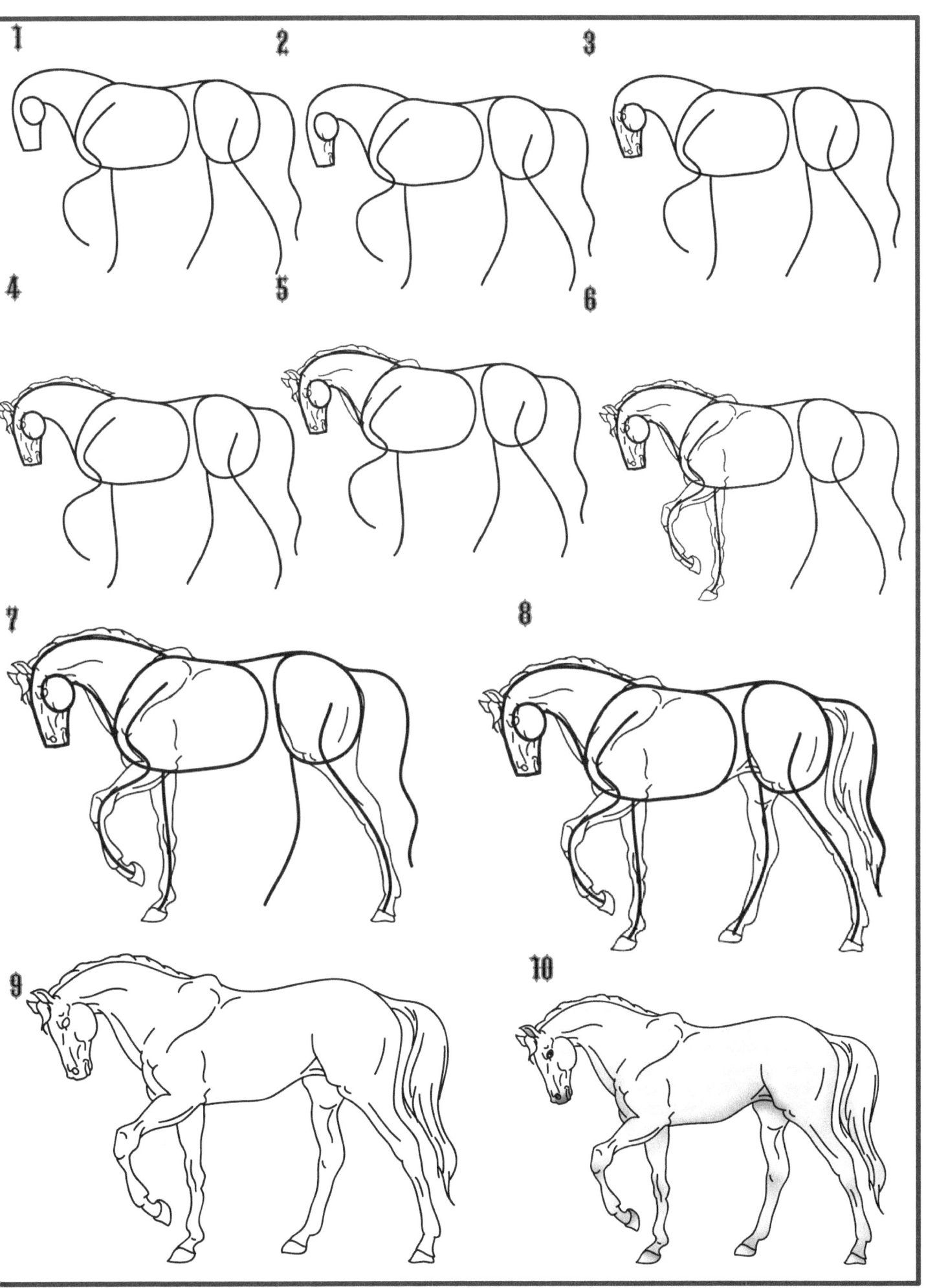

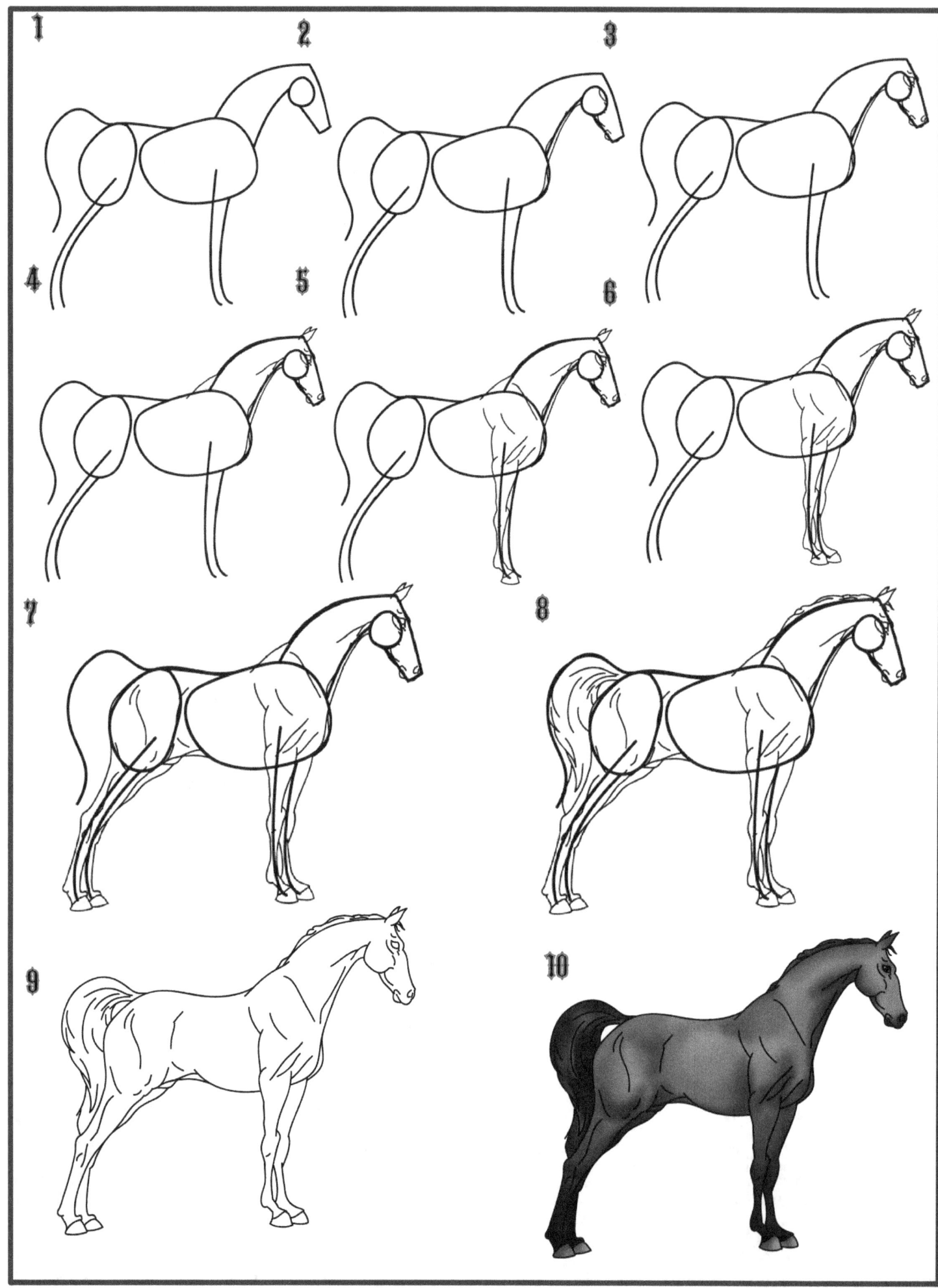

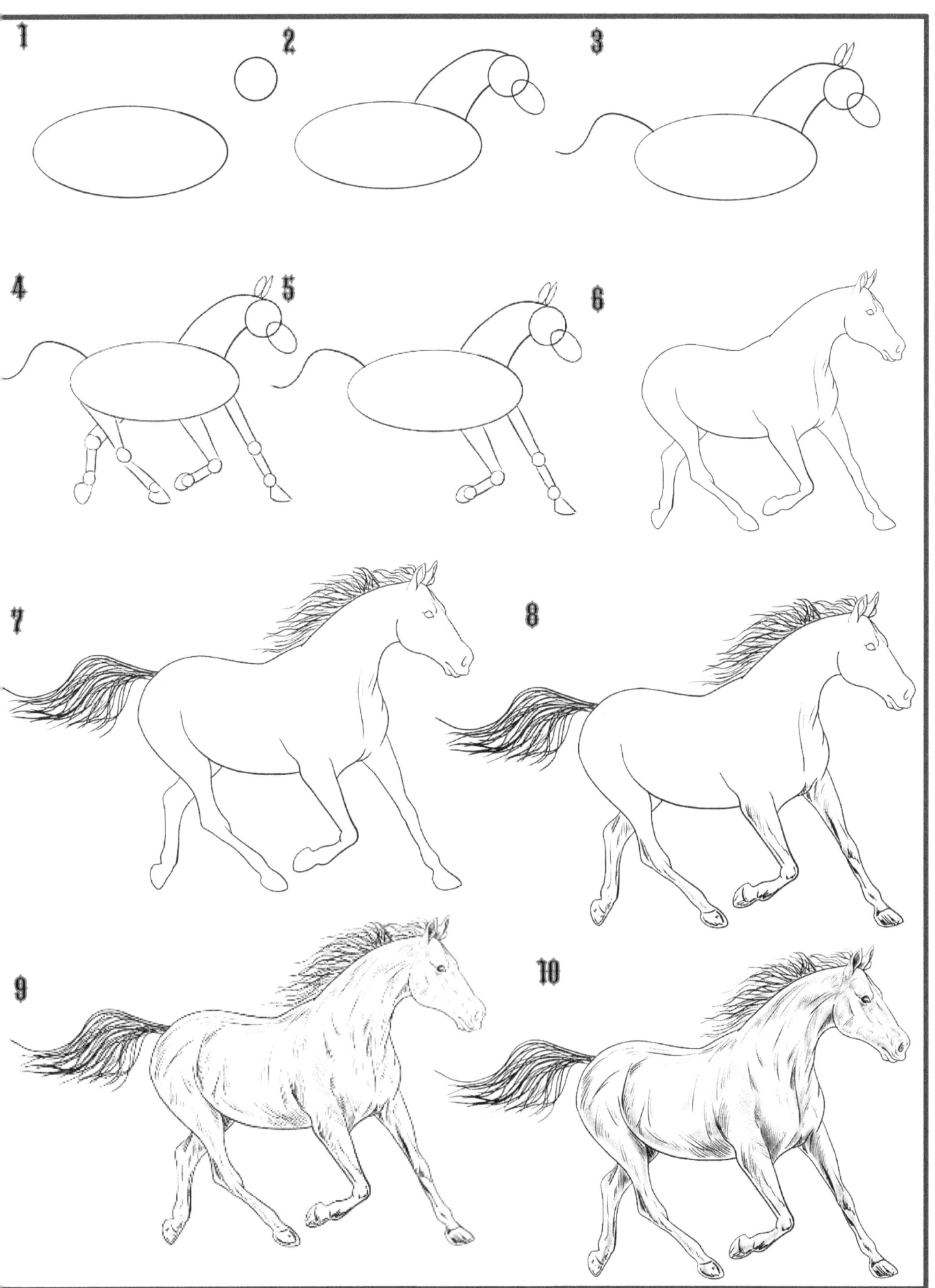

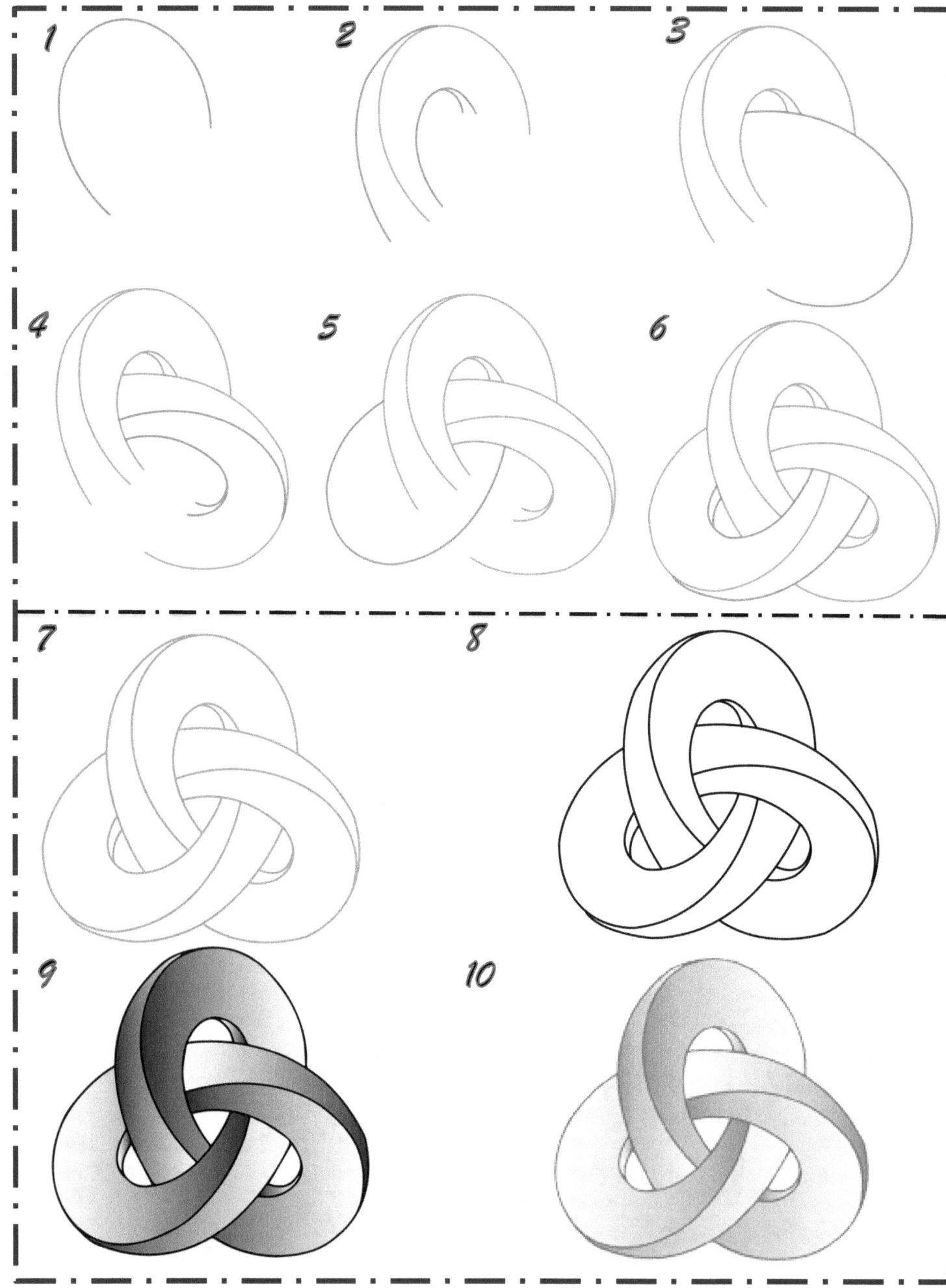

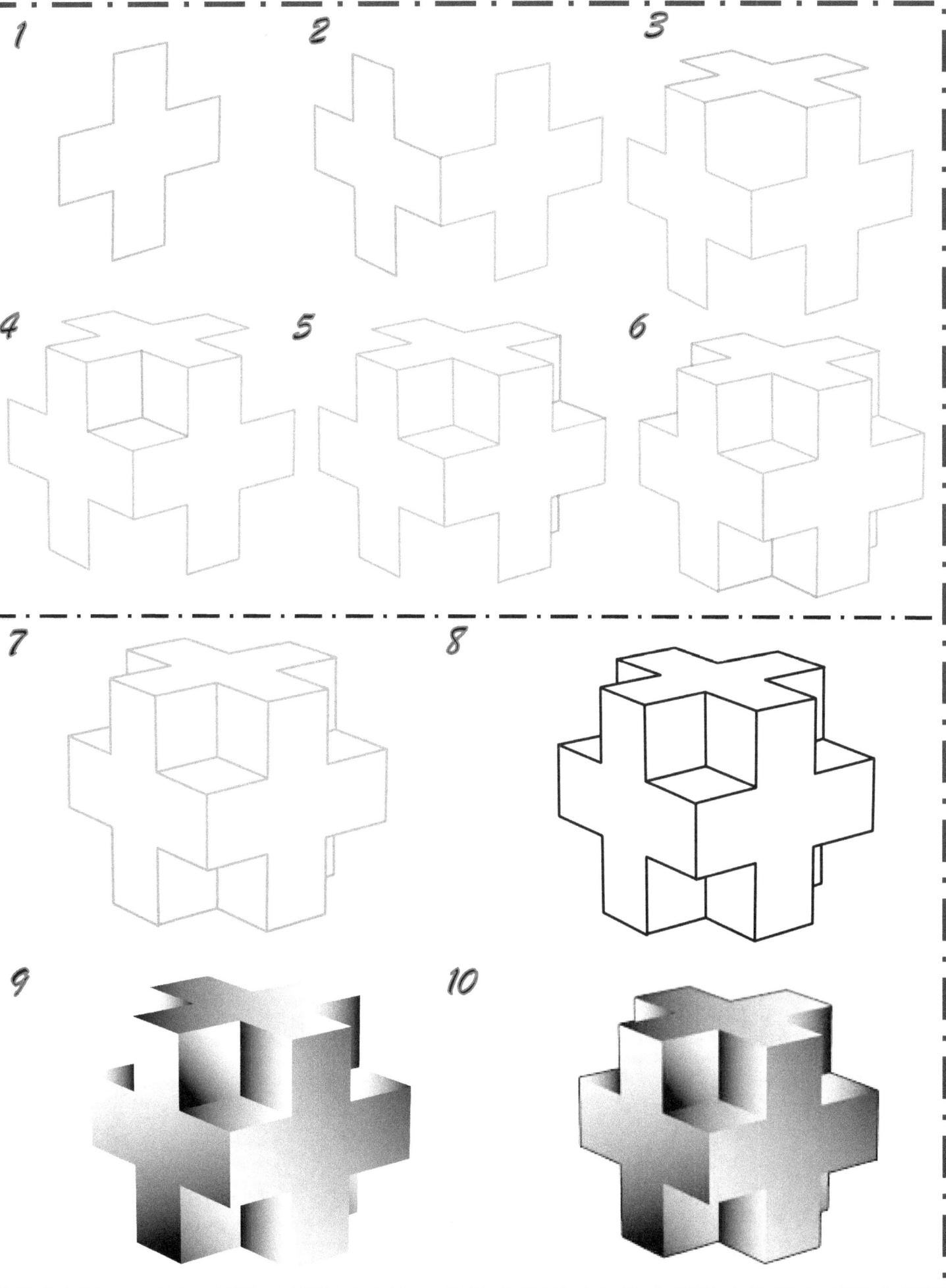

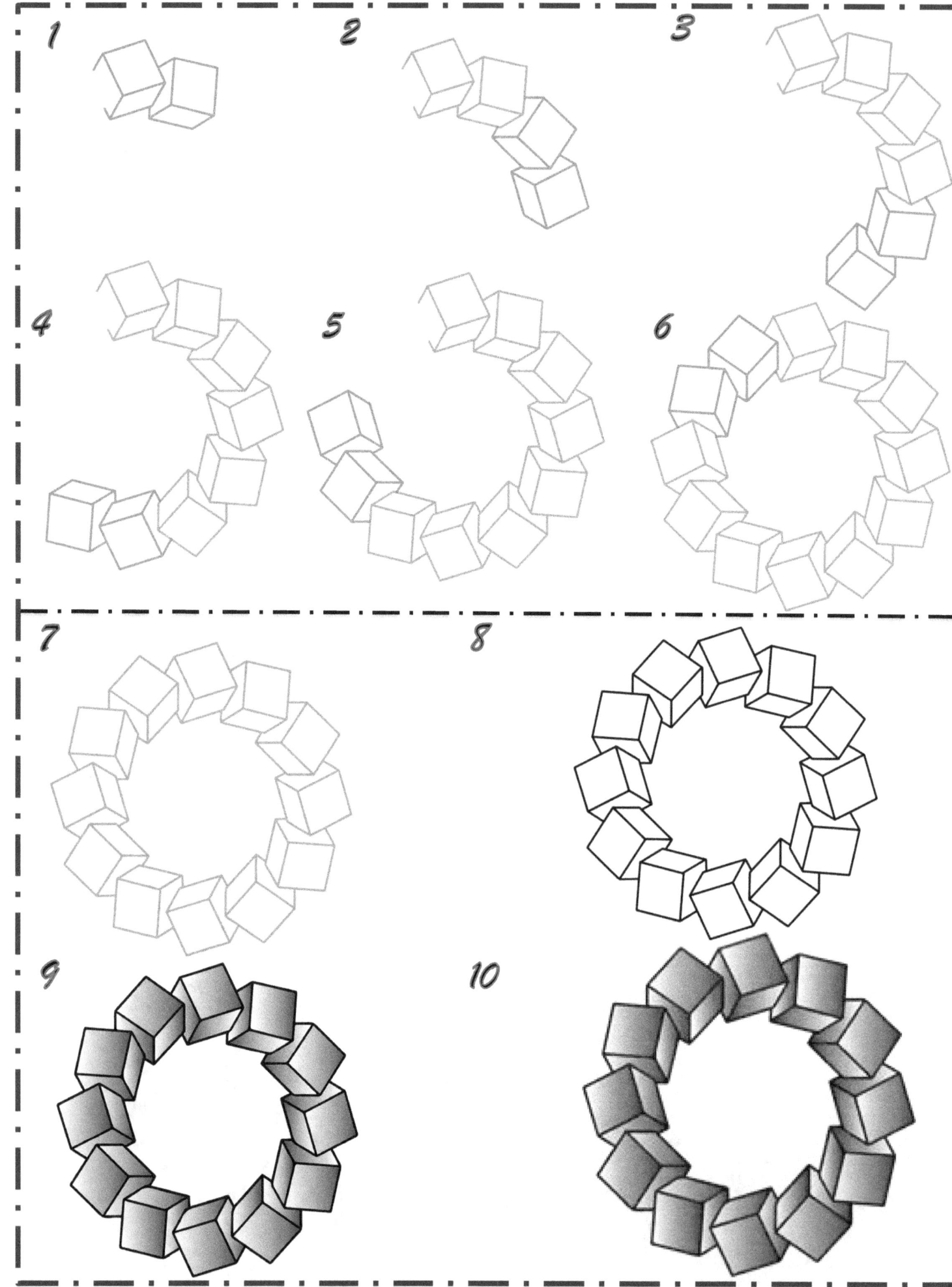

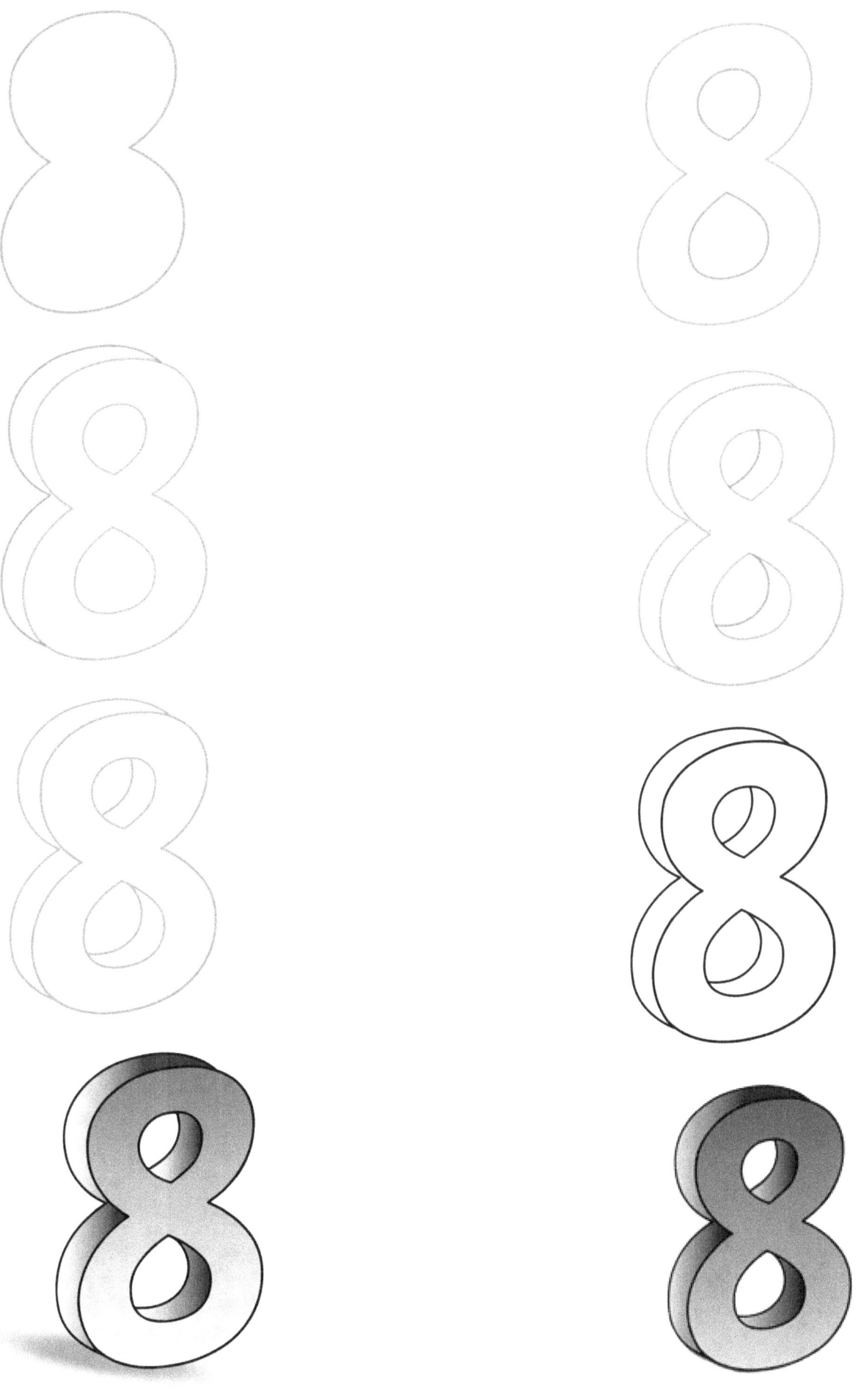

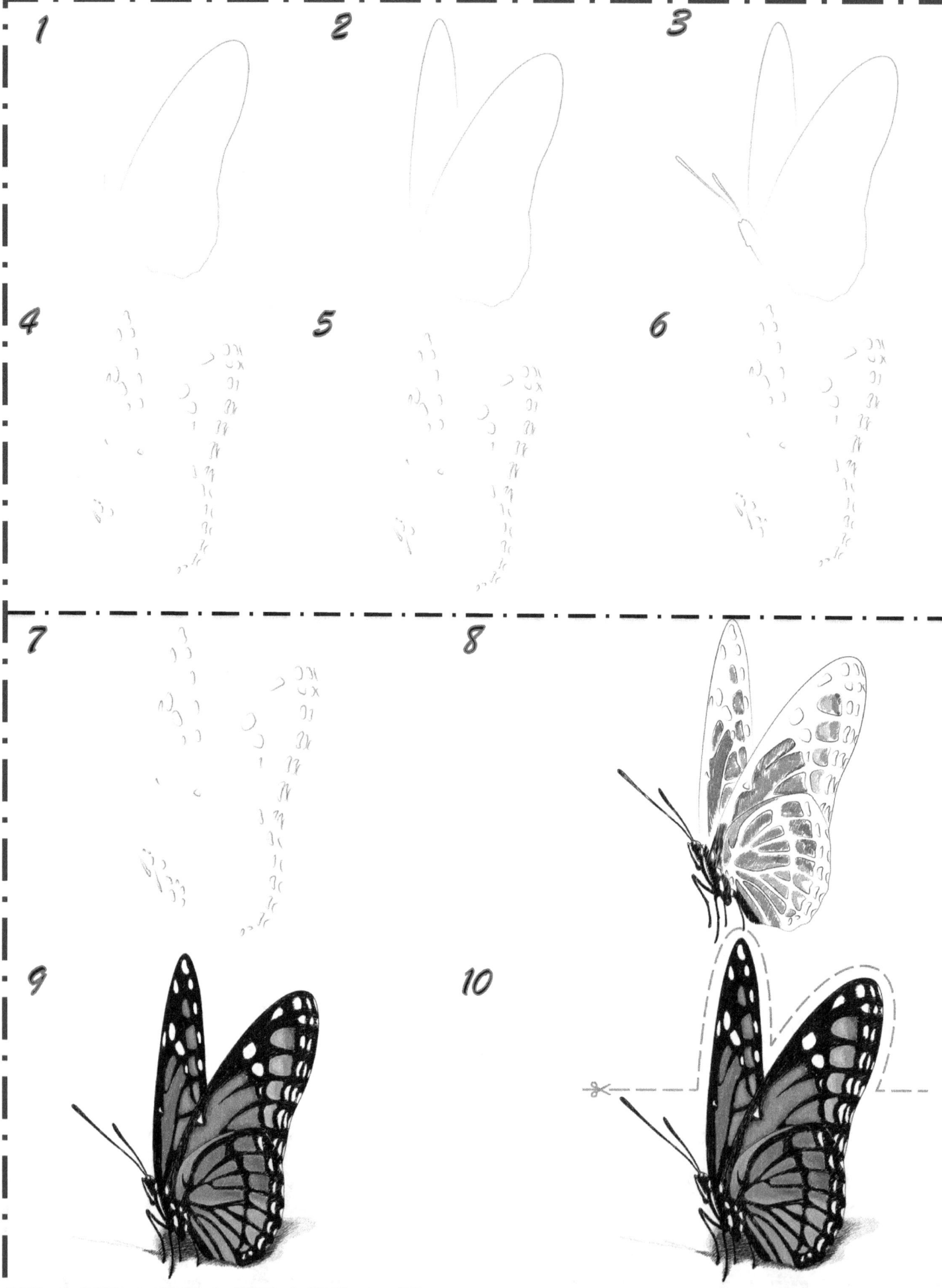

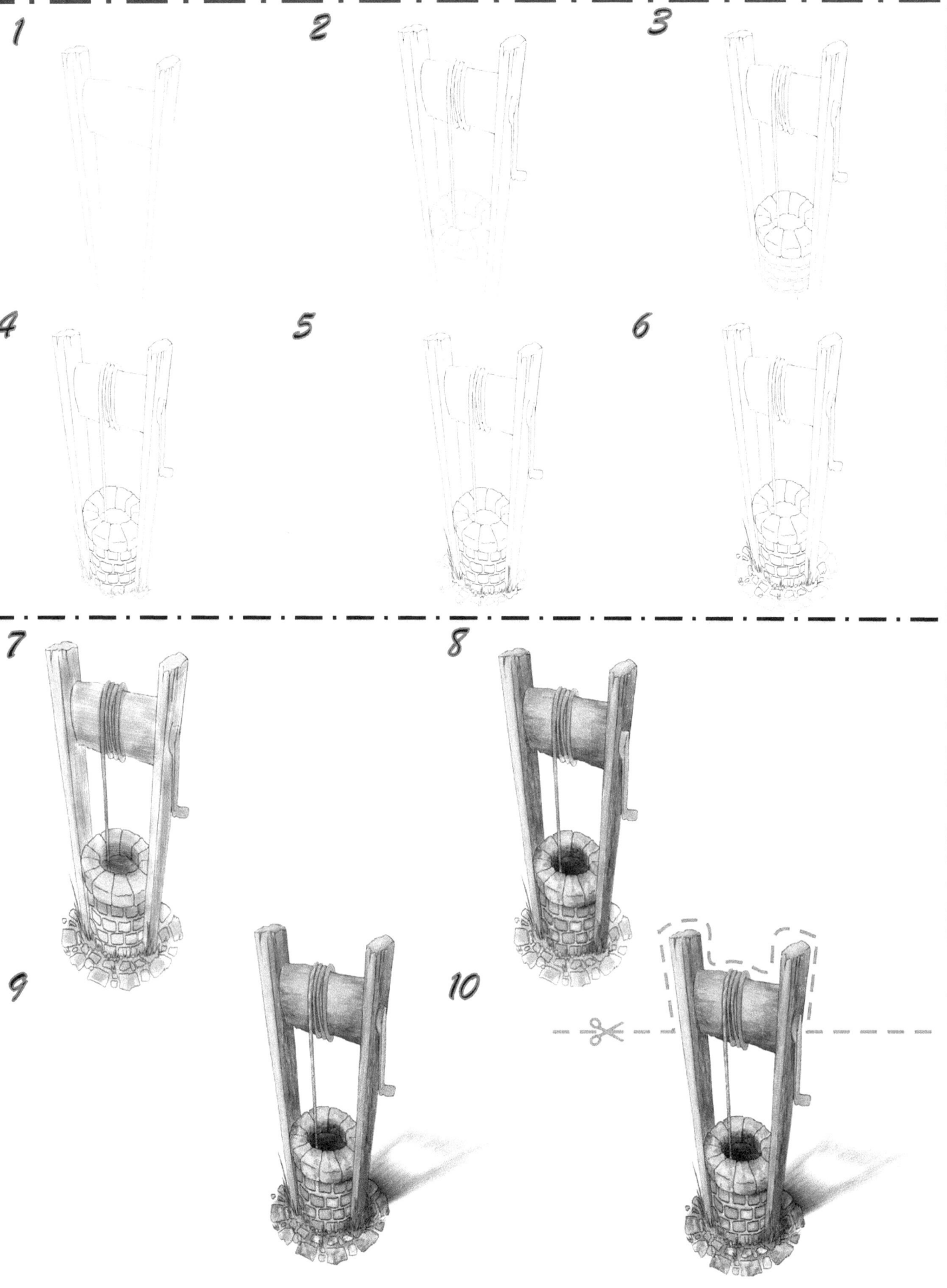

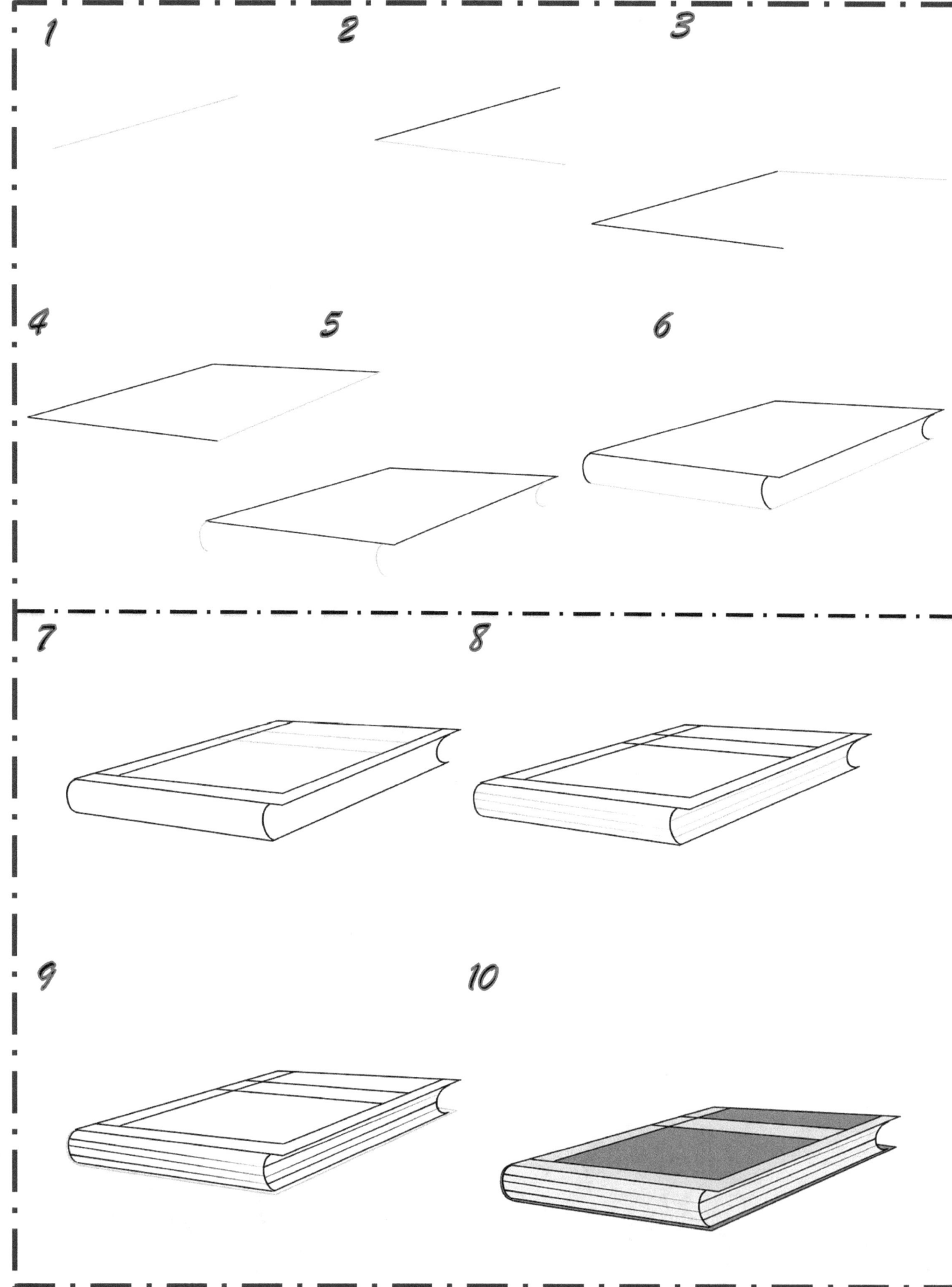

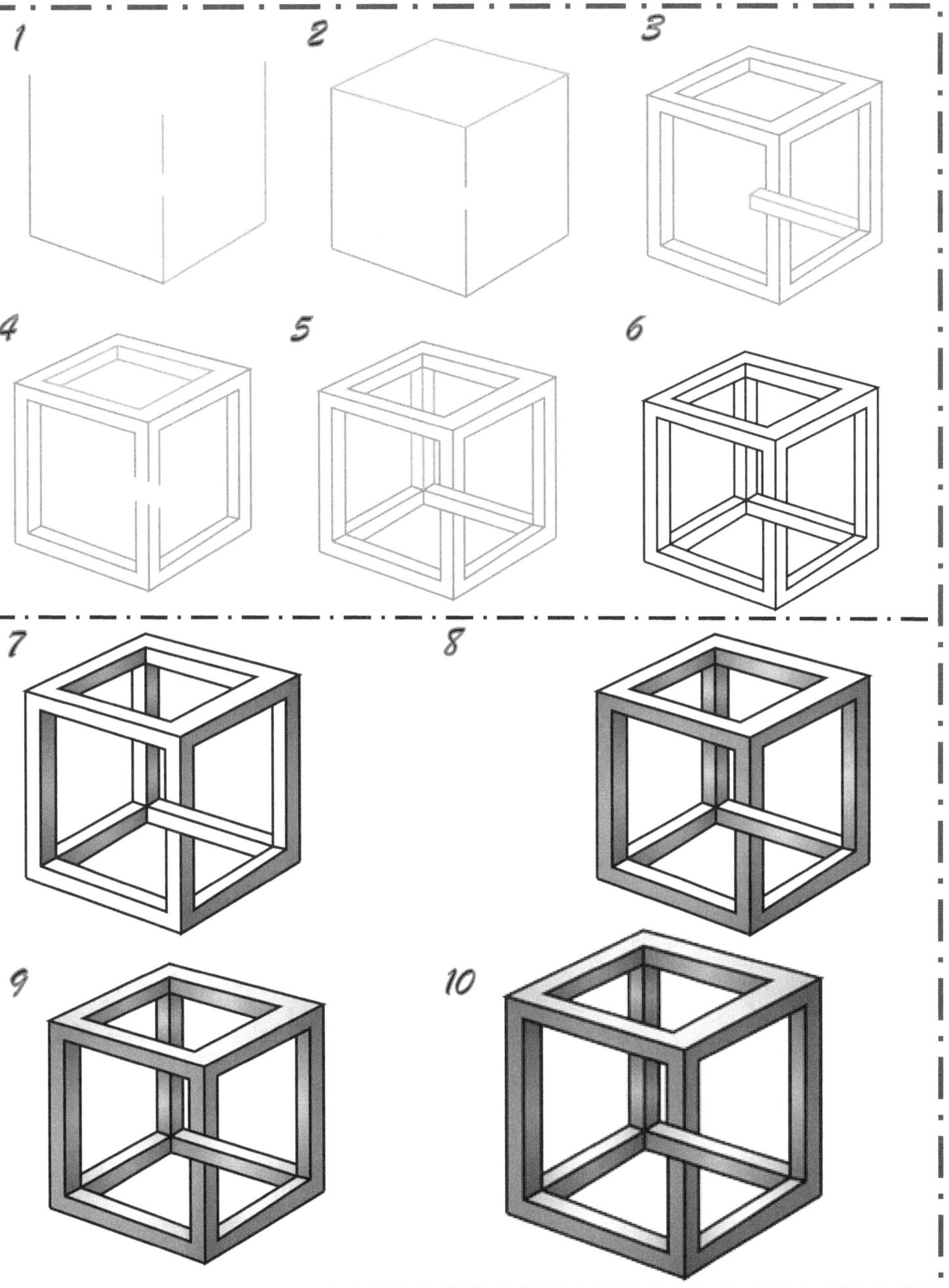

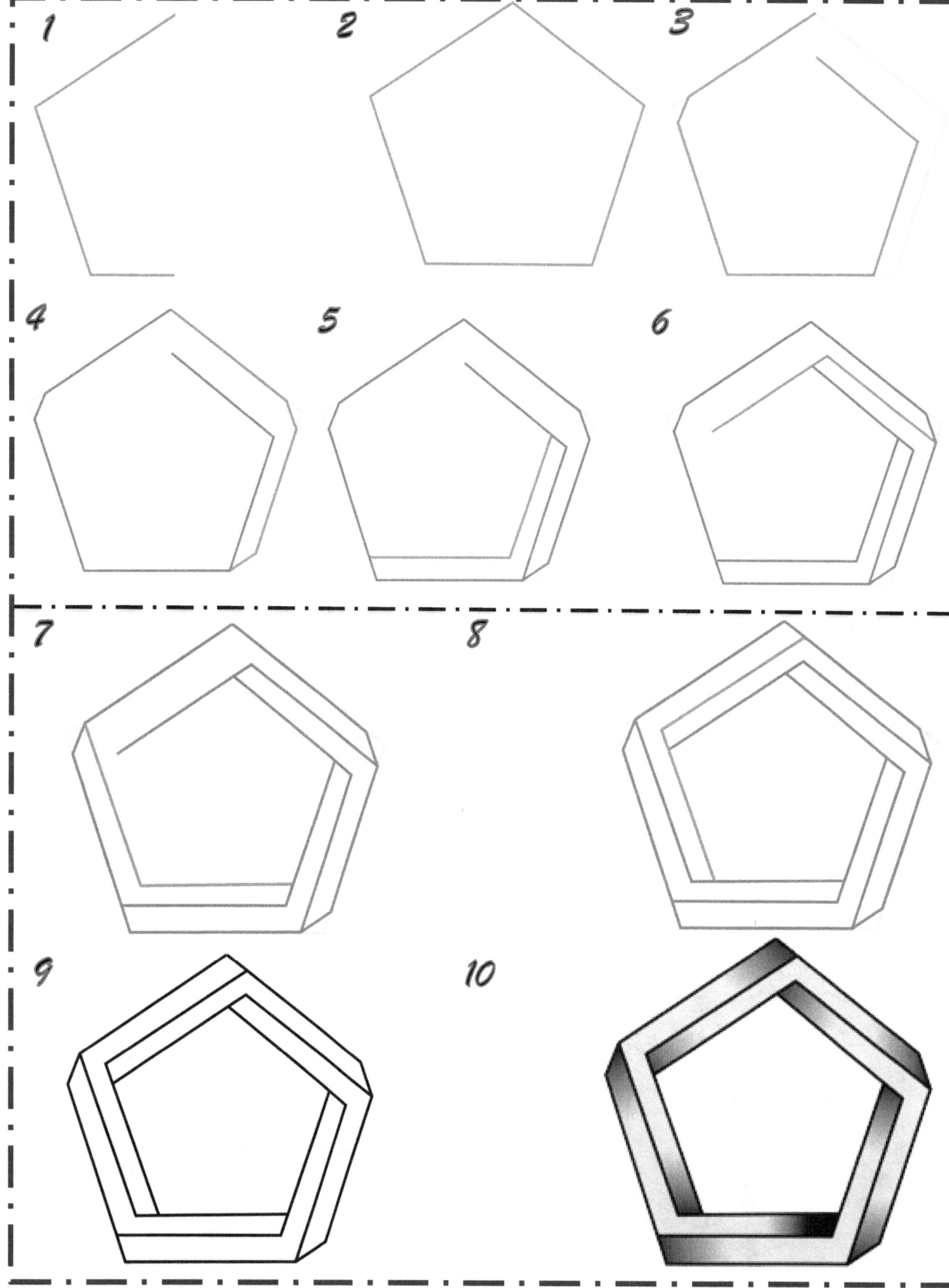

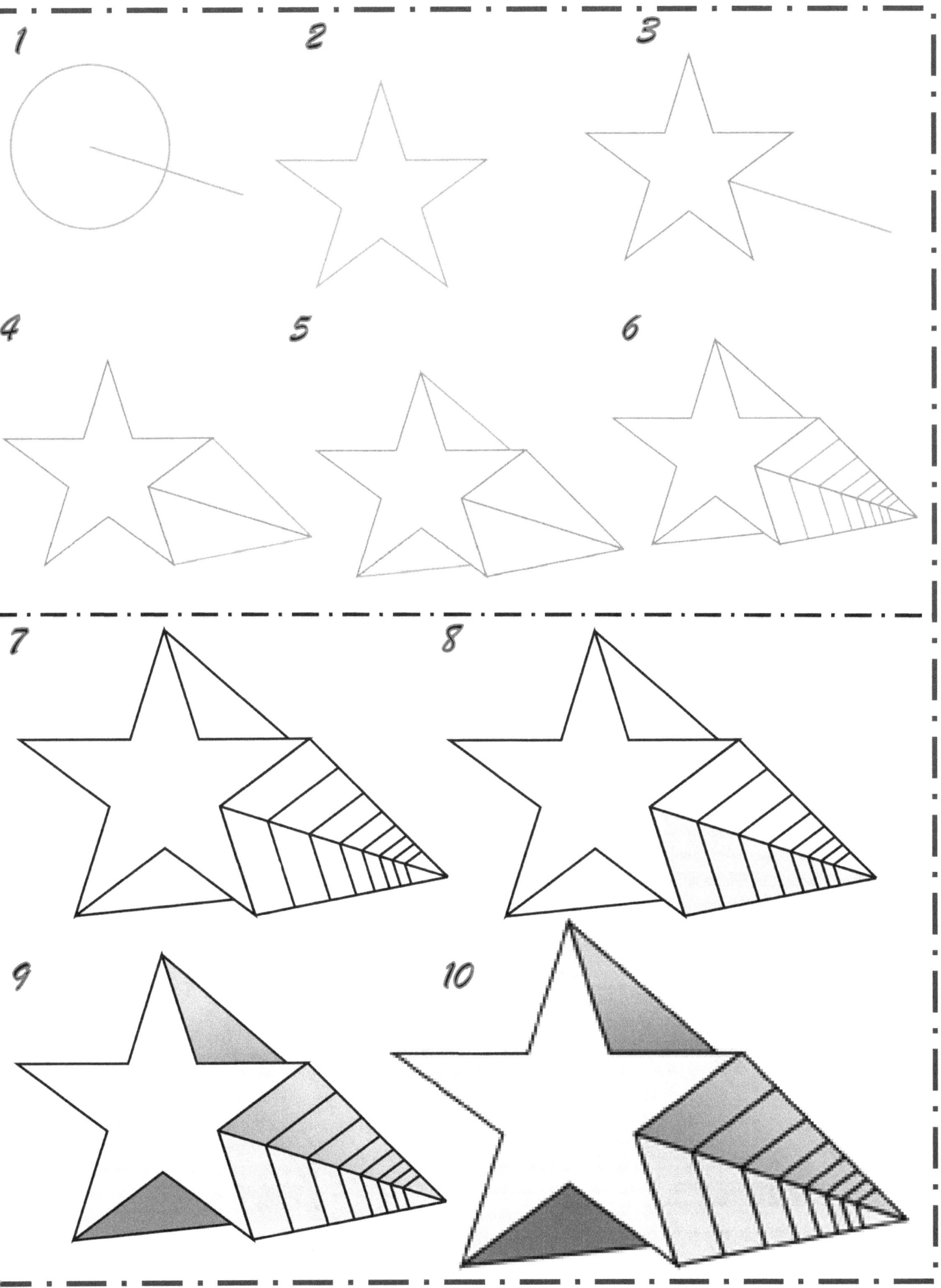

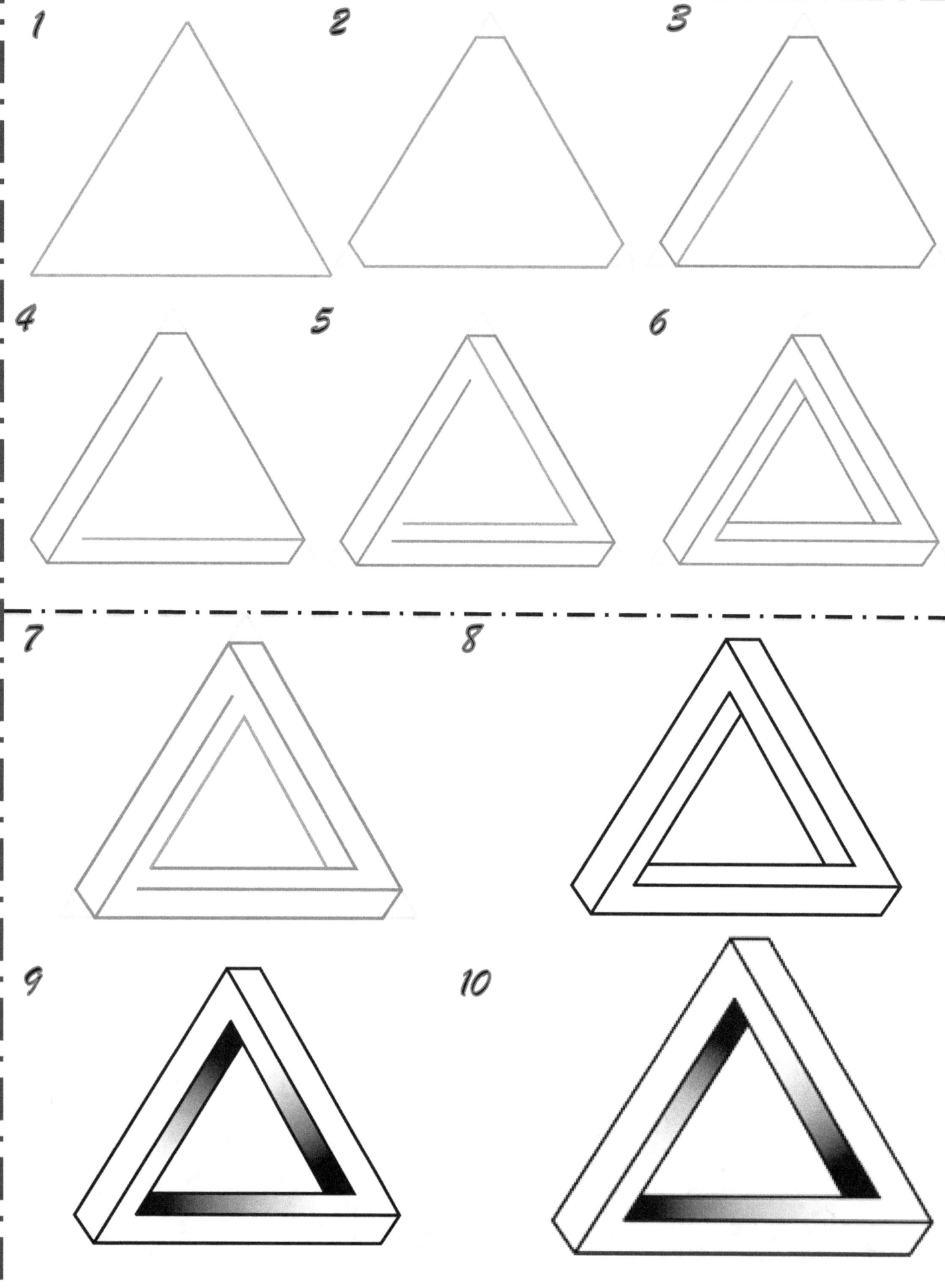

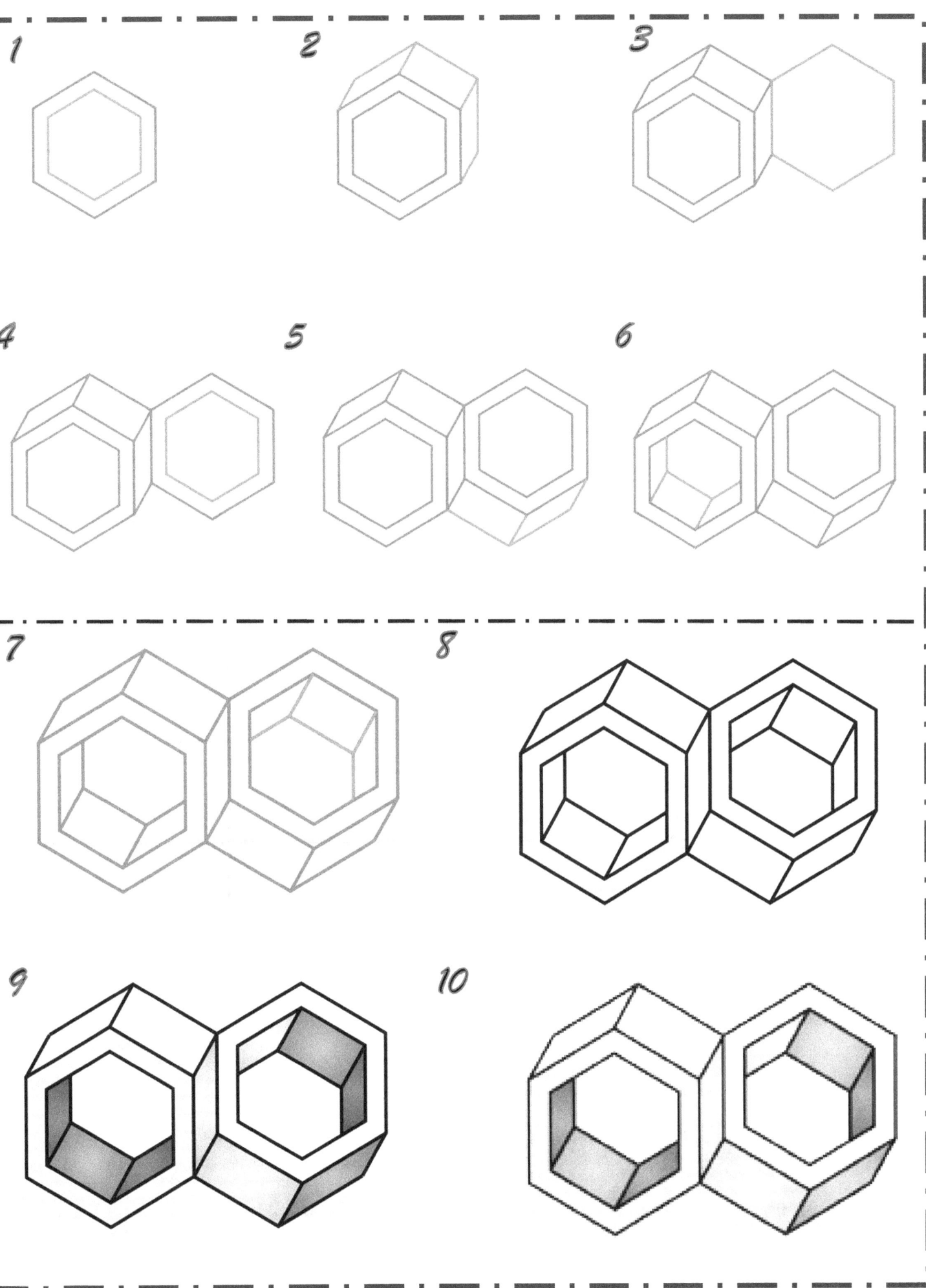

1

2

3

4

5

6

7

8

9

10

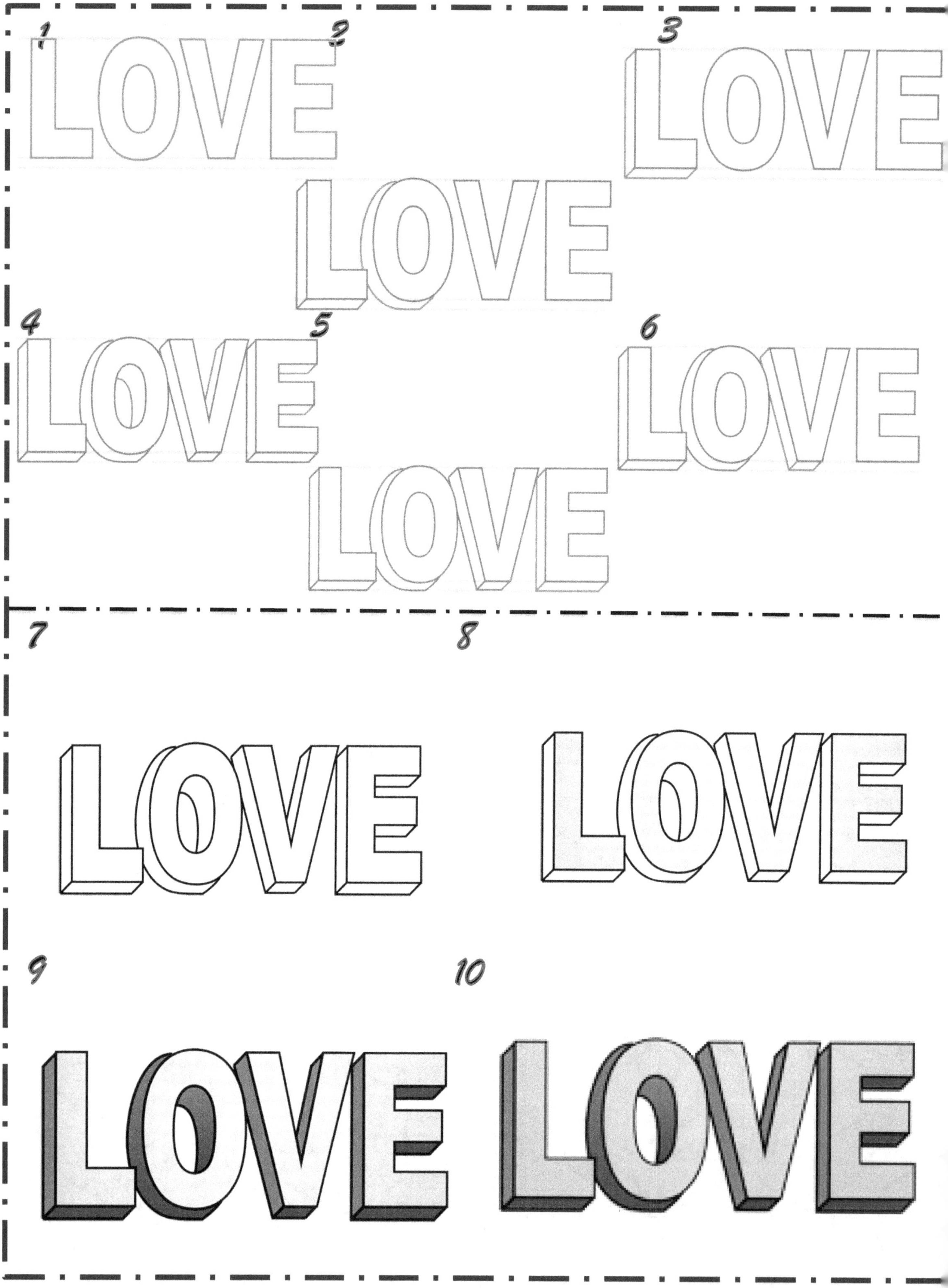

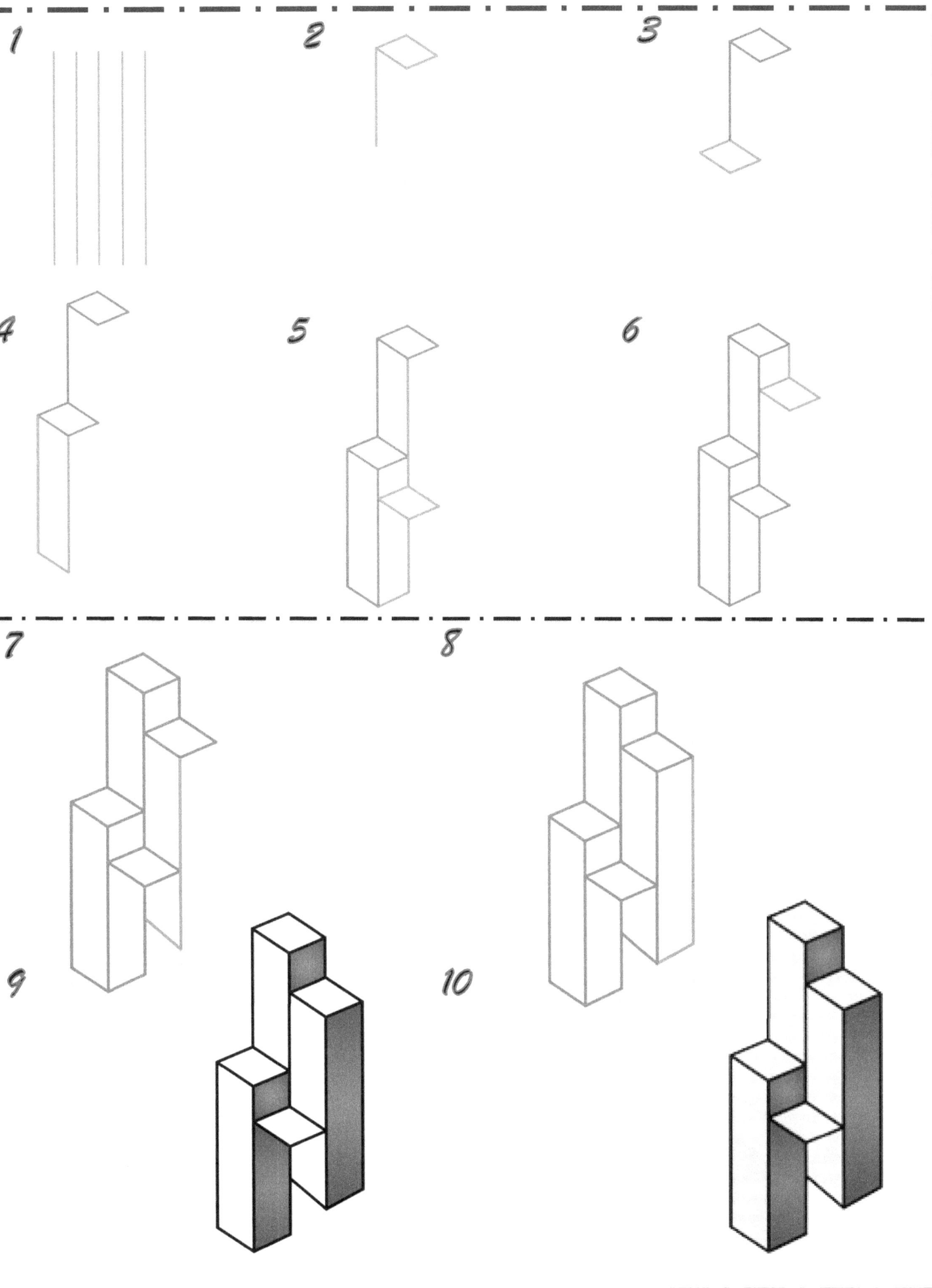

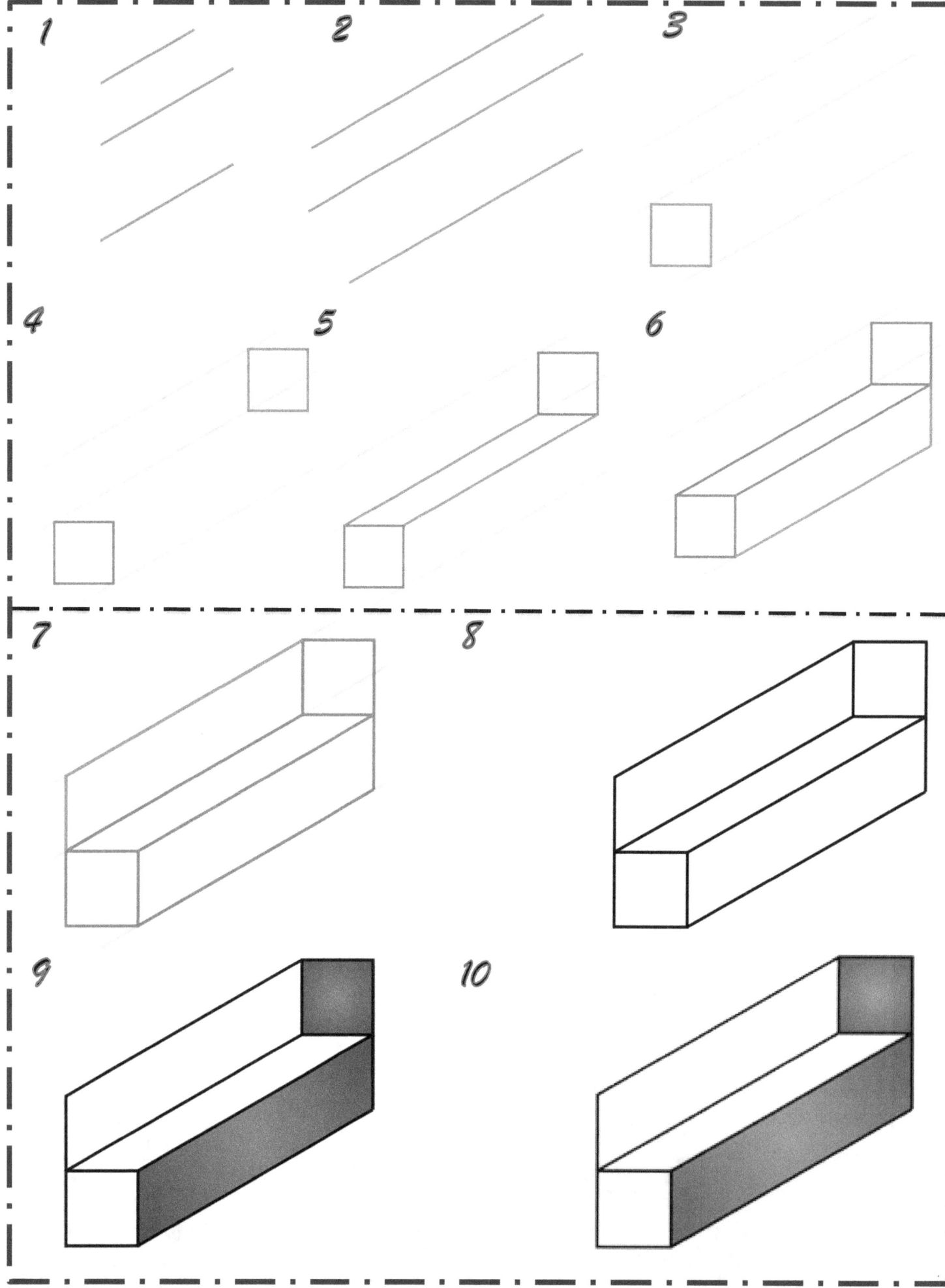

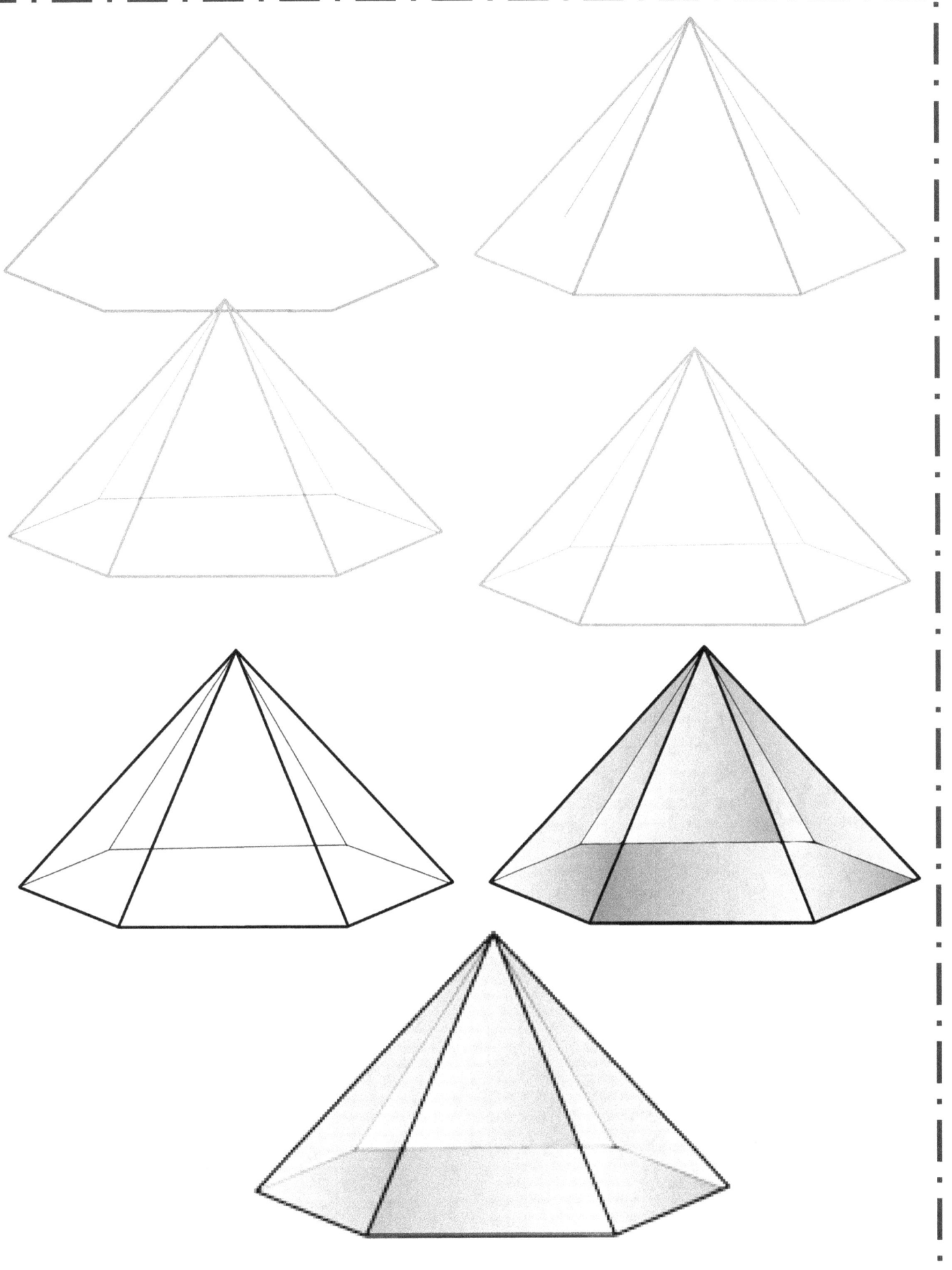

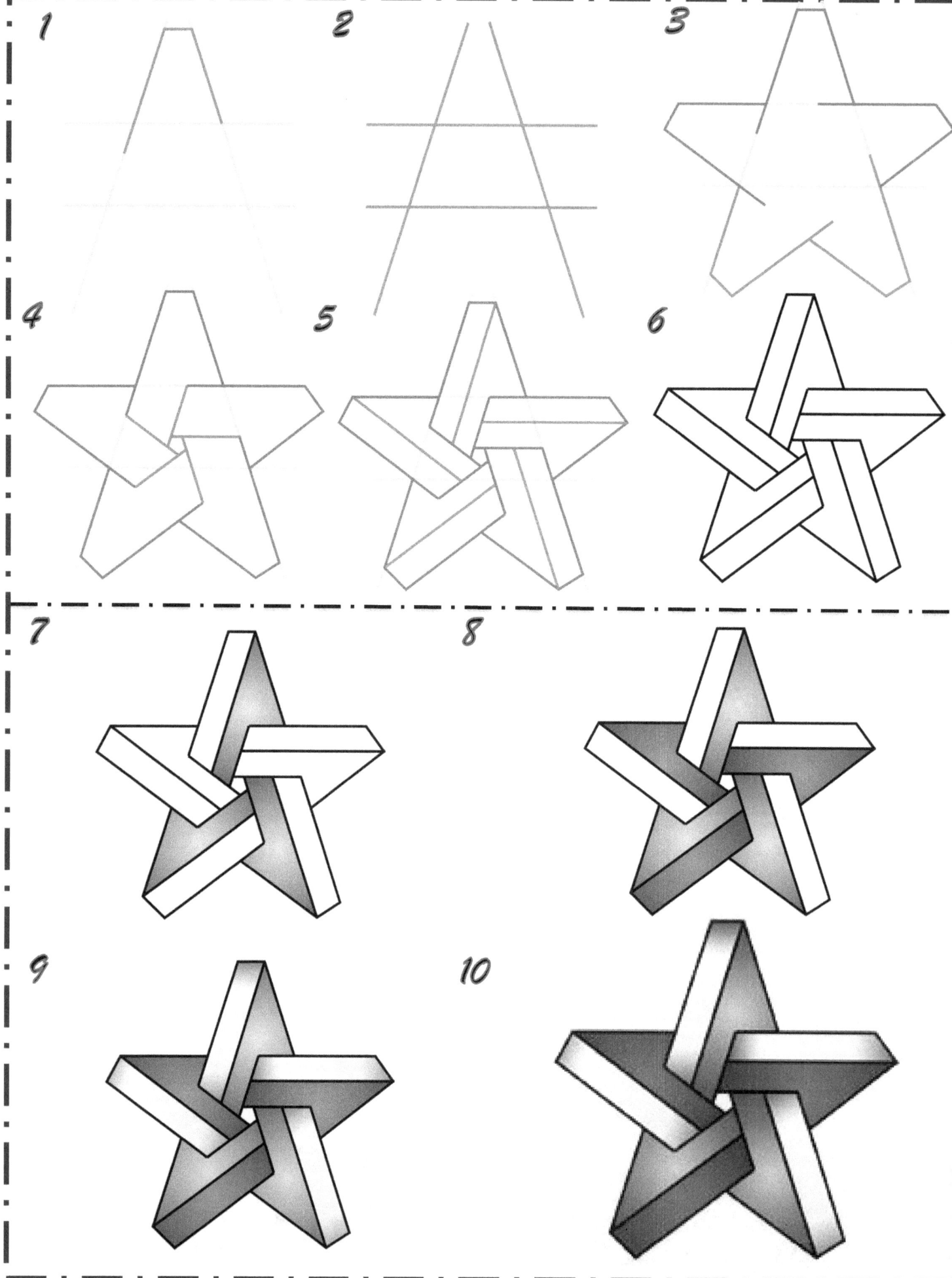

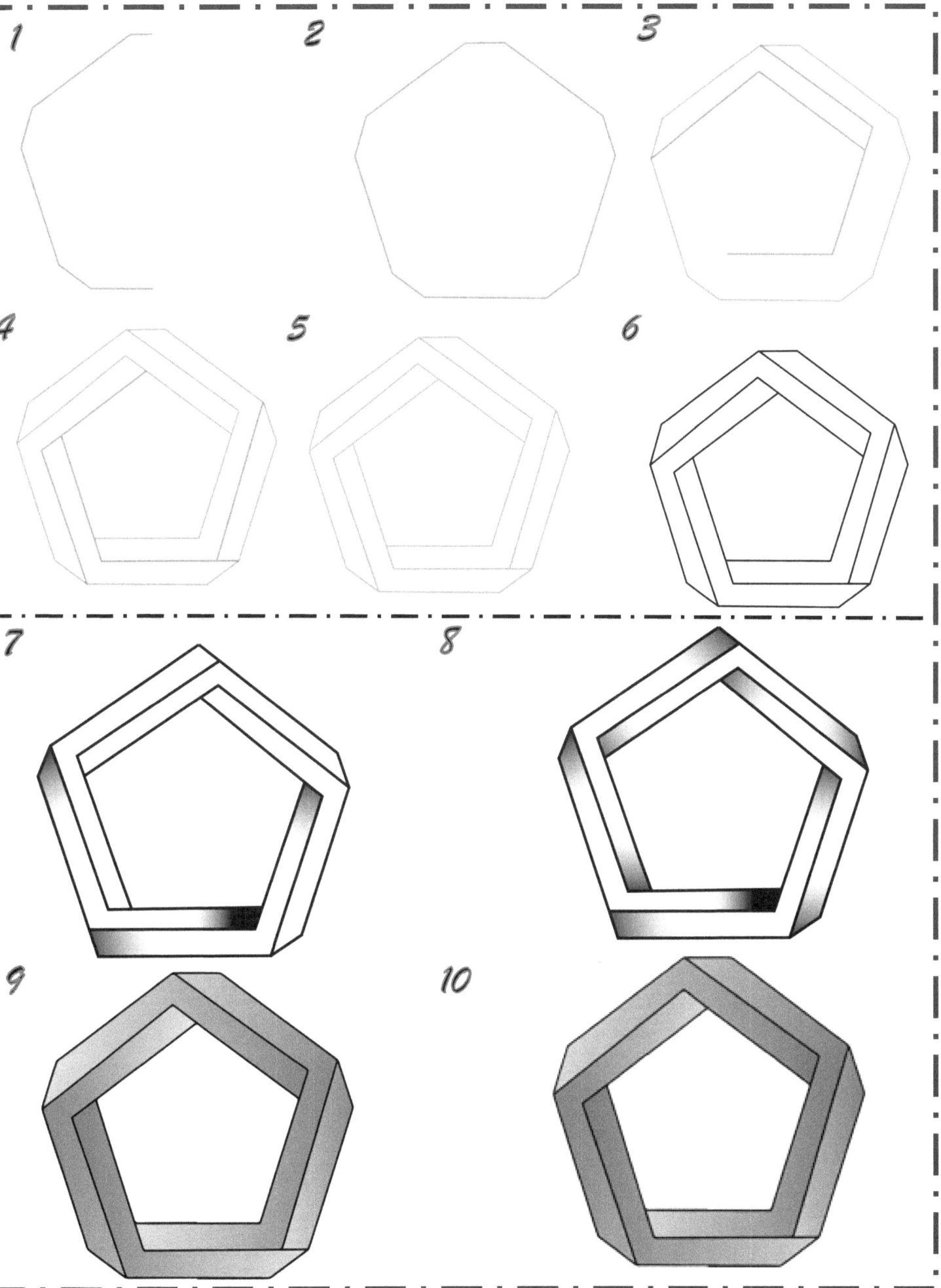

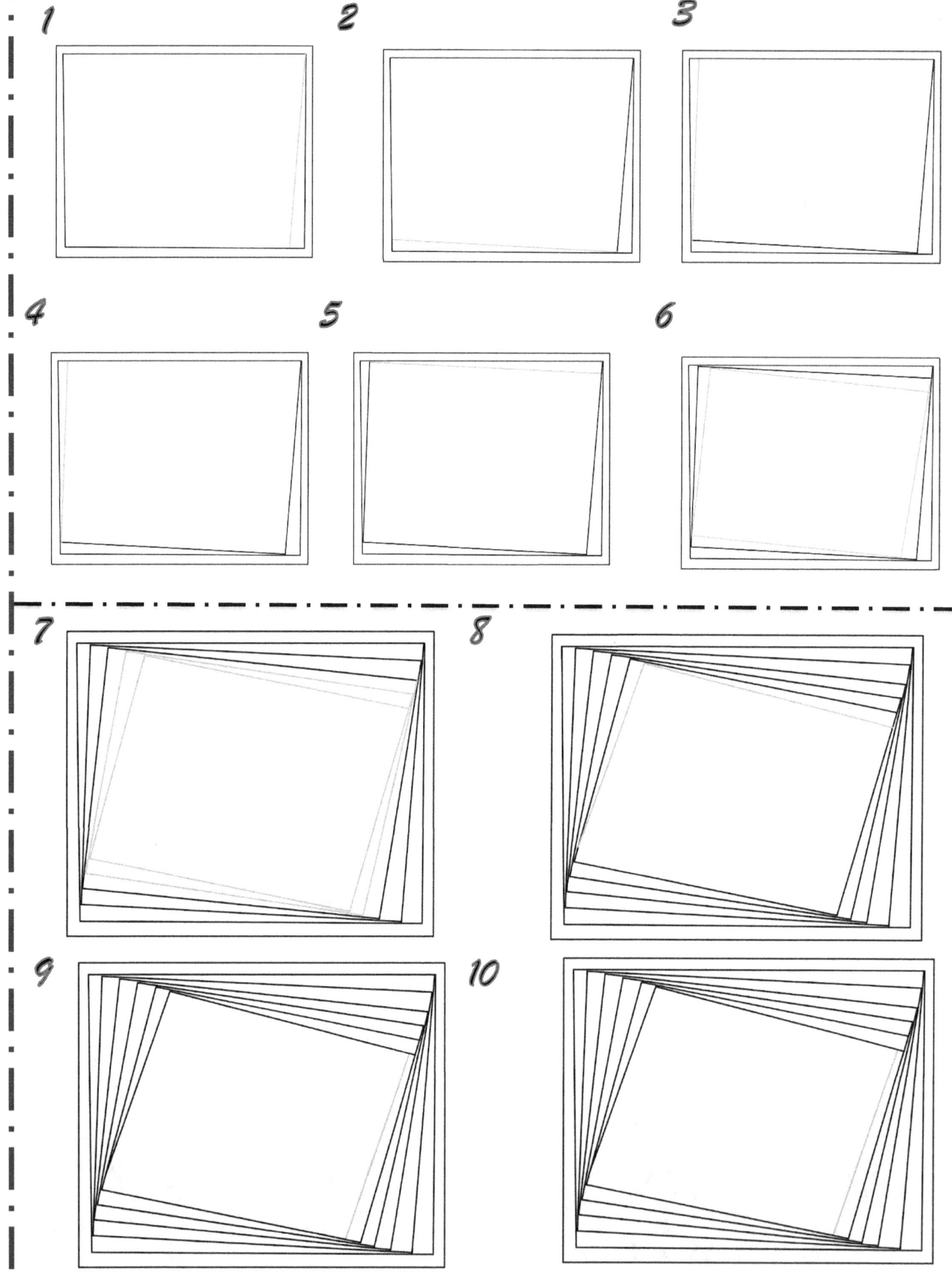

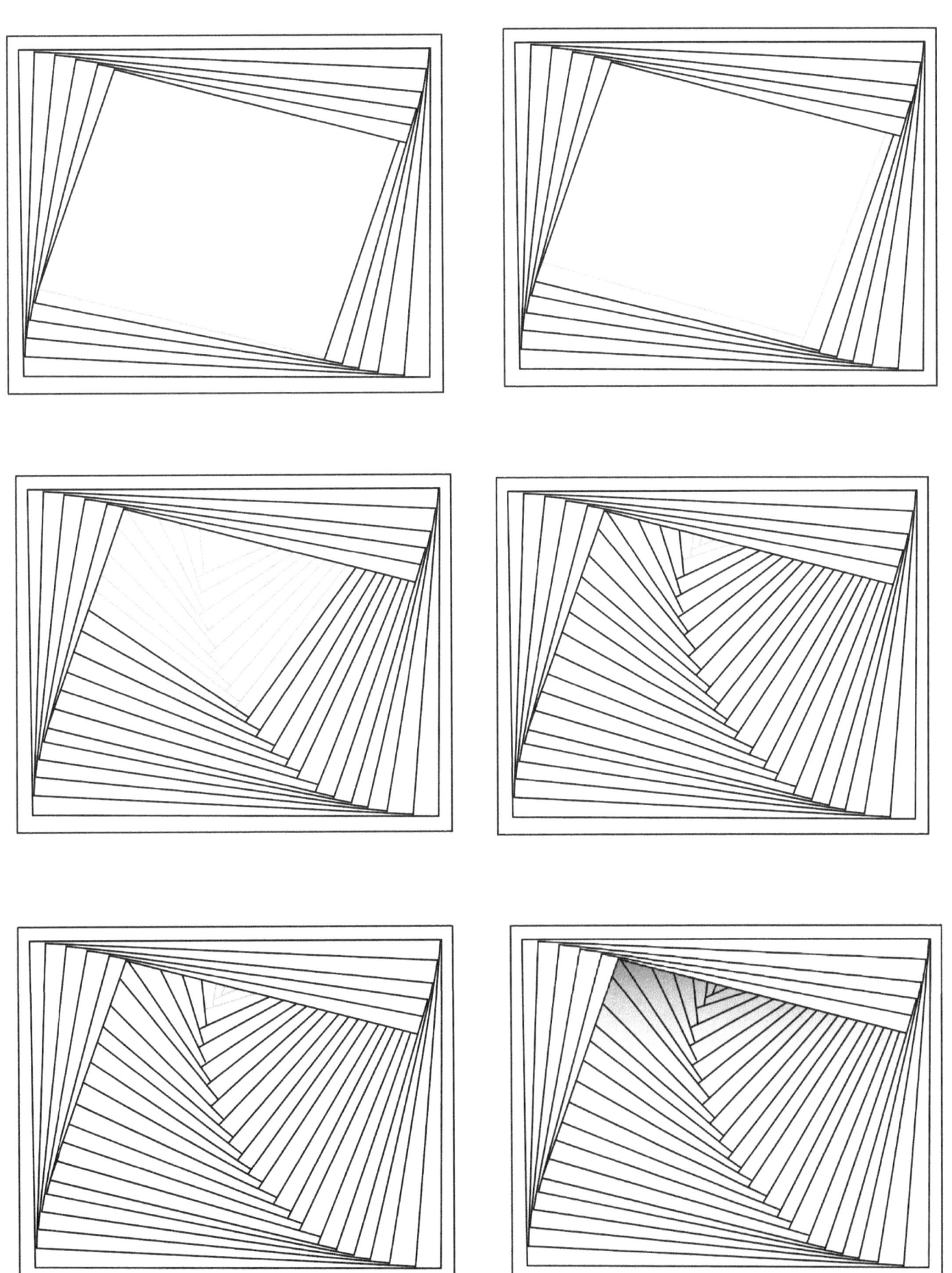

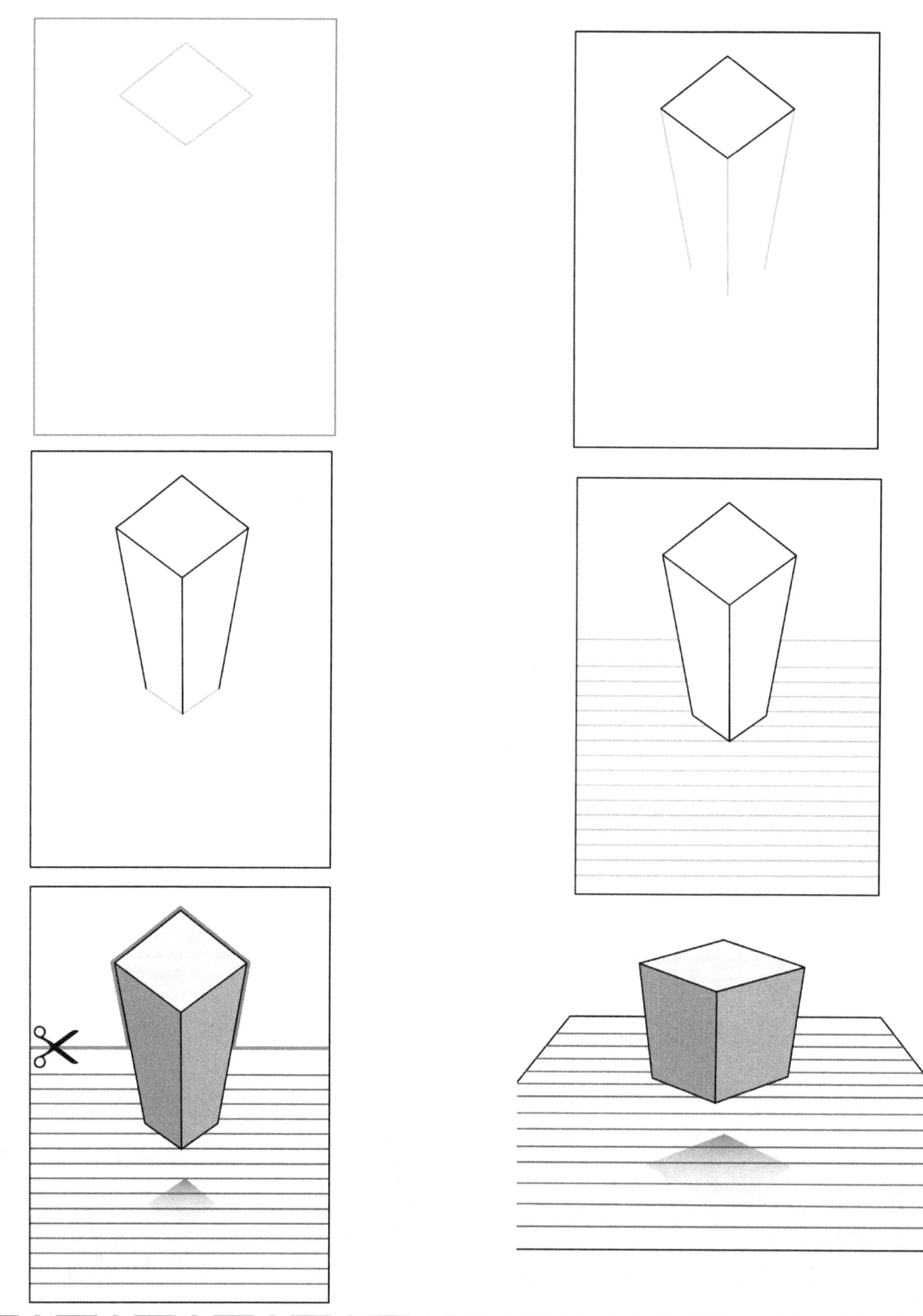

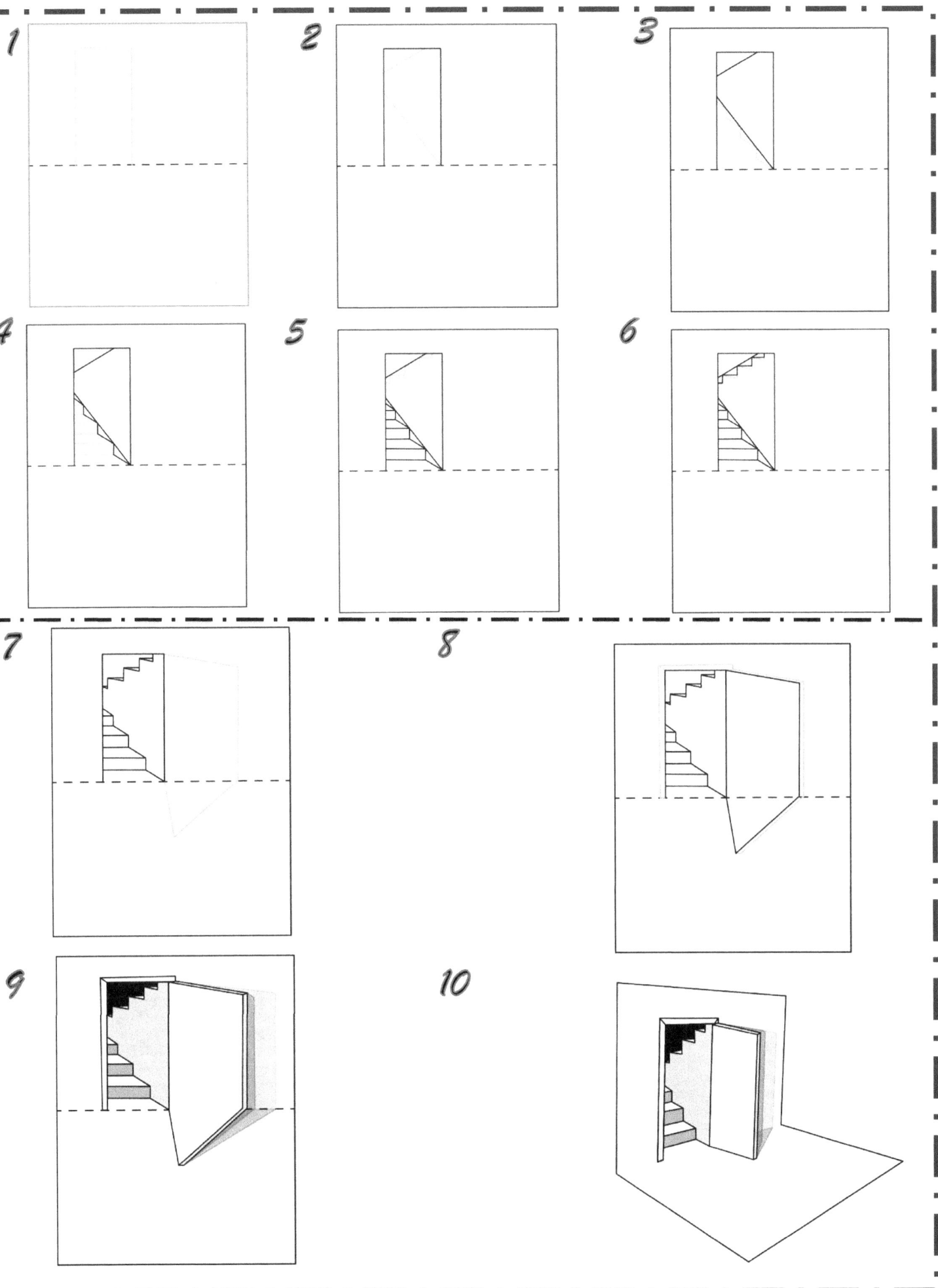

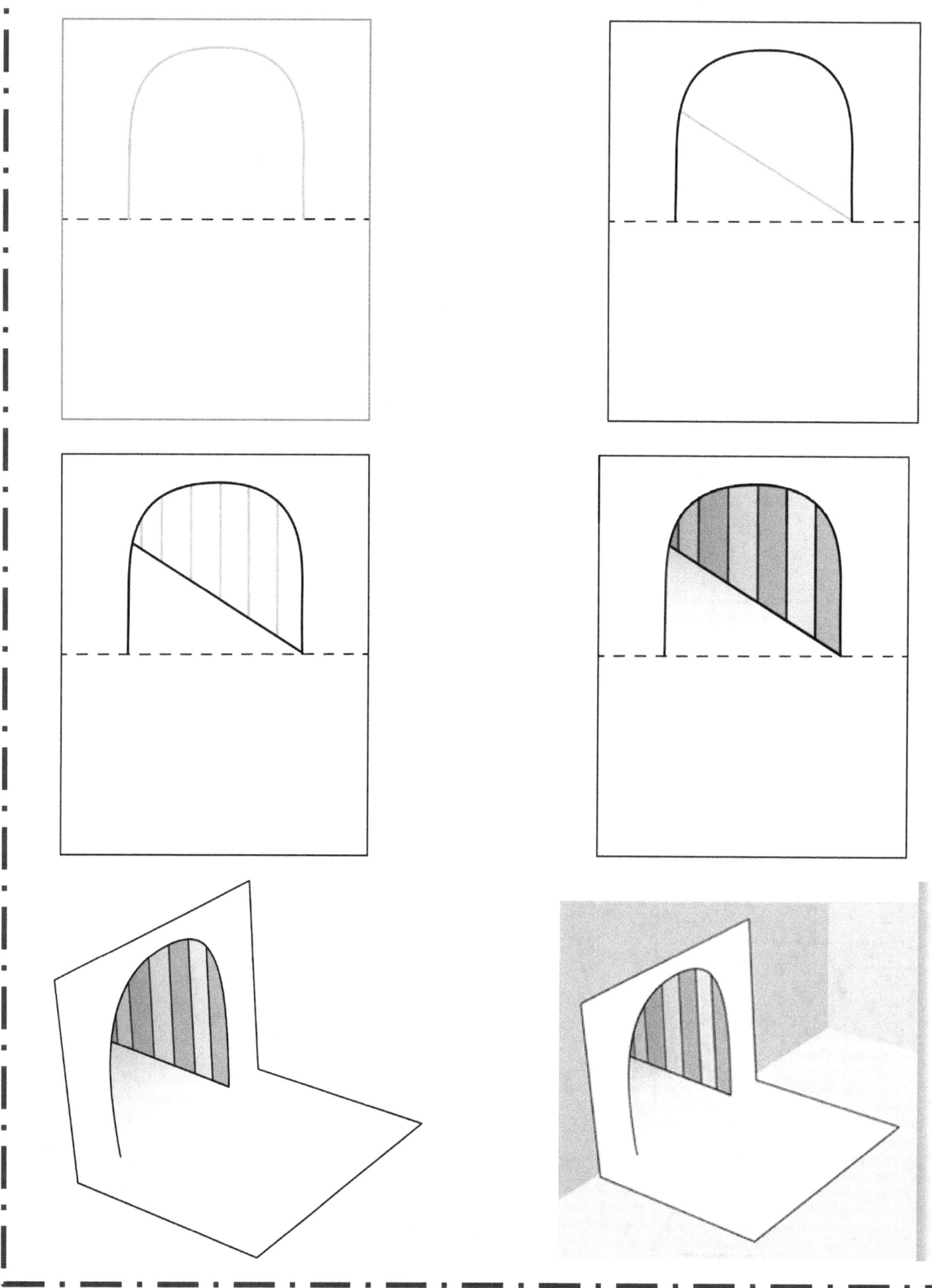

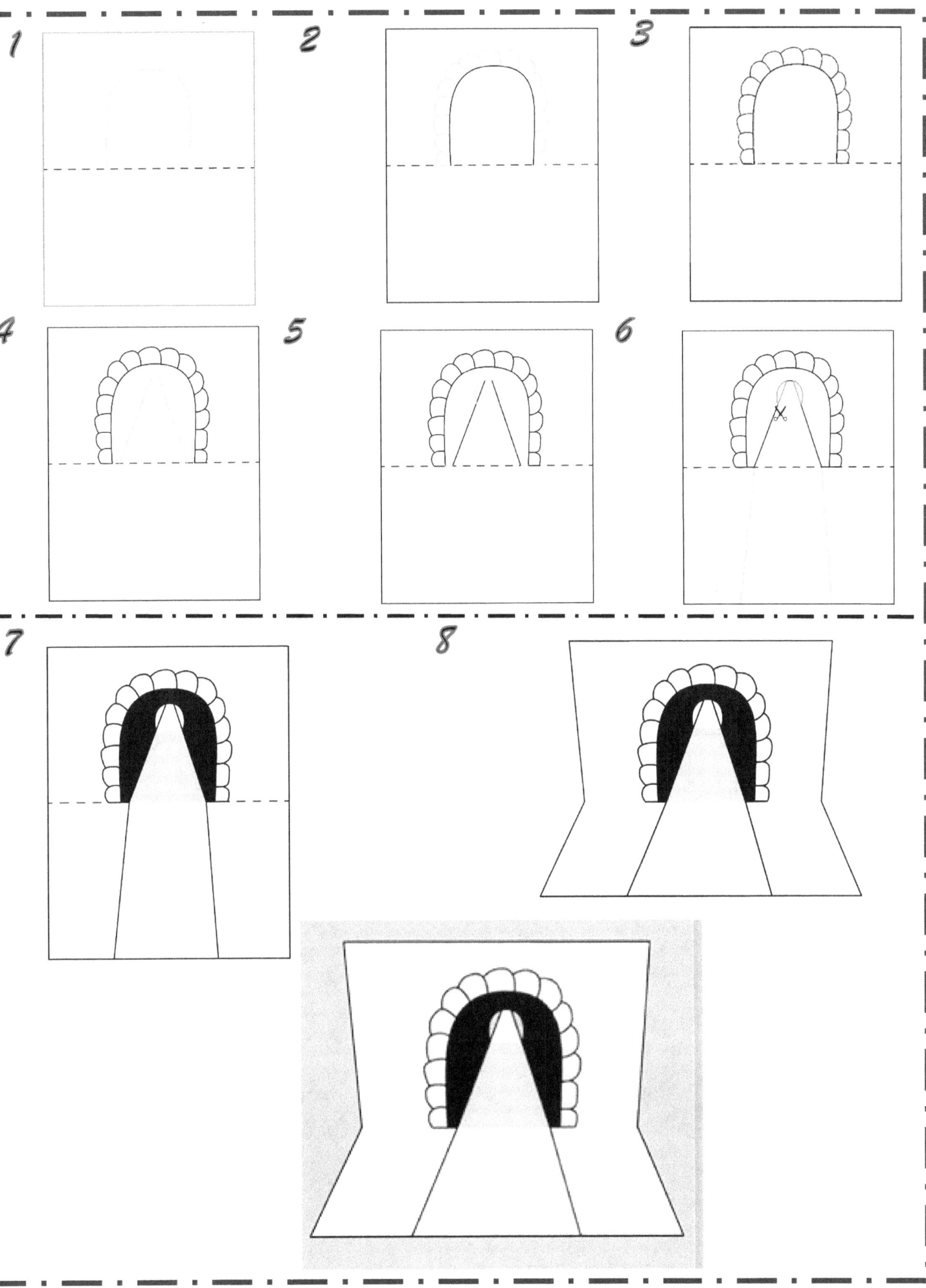

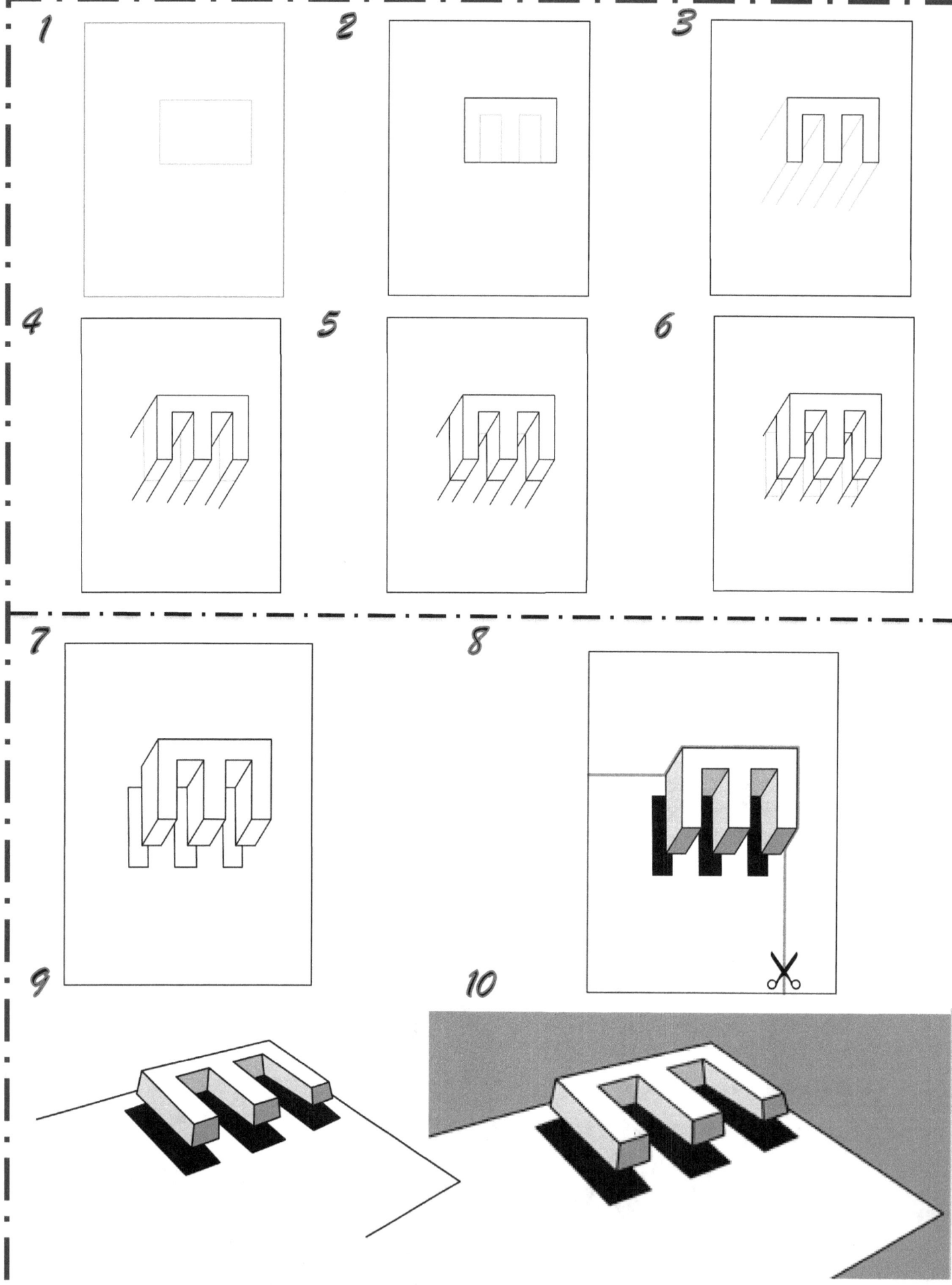

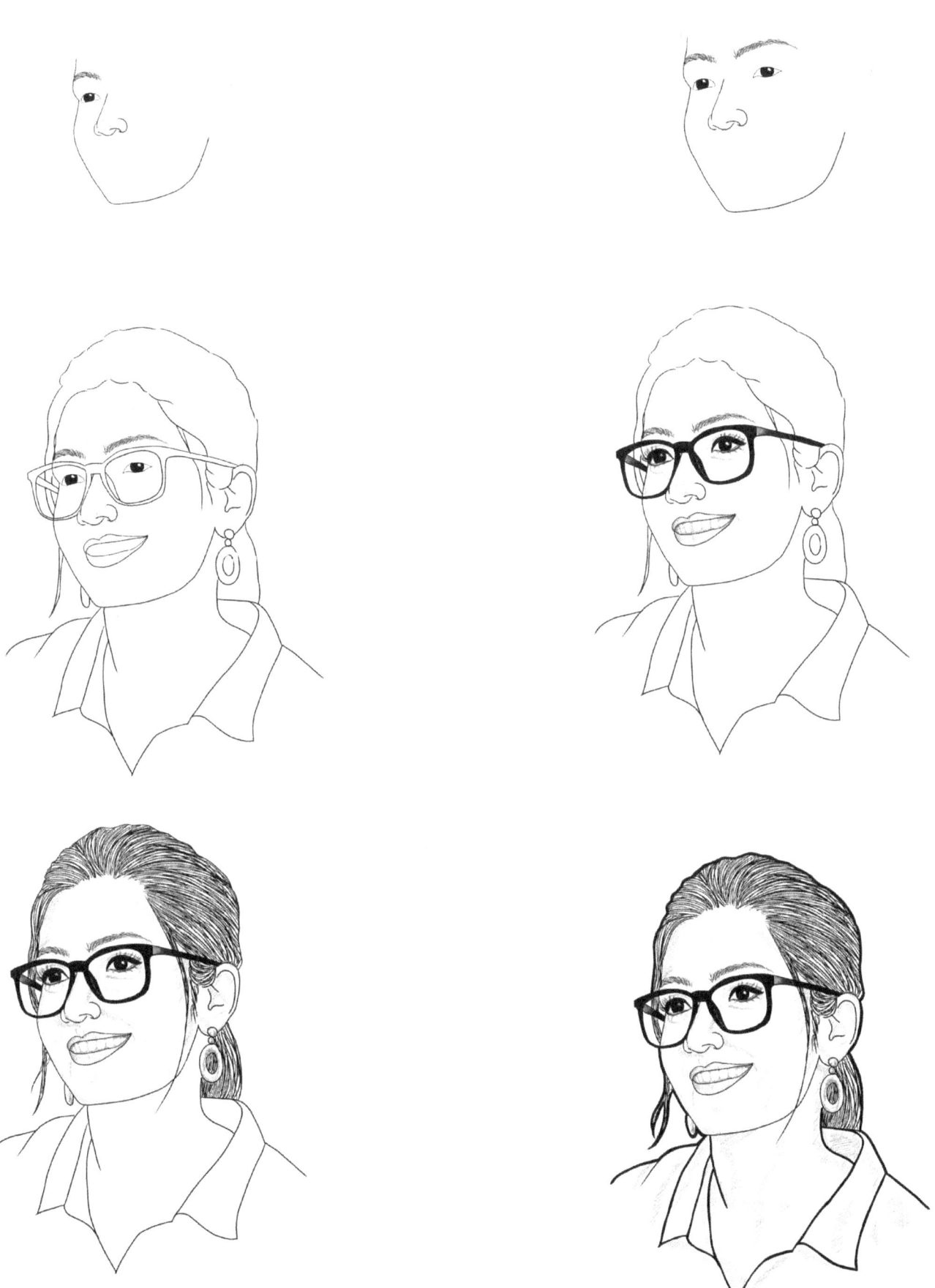

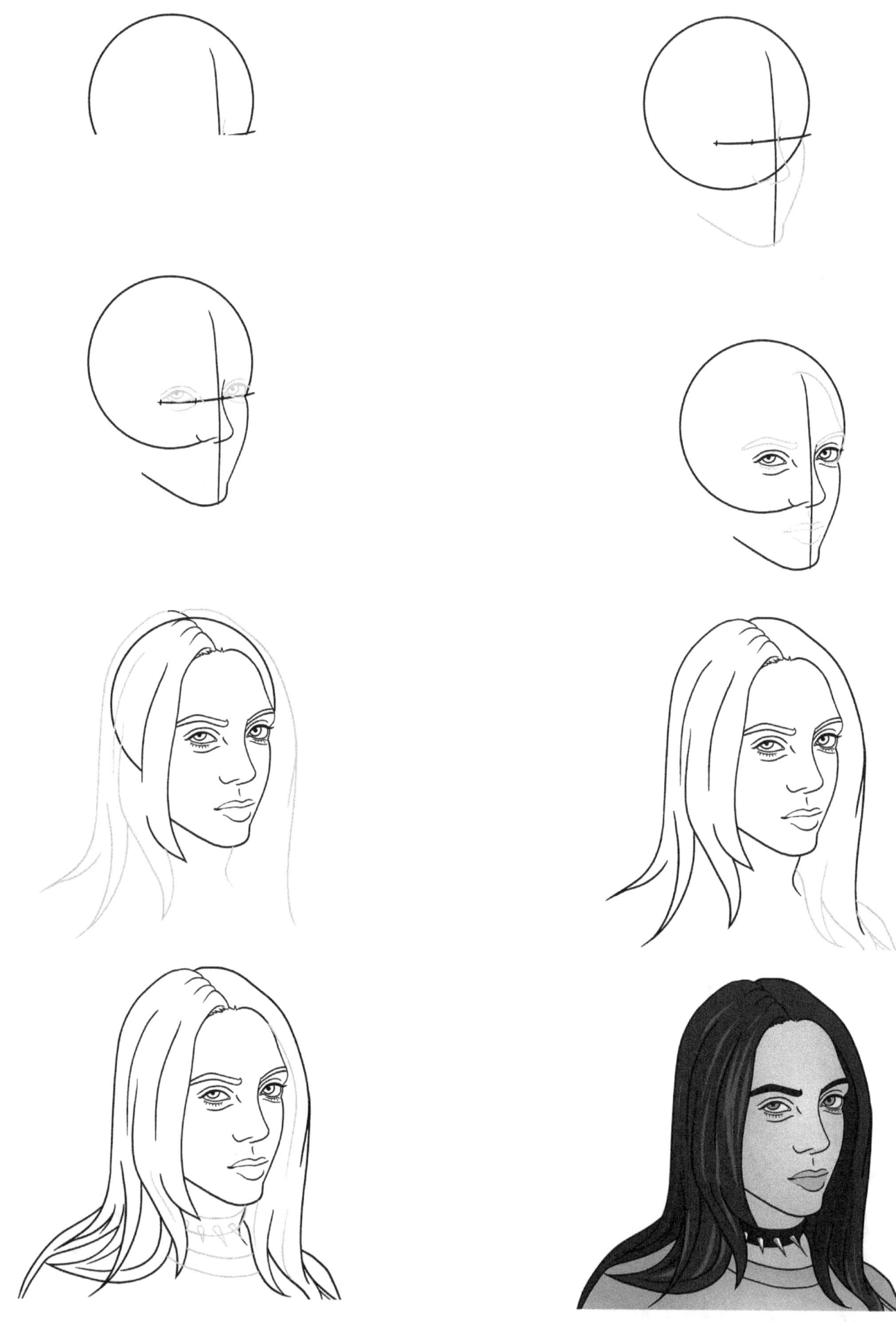

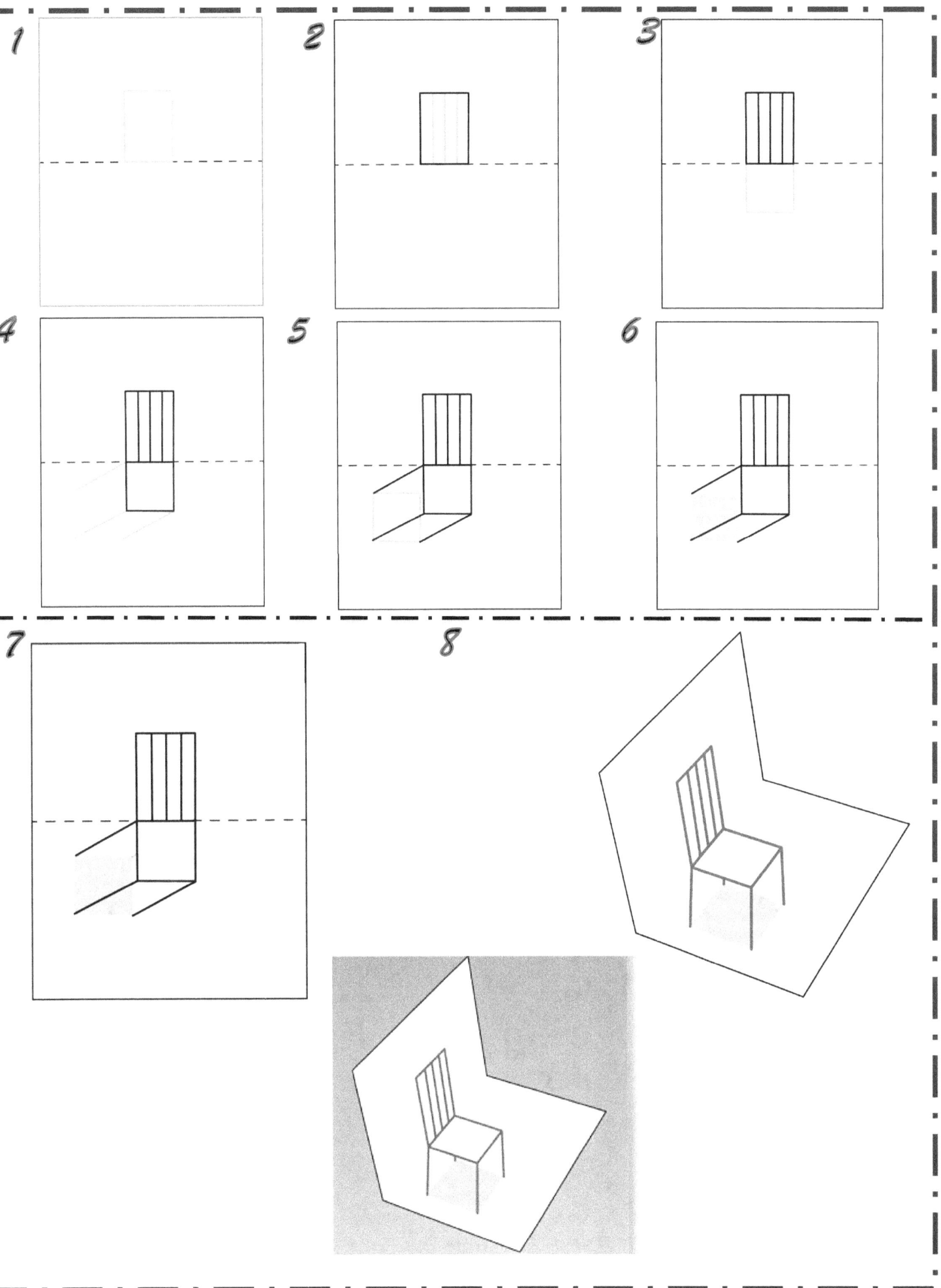

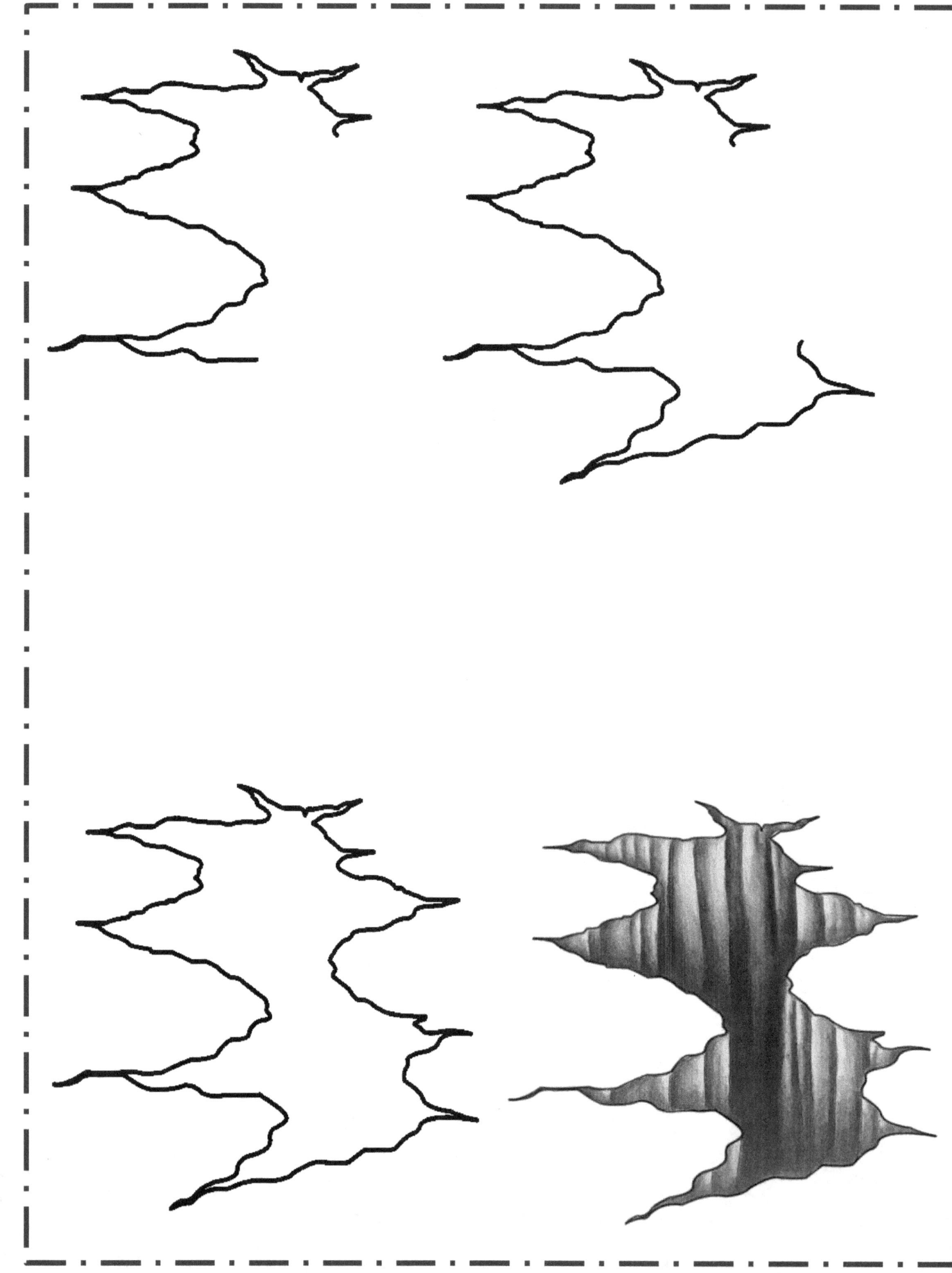

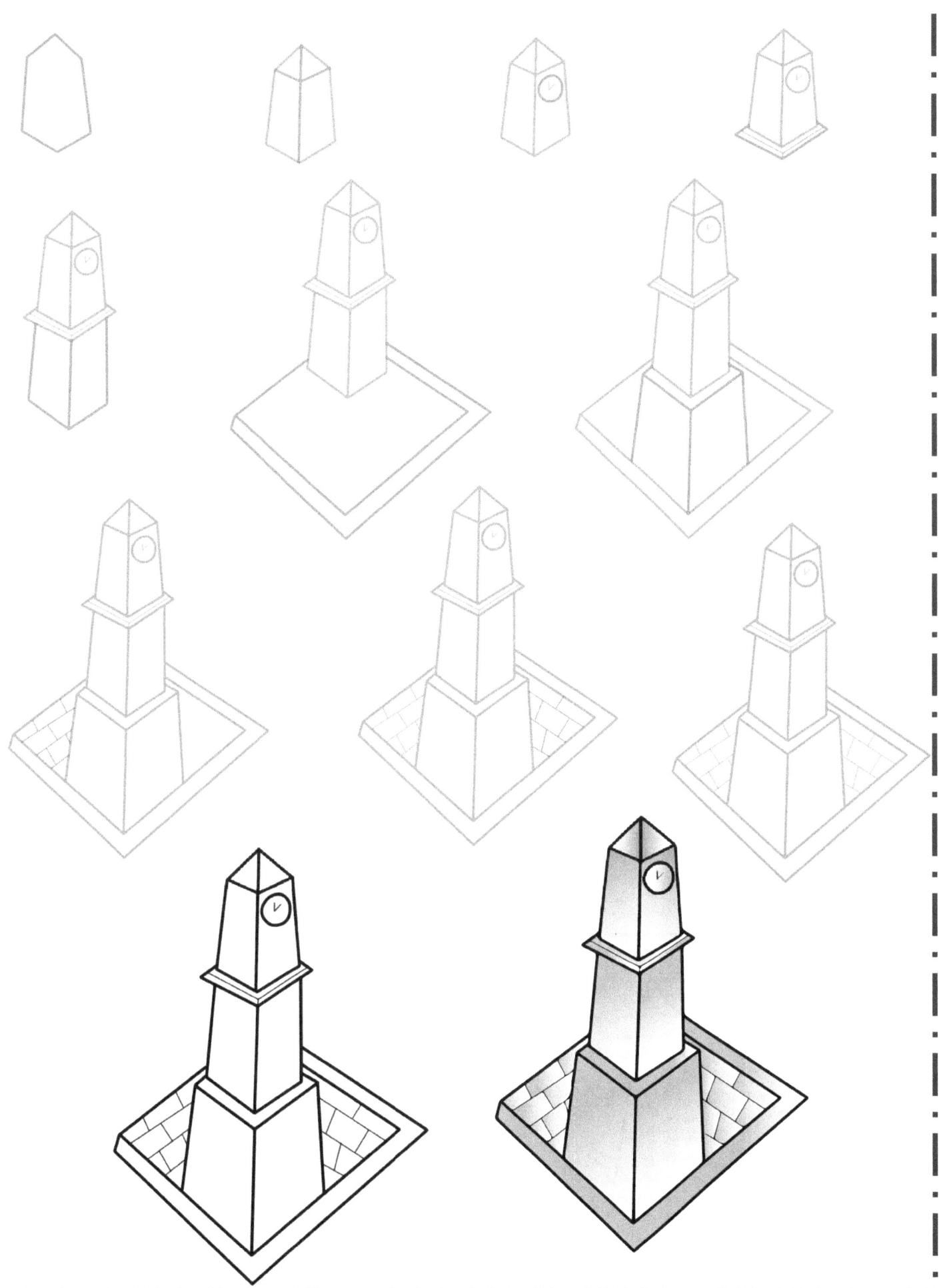

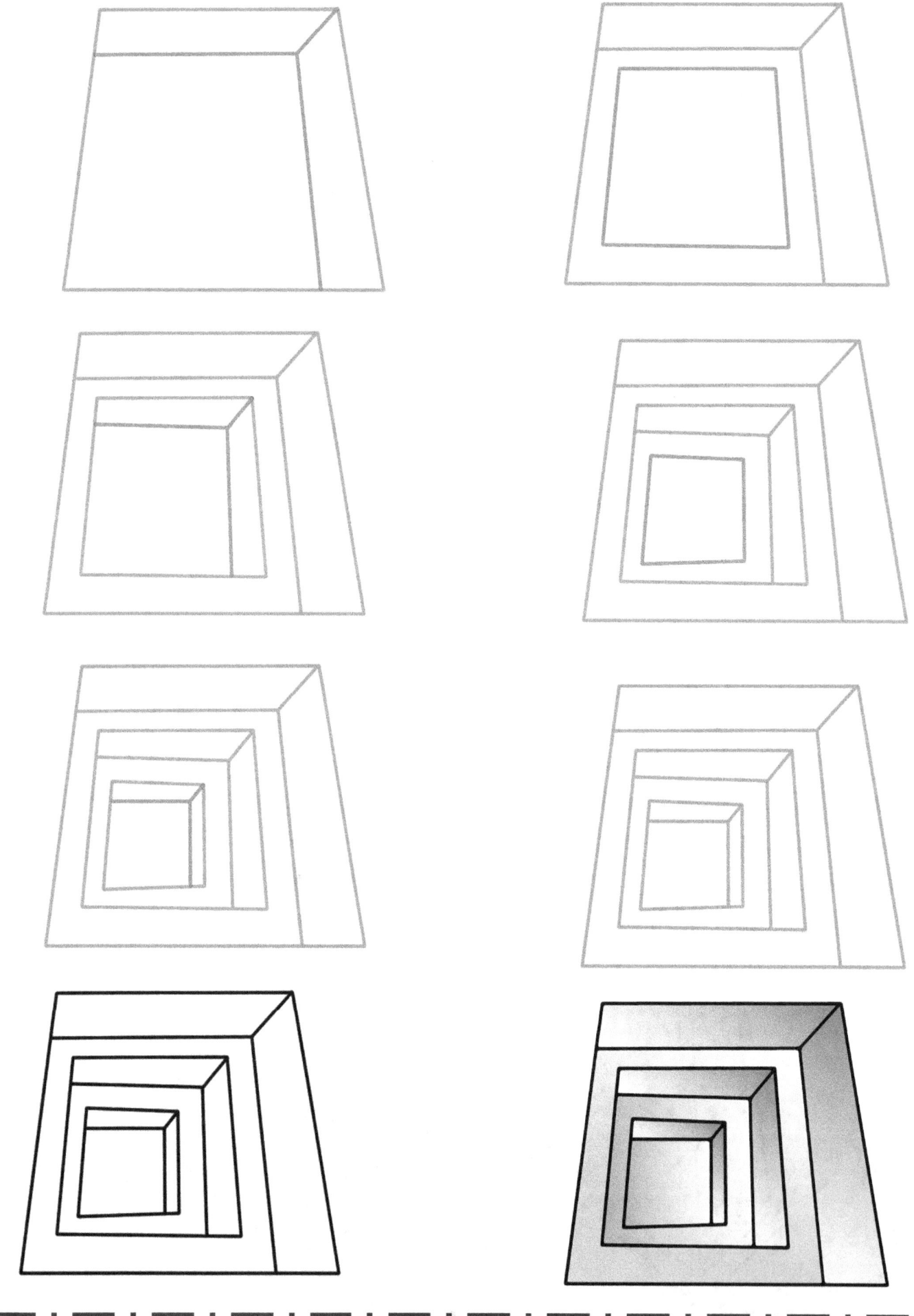

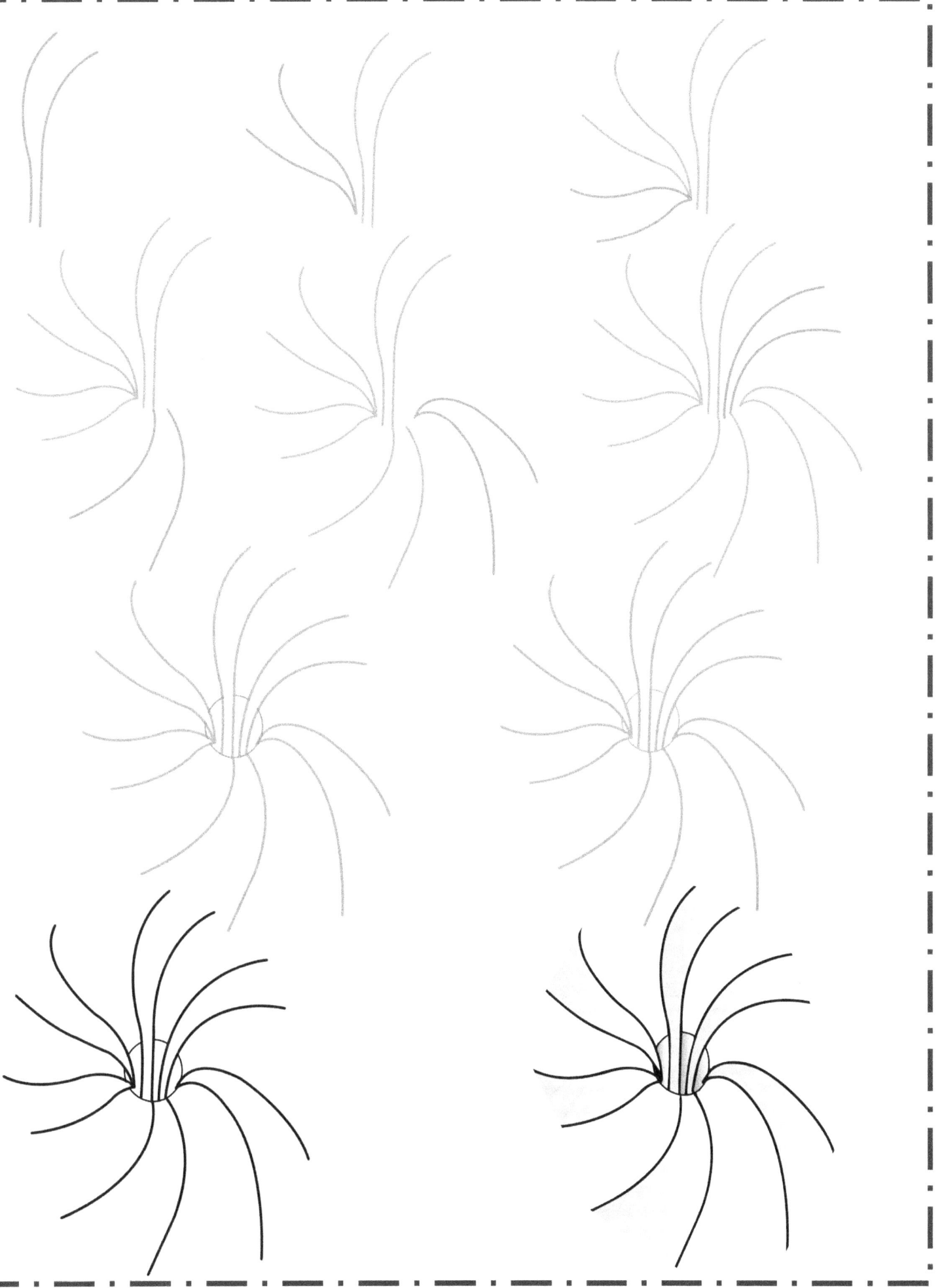

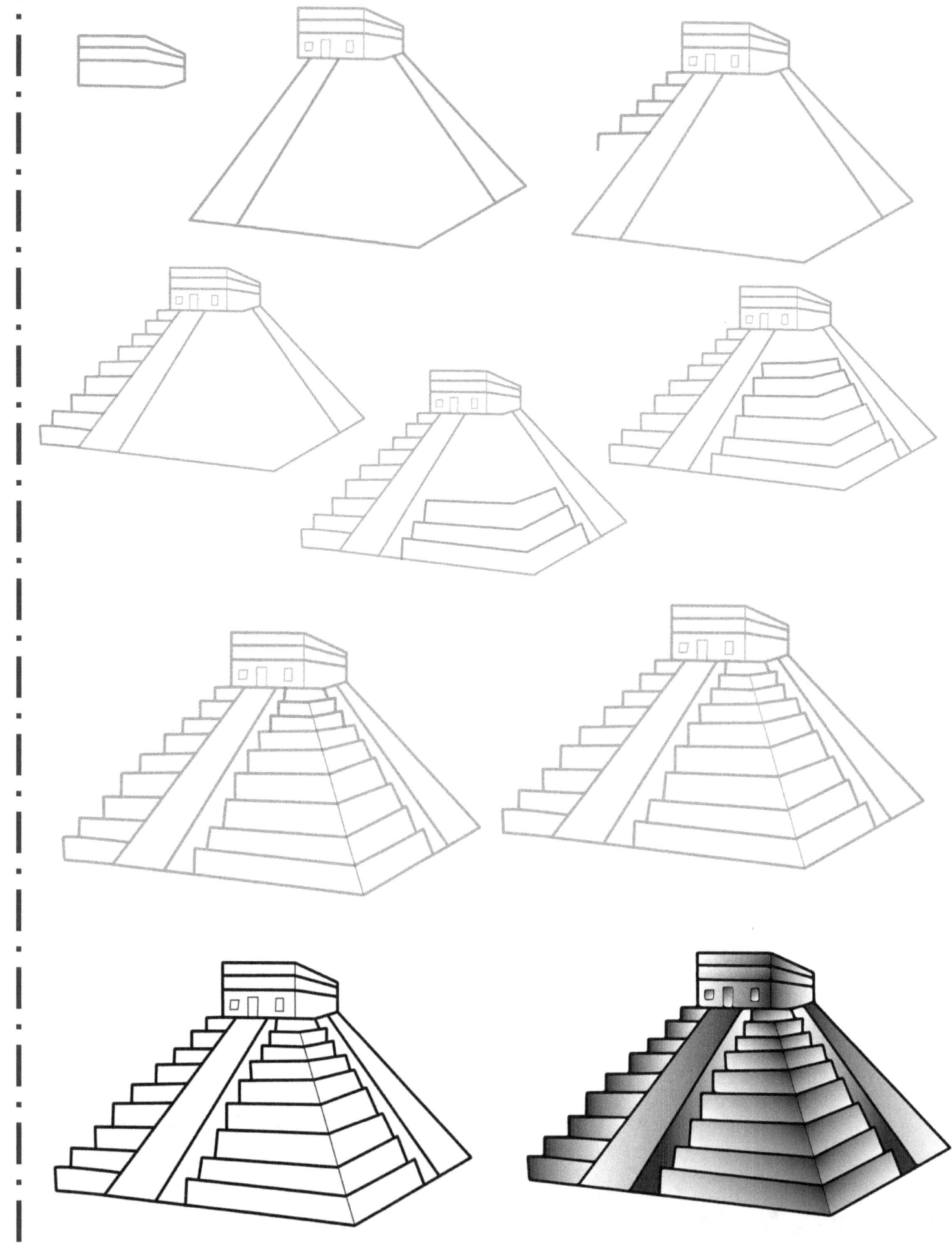

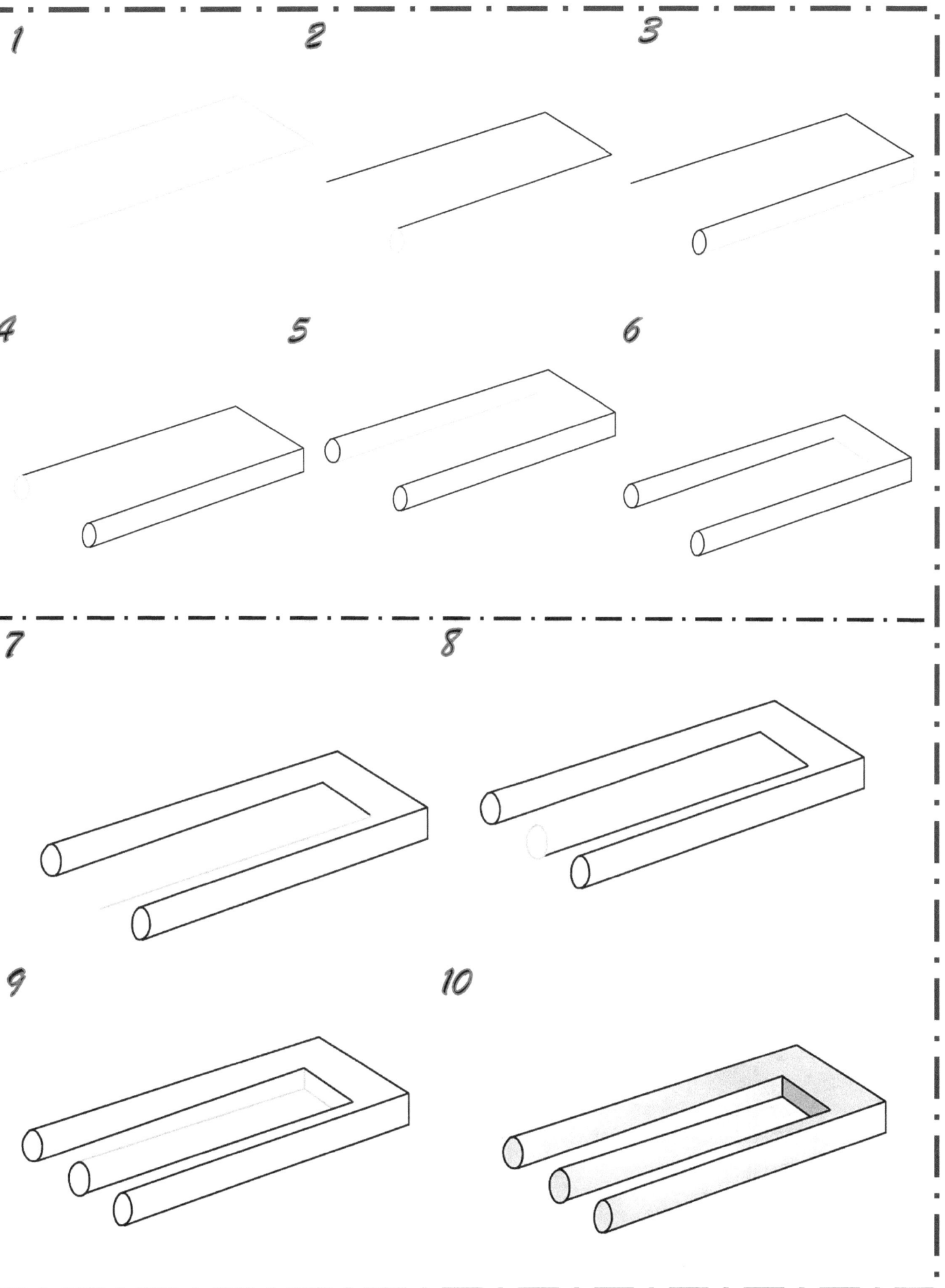

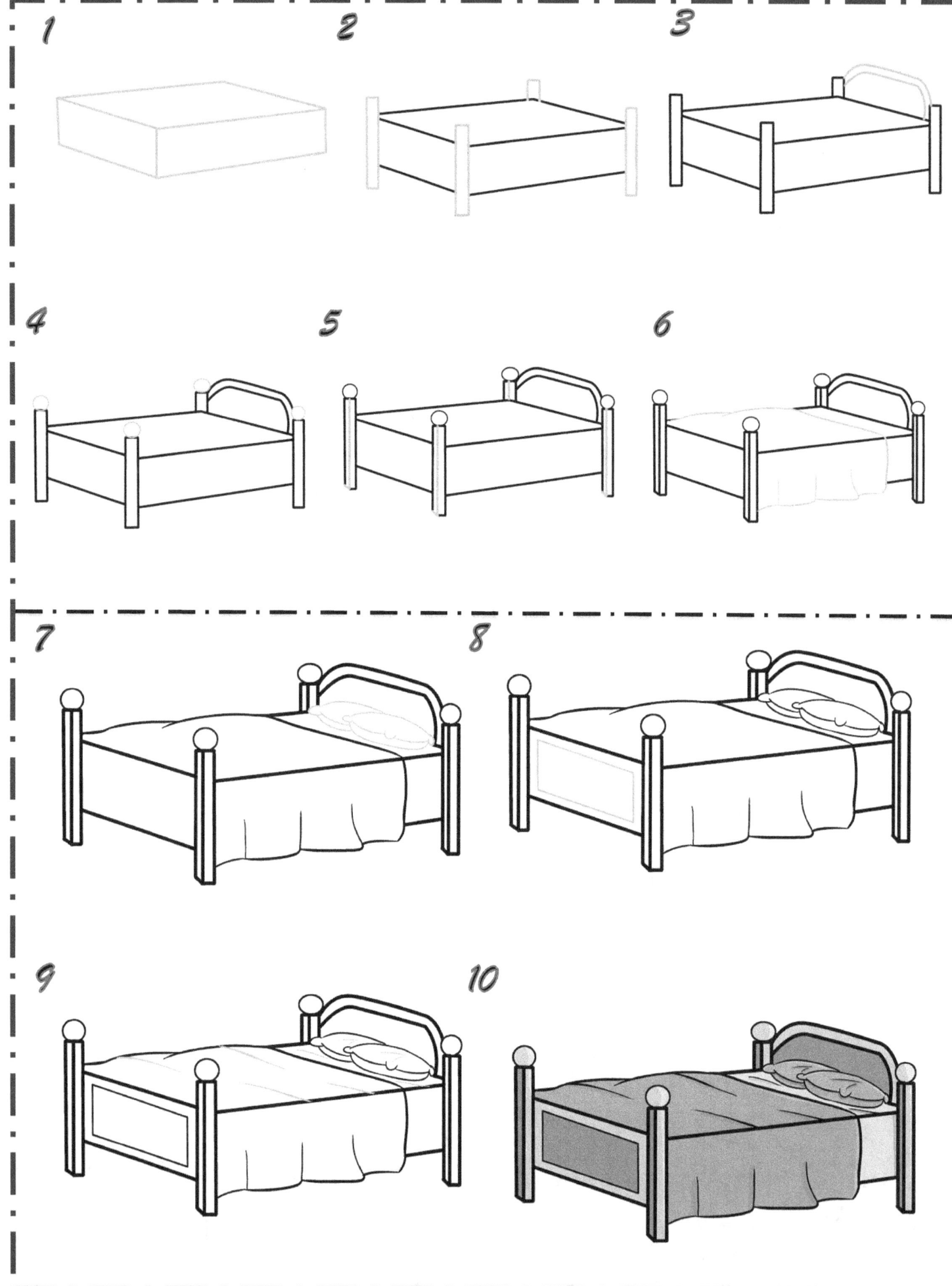

1

2

3

4

5

6

7

8

9

10

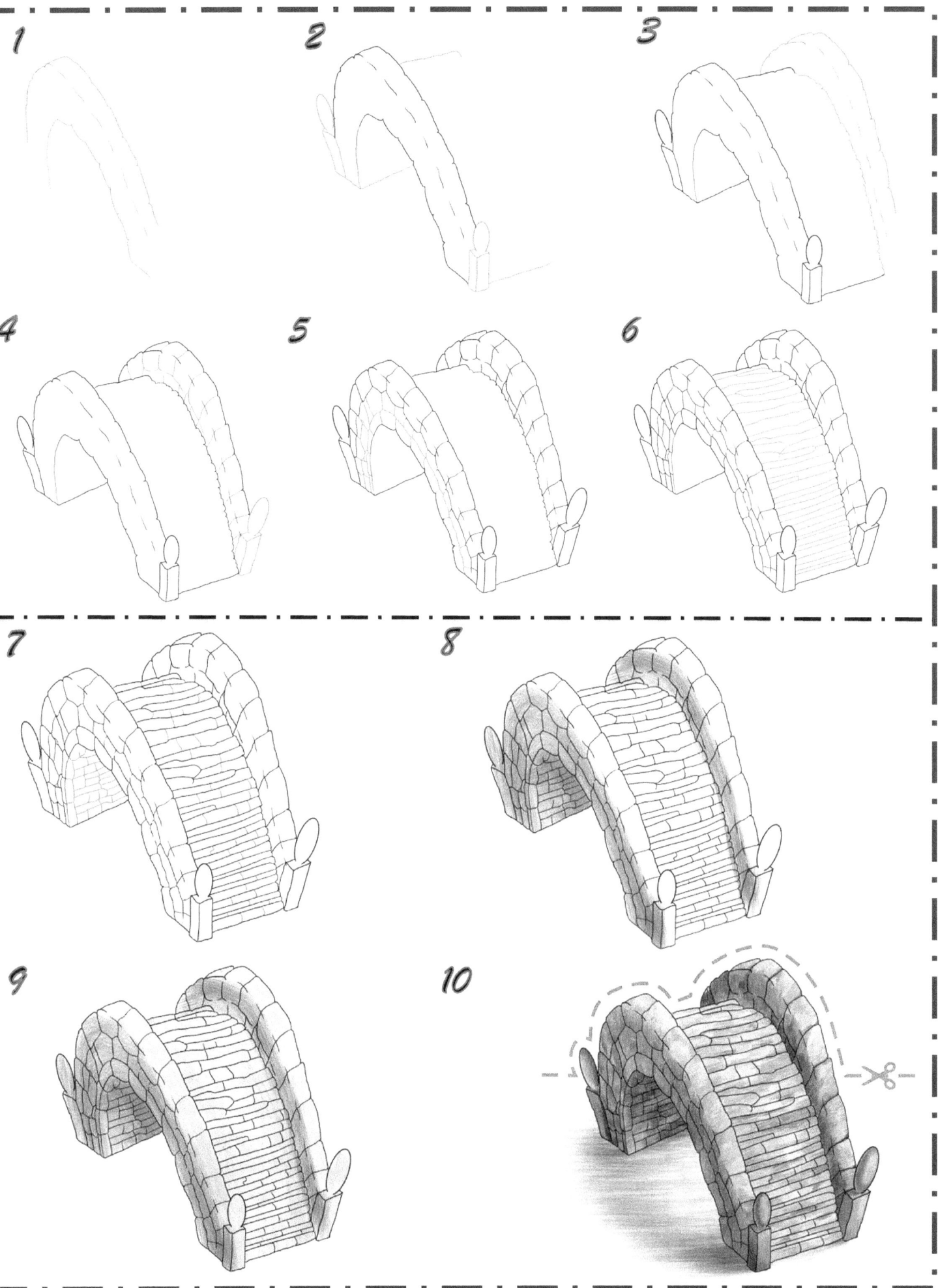

1

2

3

4

5

6

7

8

9

10

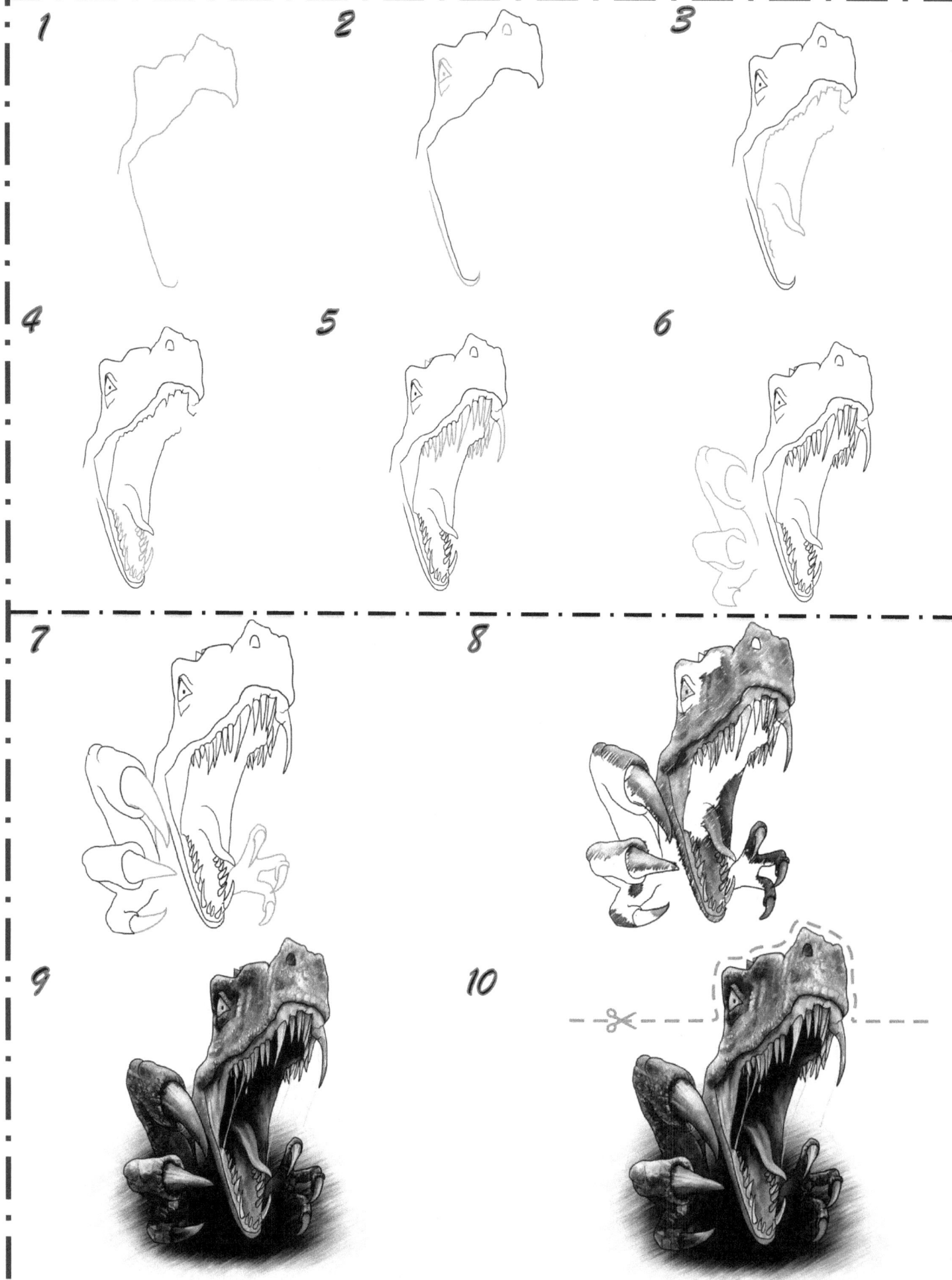

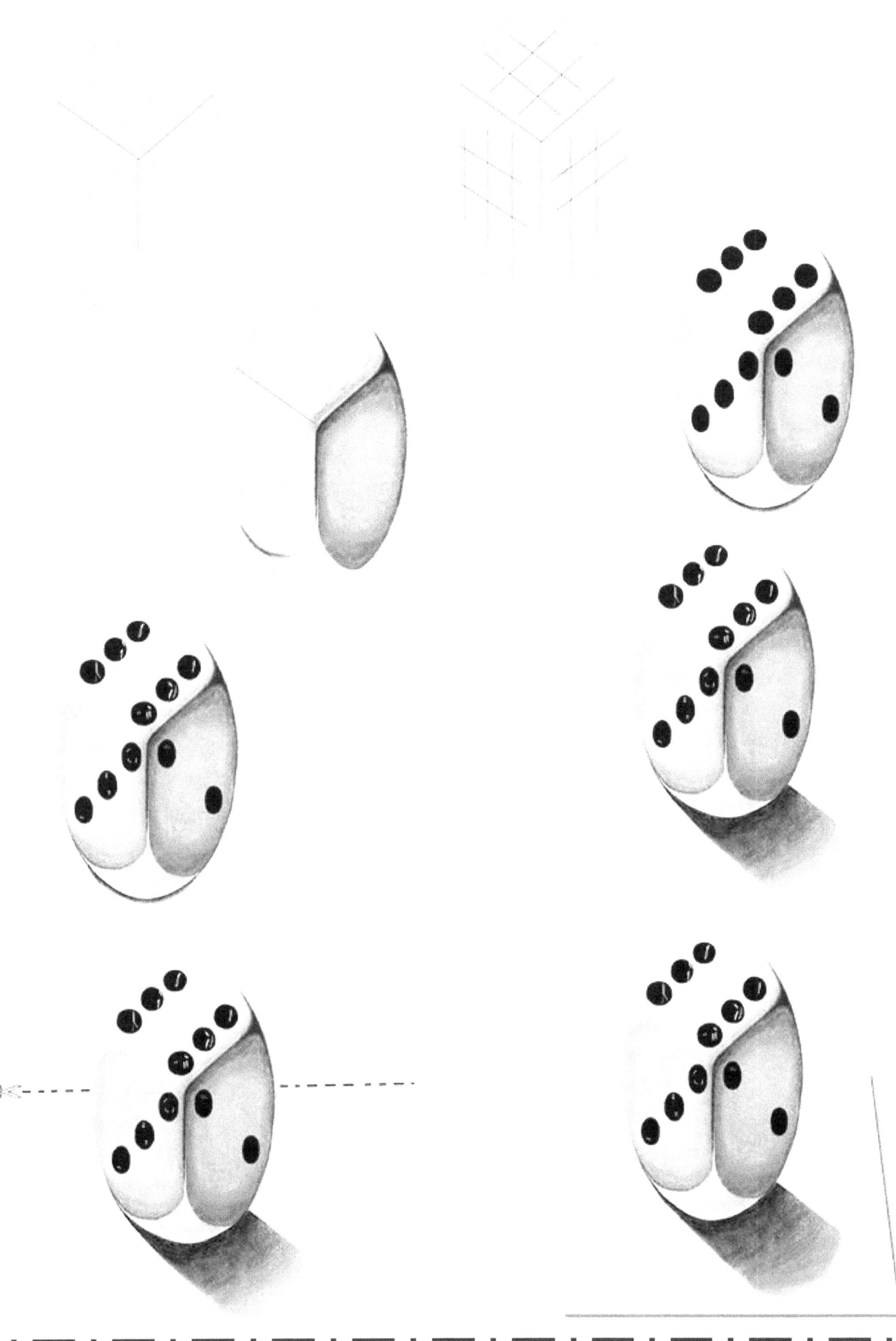

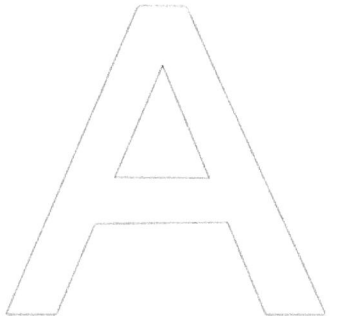
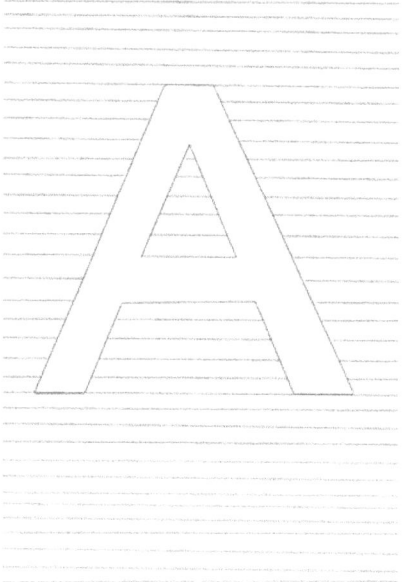
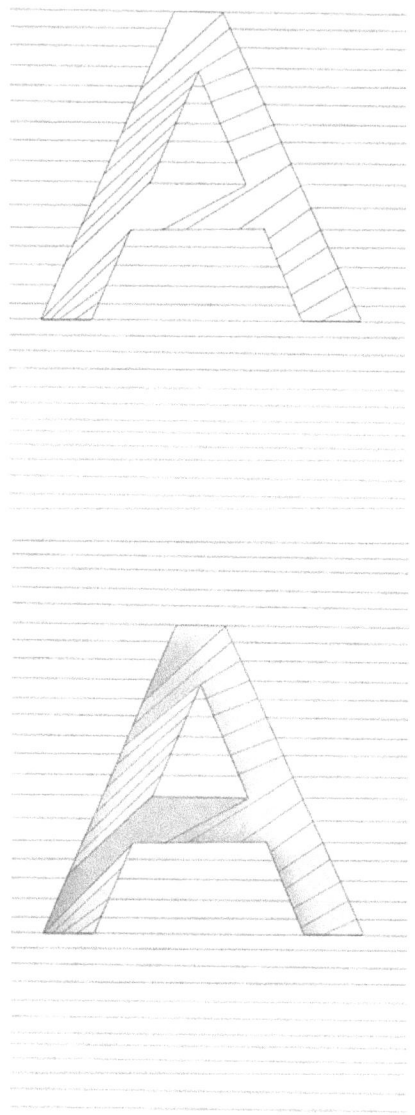
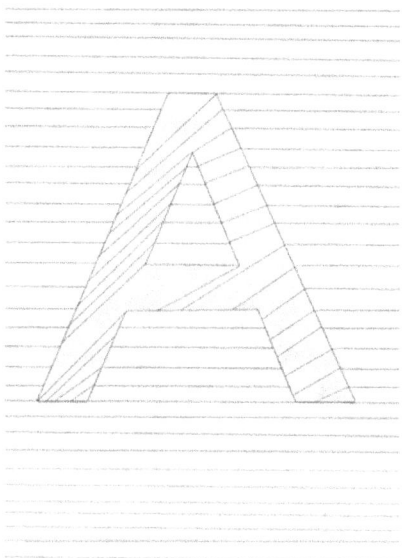
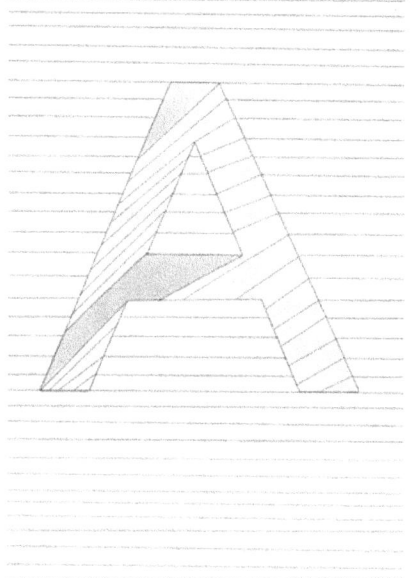
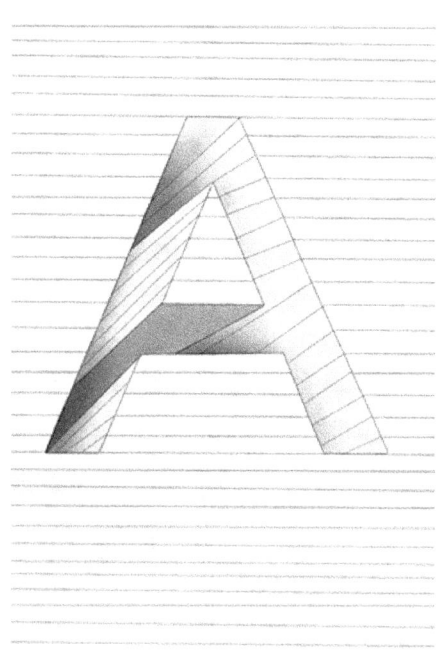
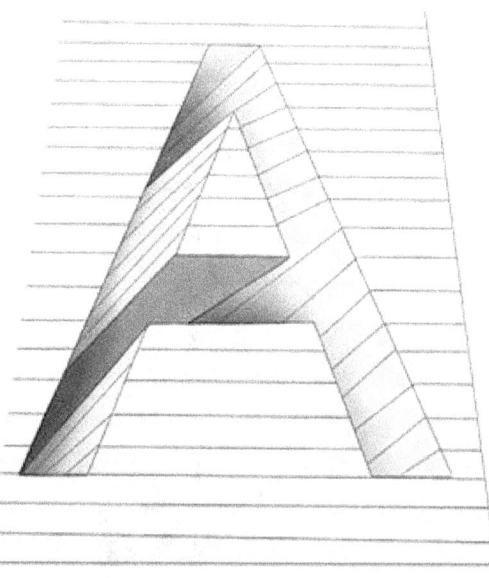

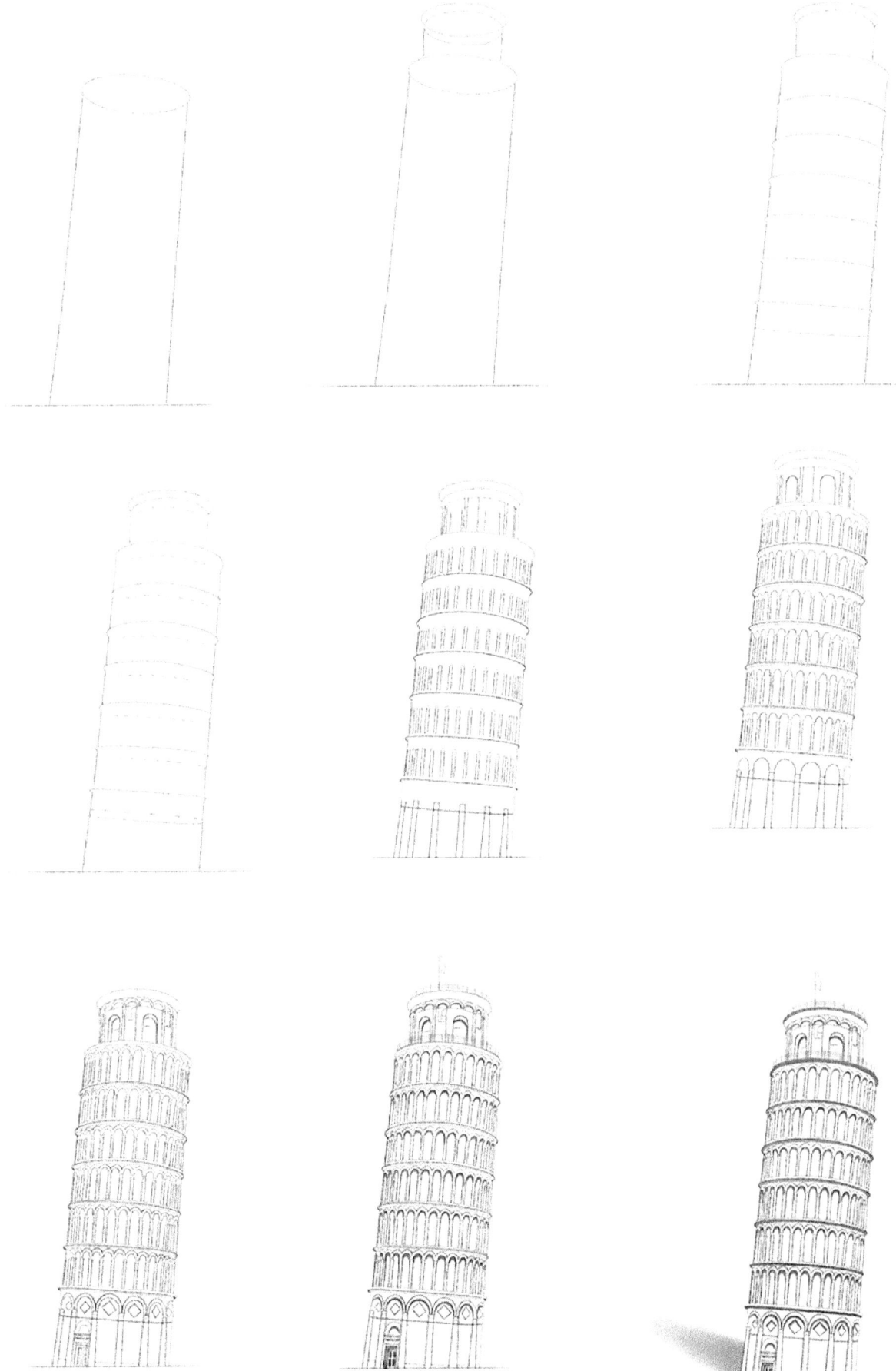

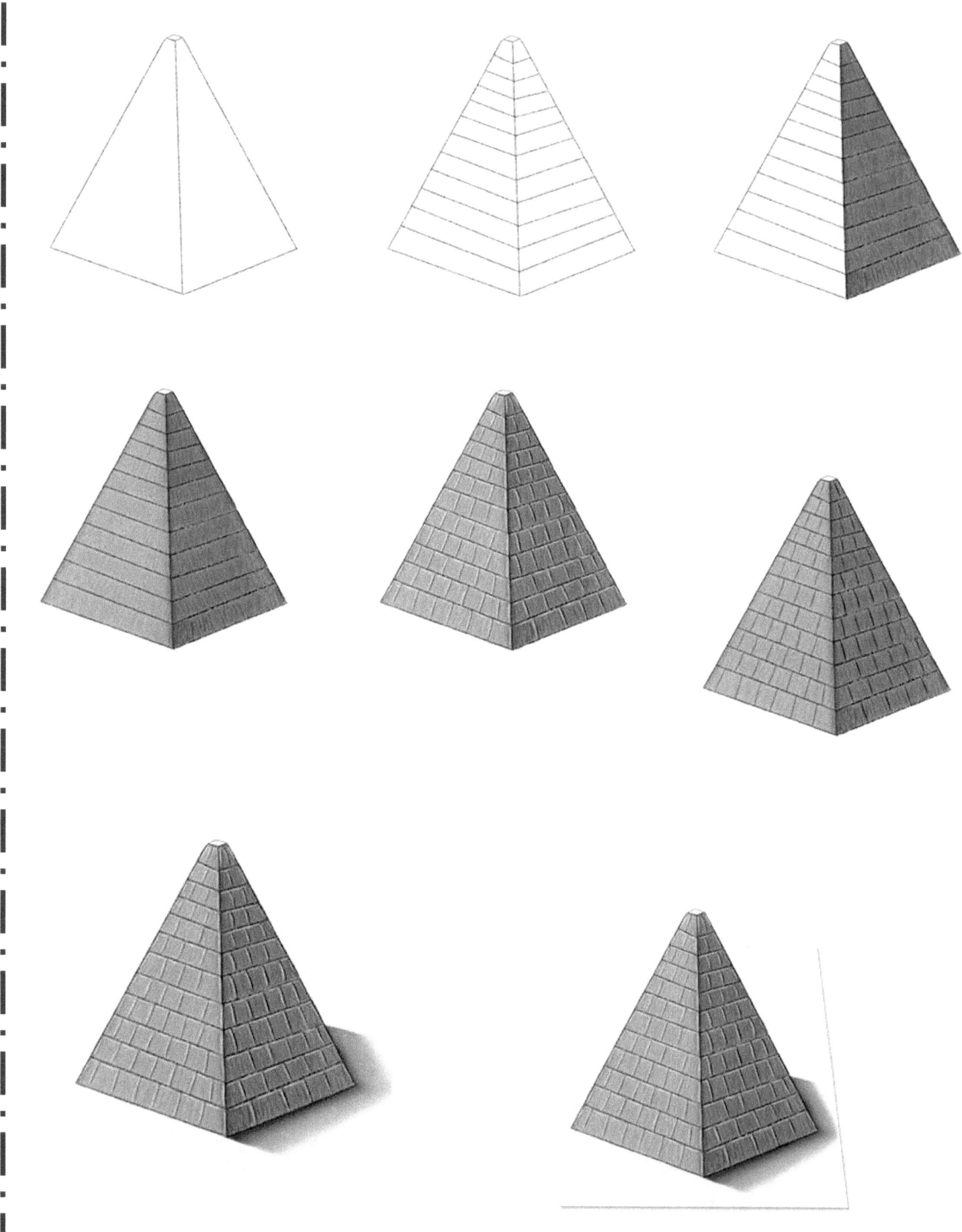

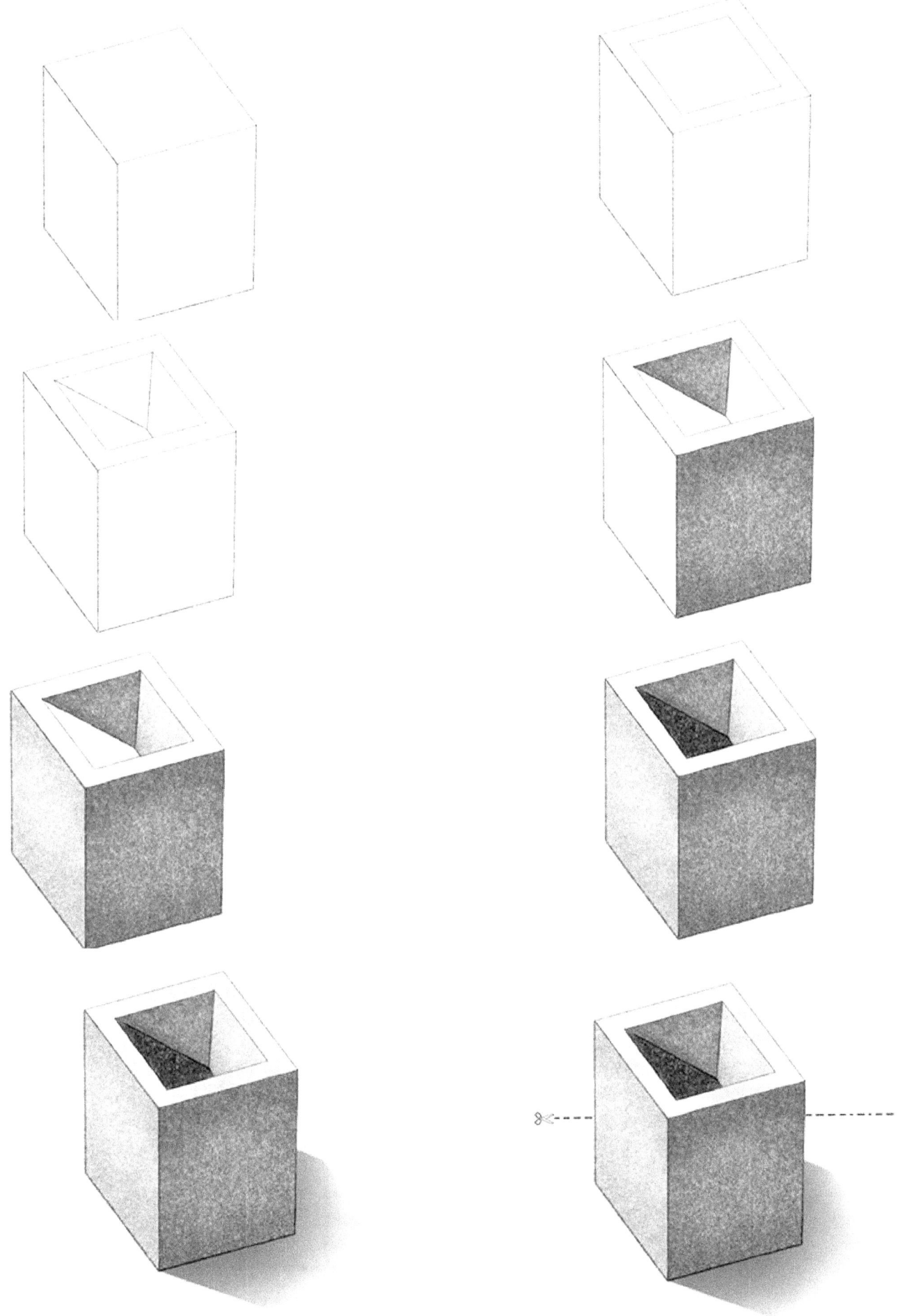

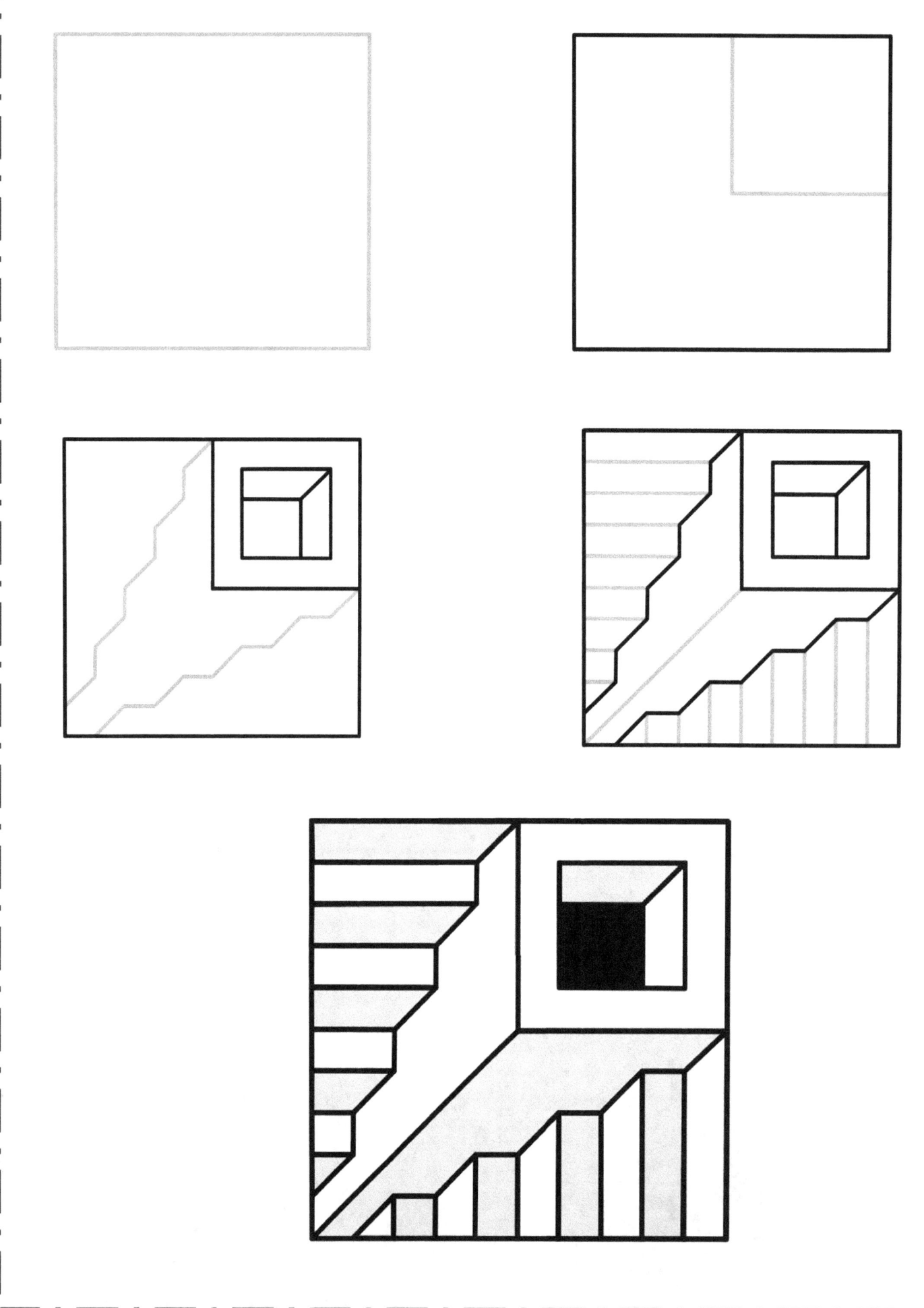

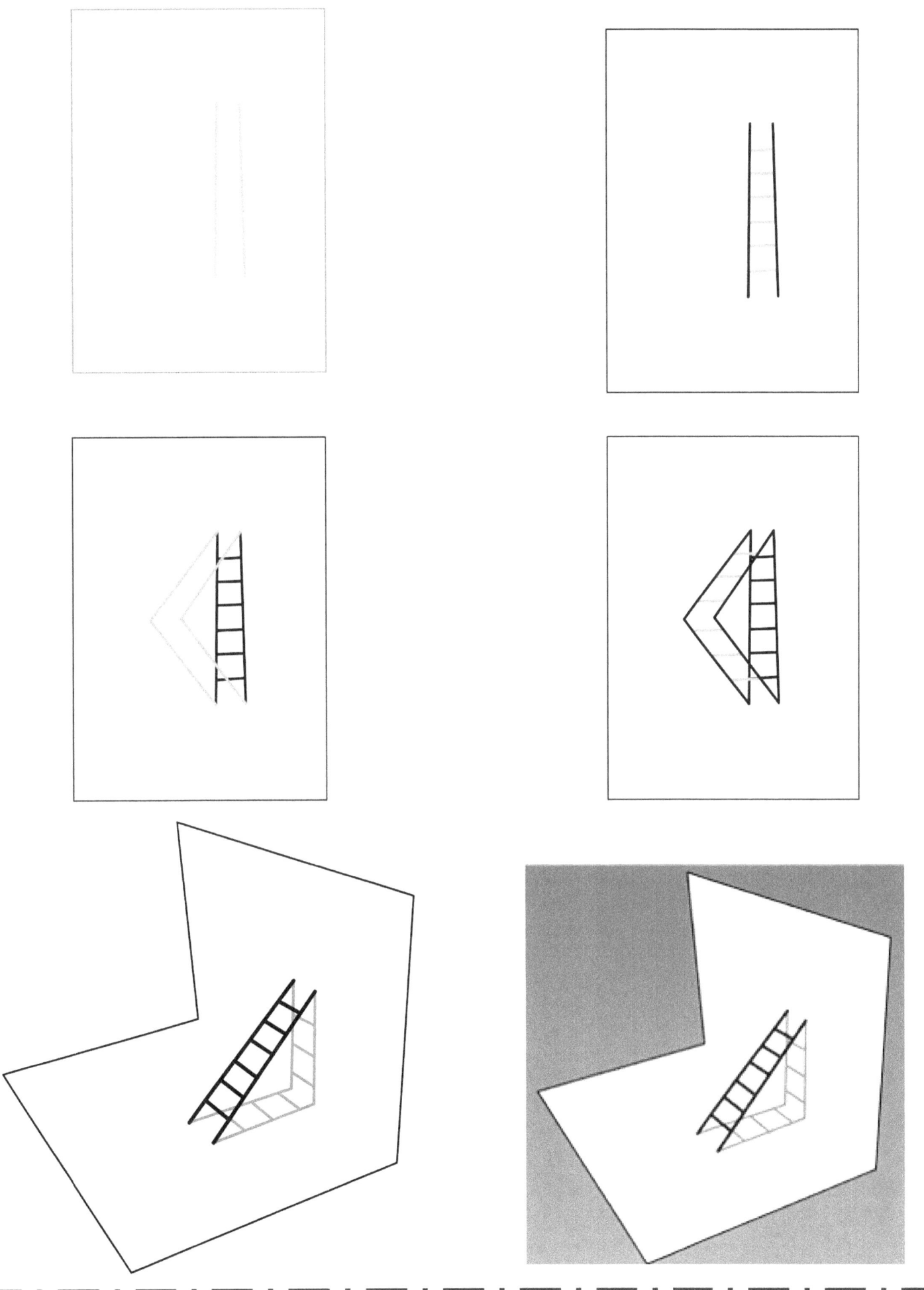

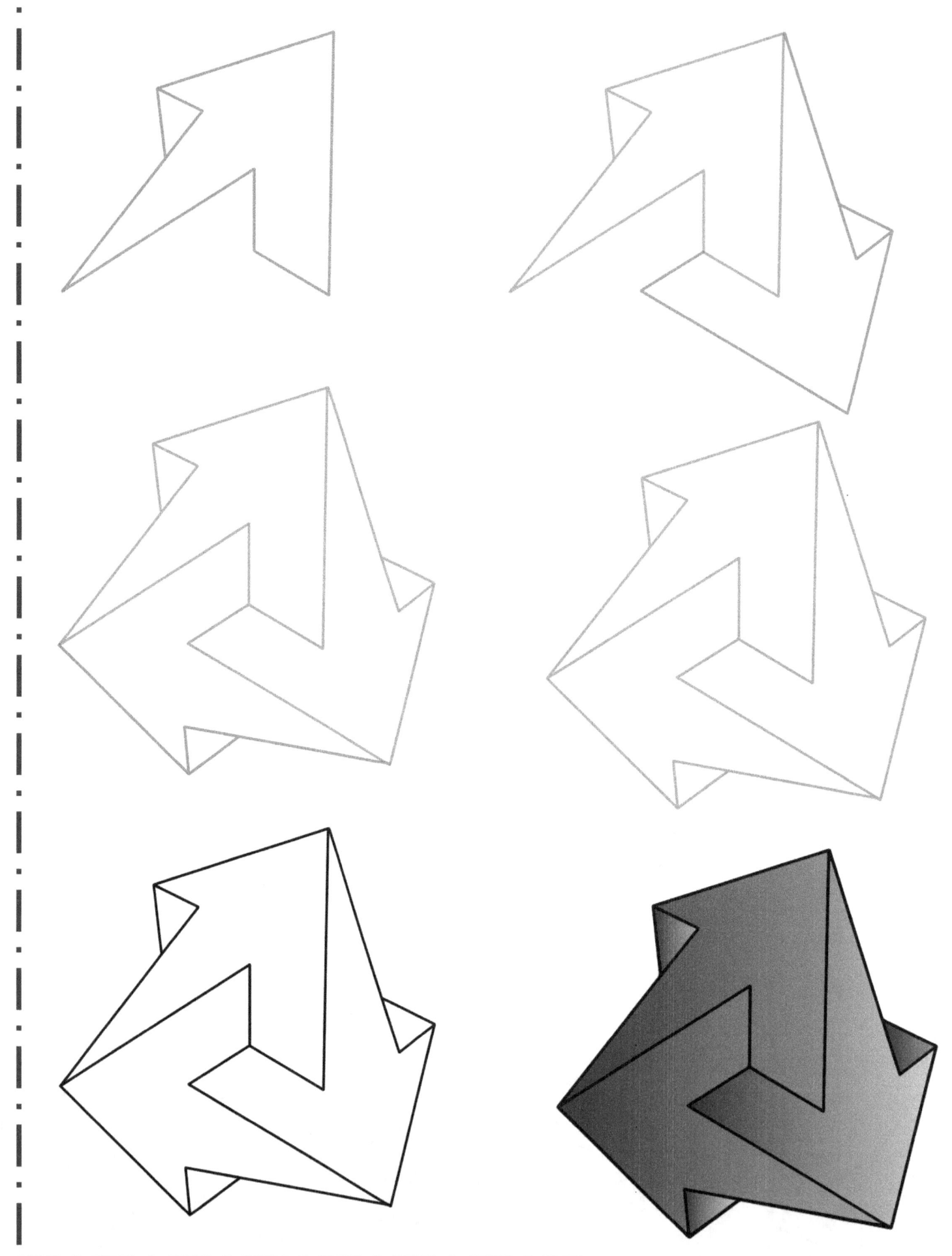

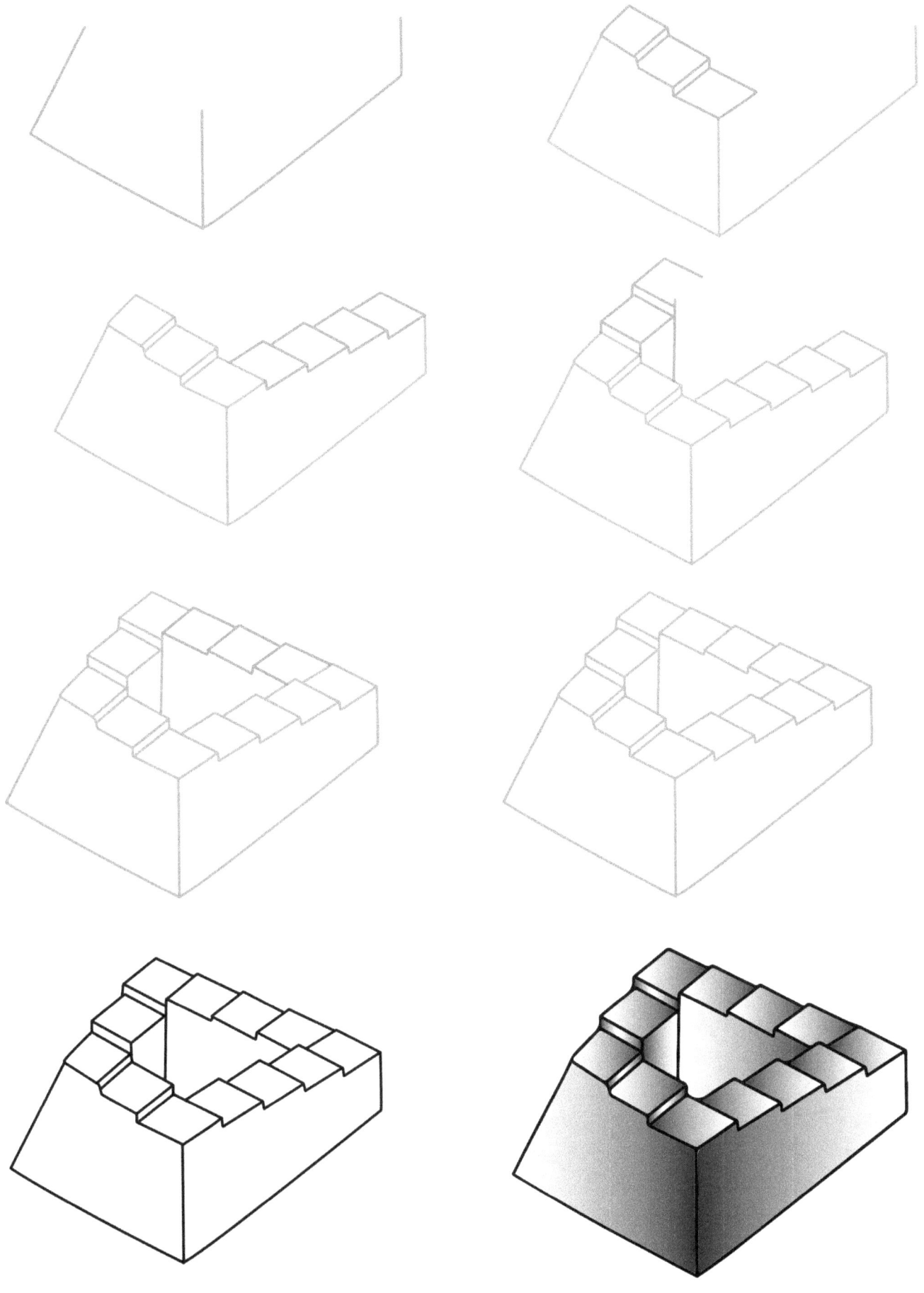

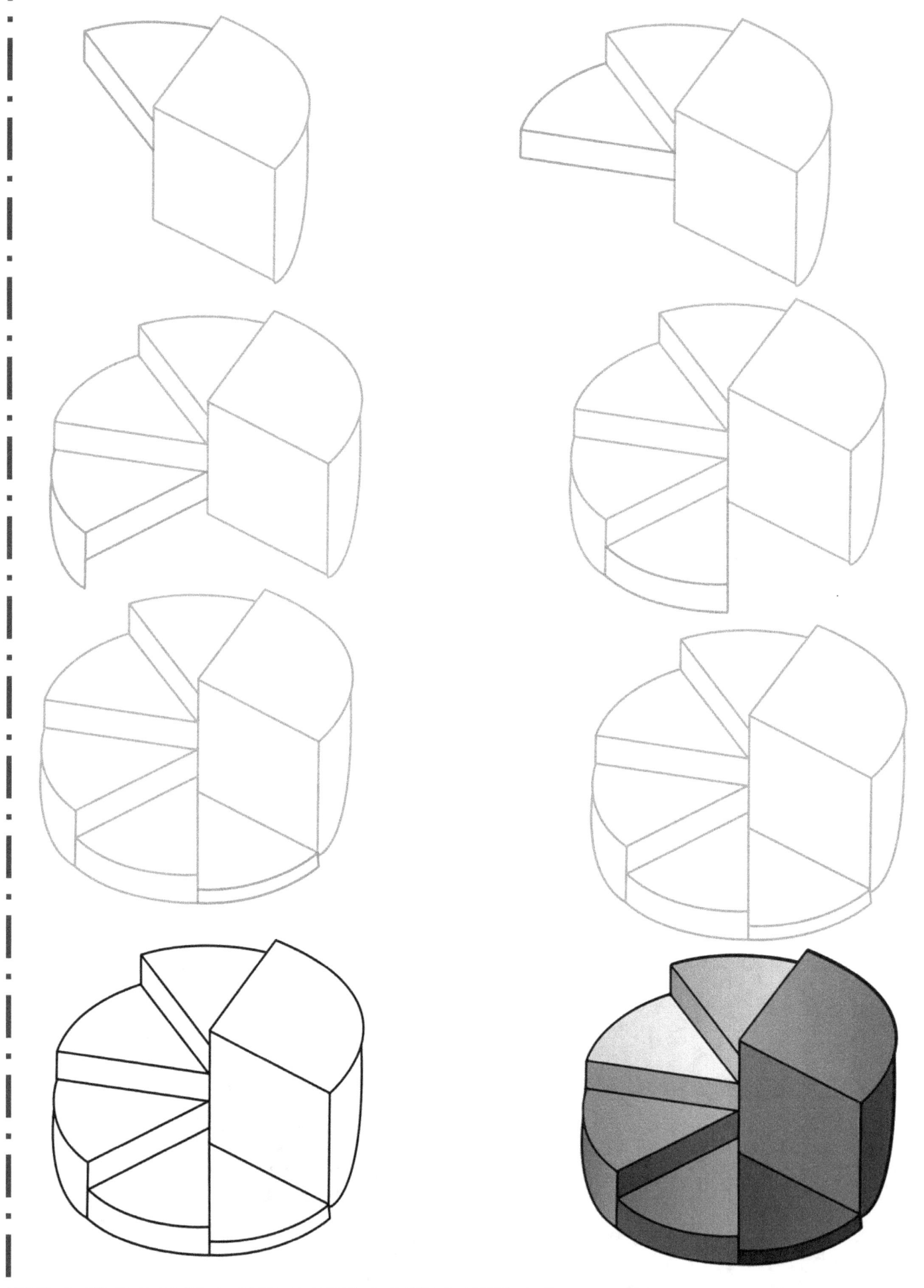

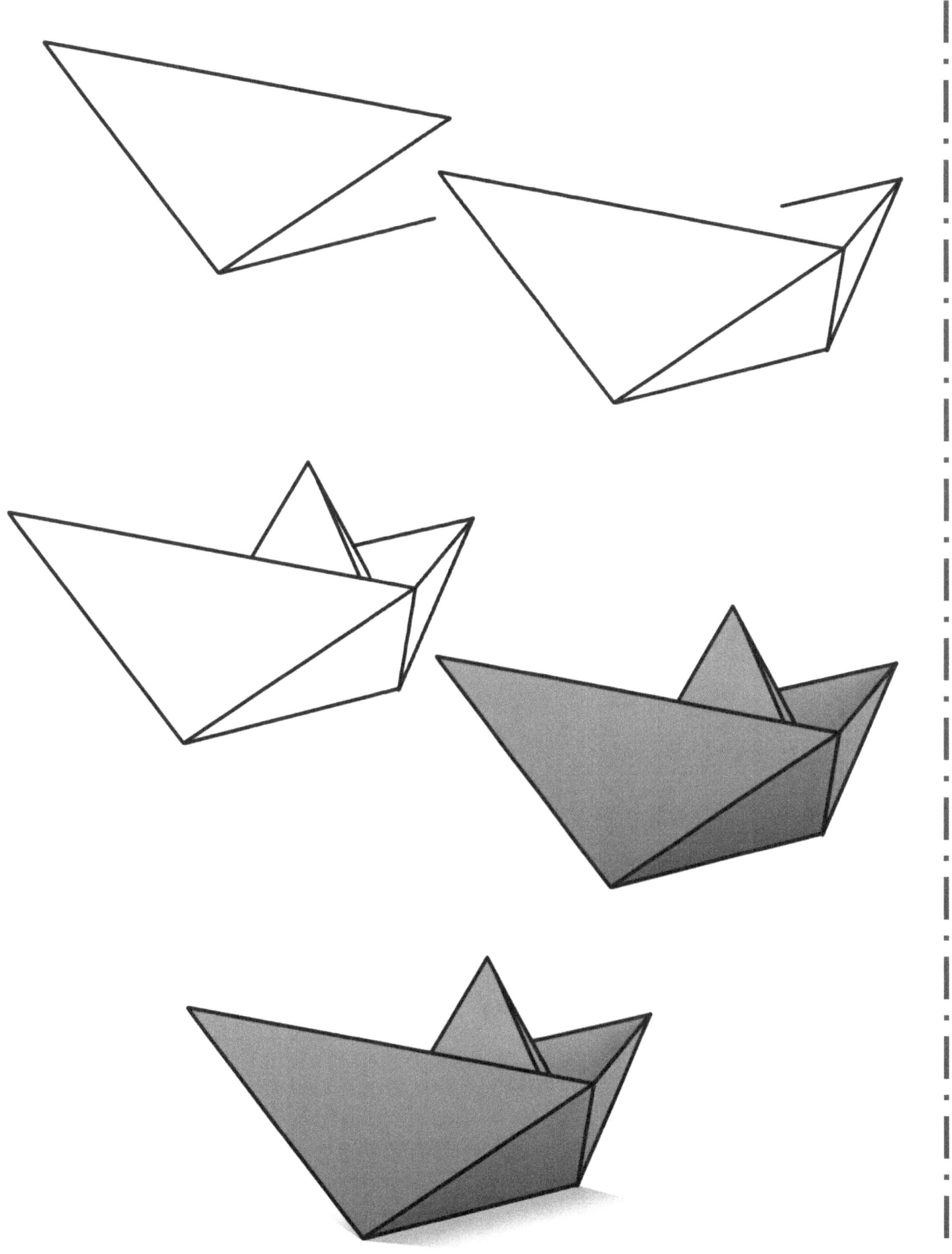

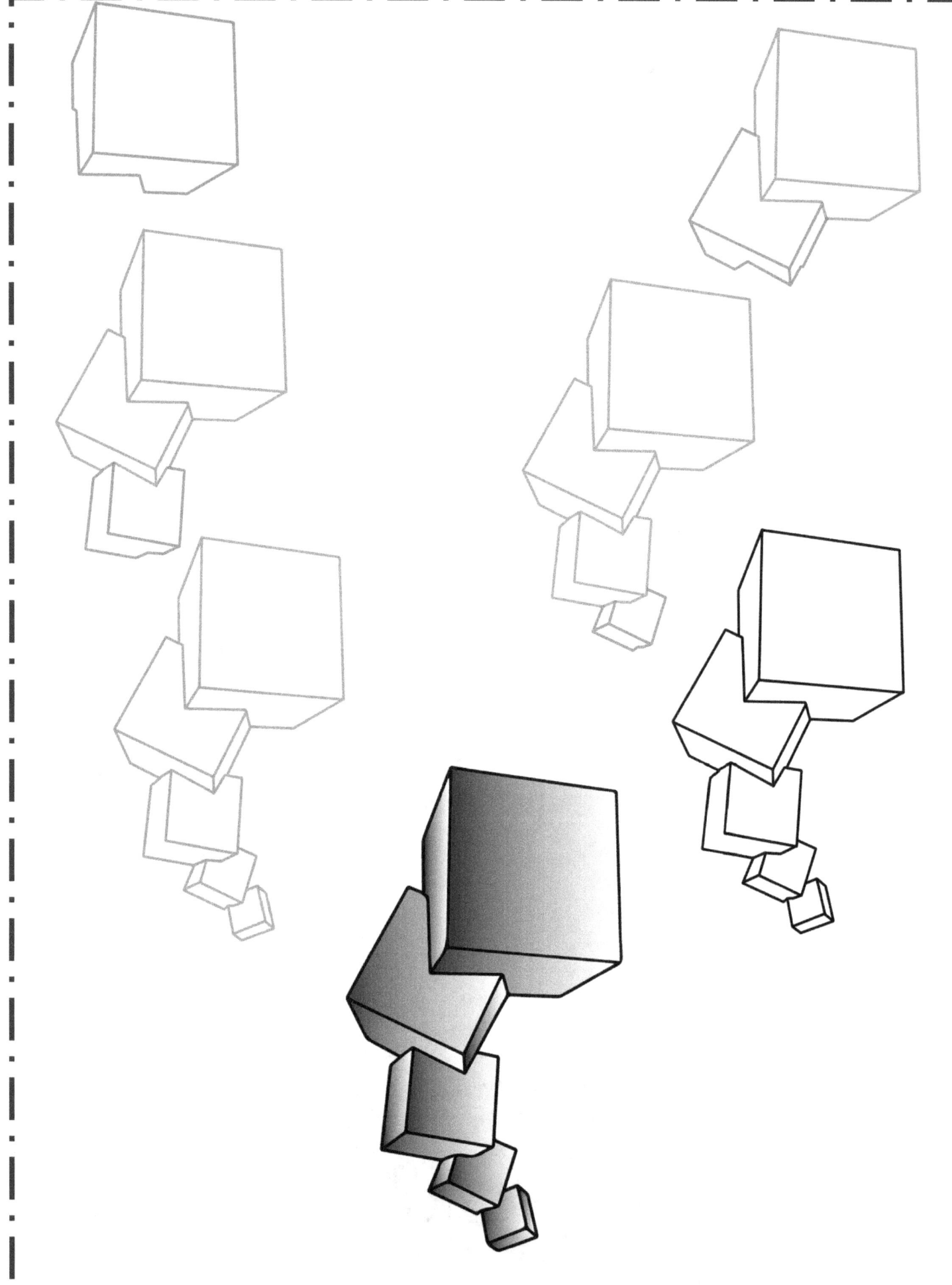

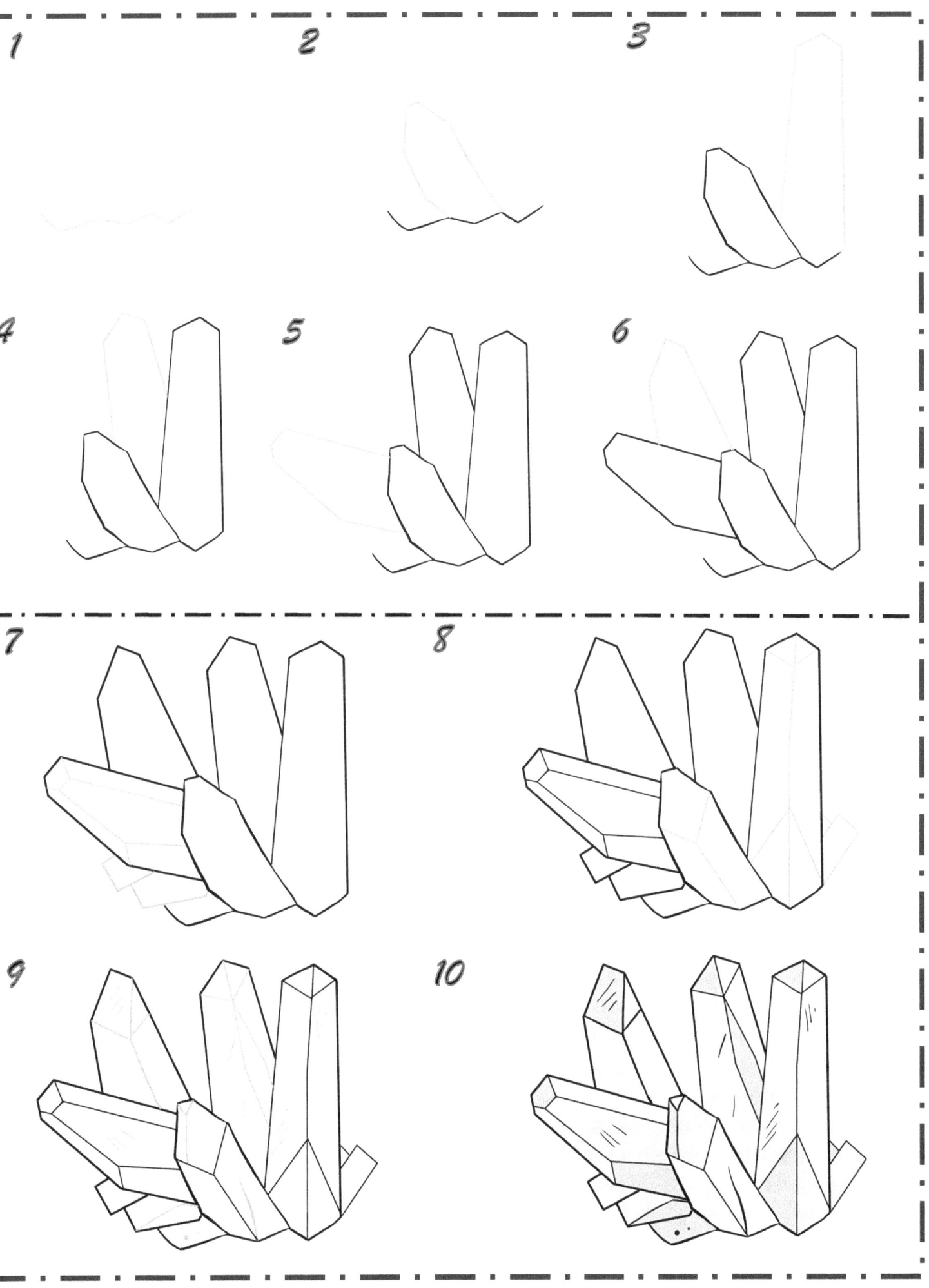

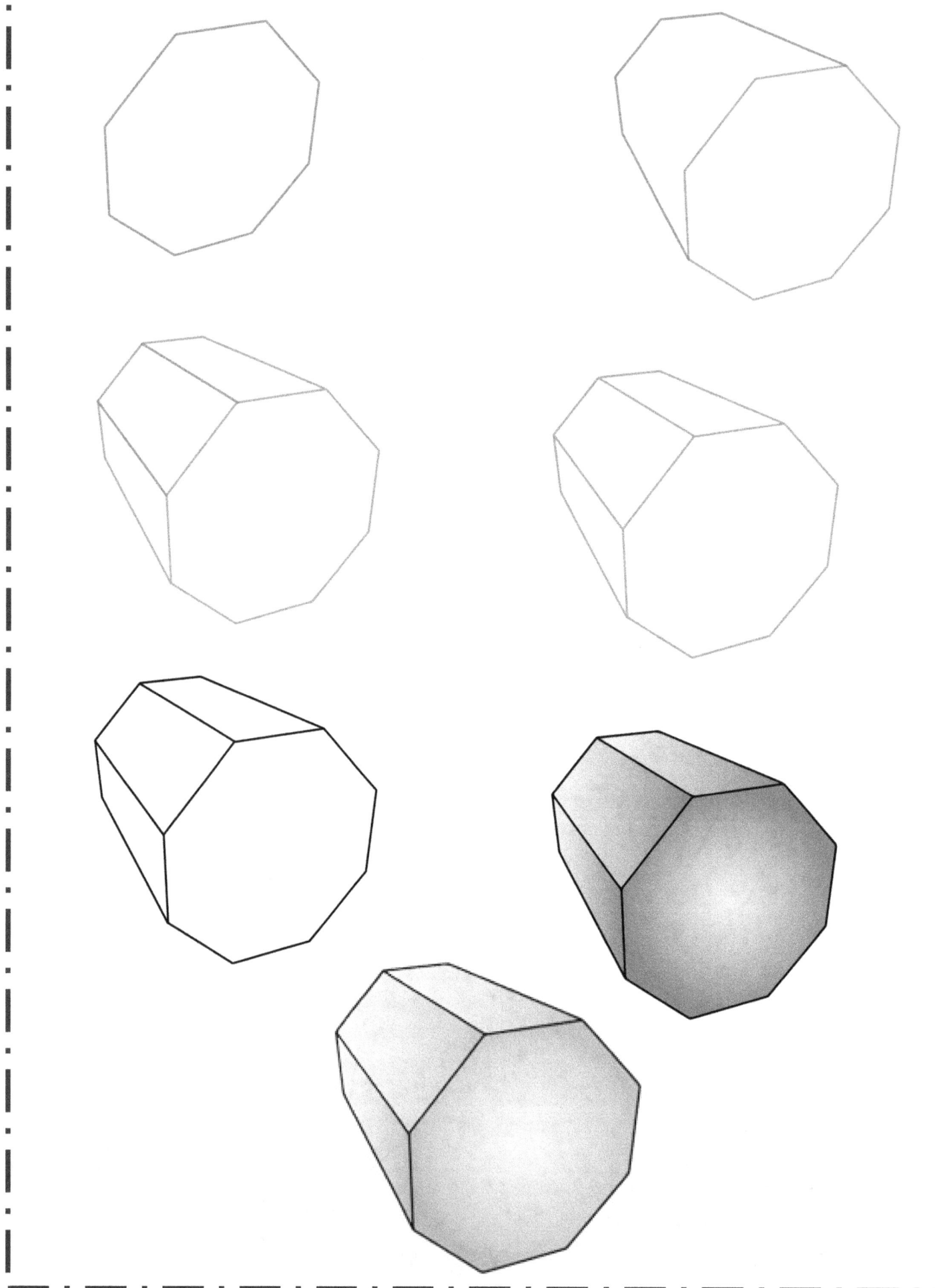

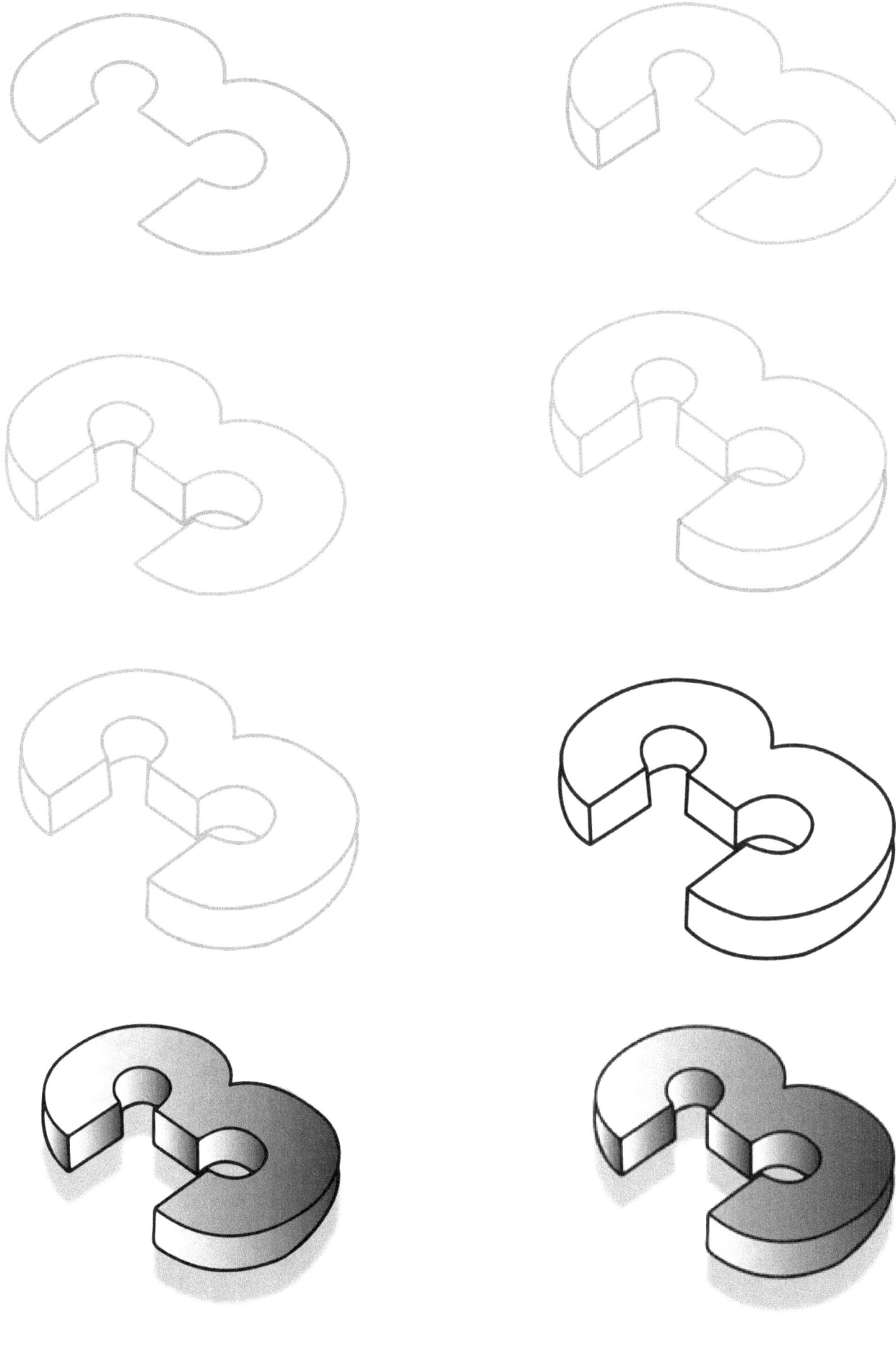

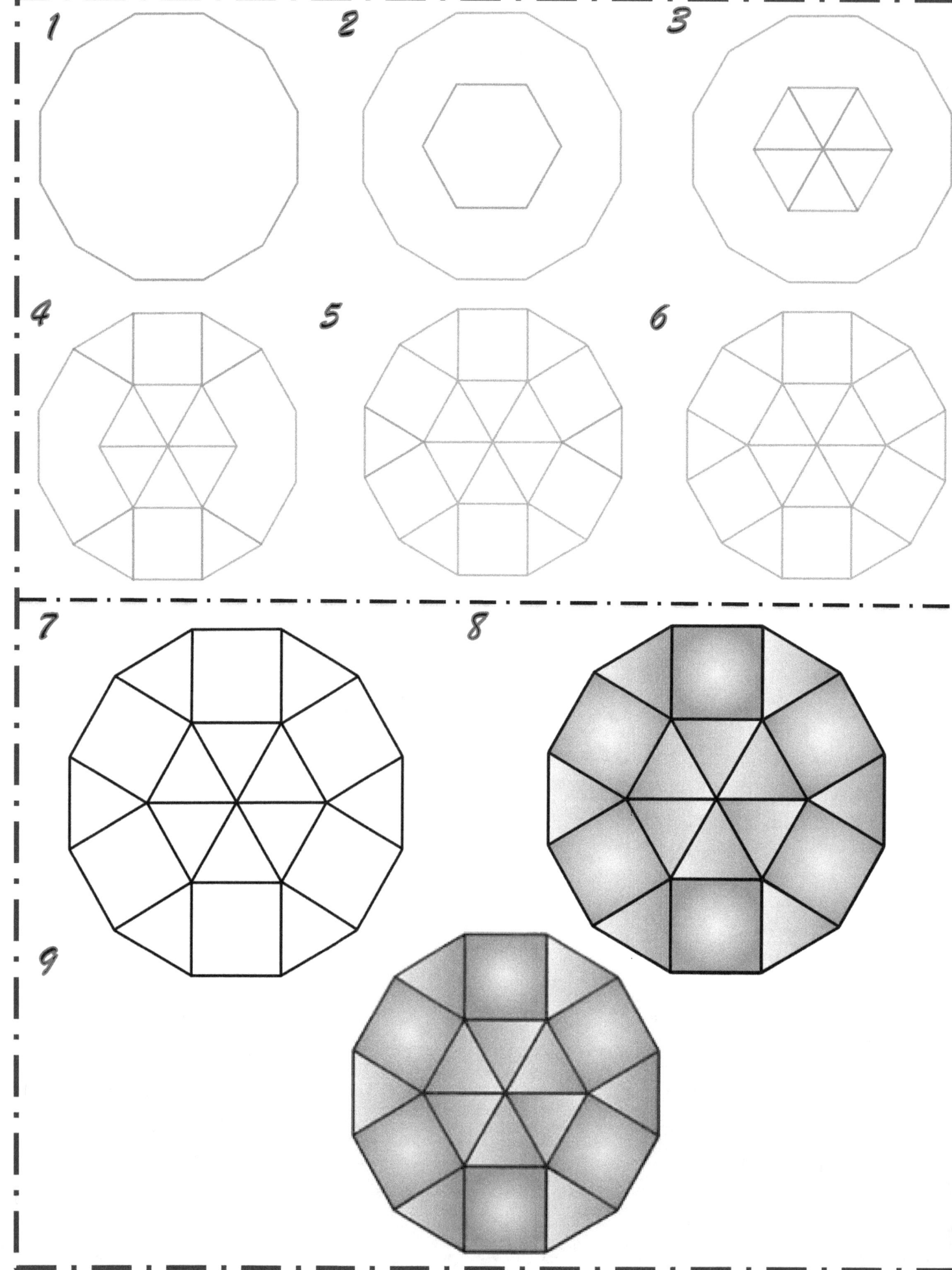

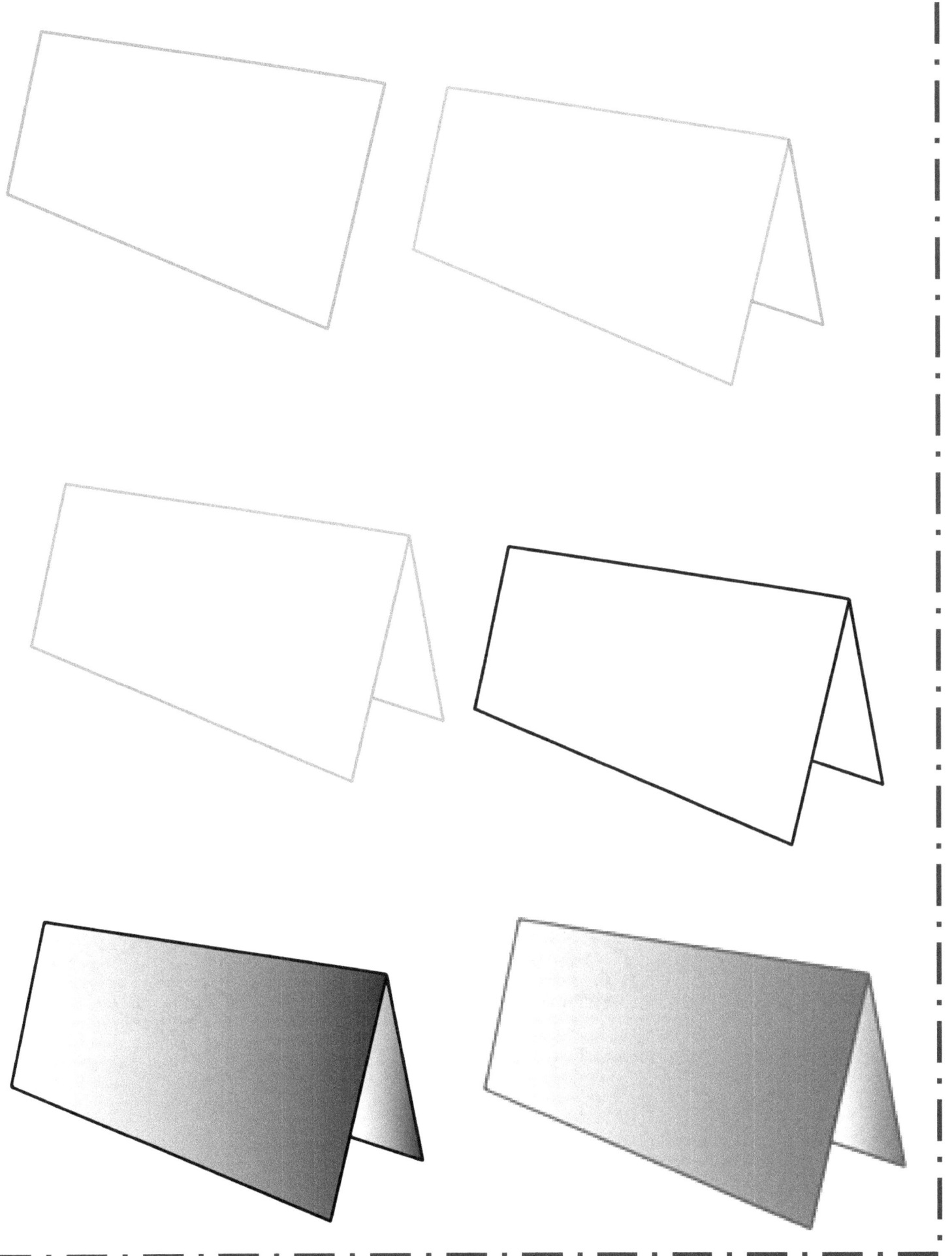

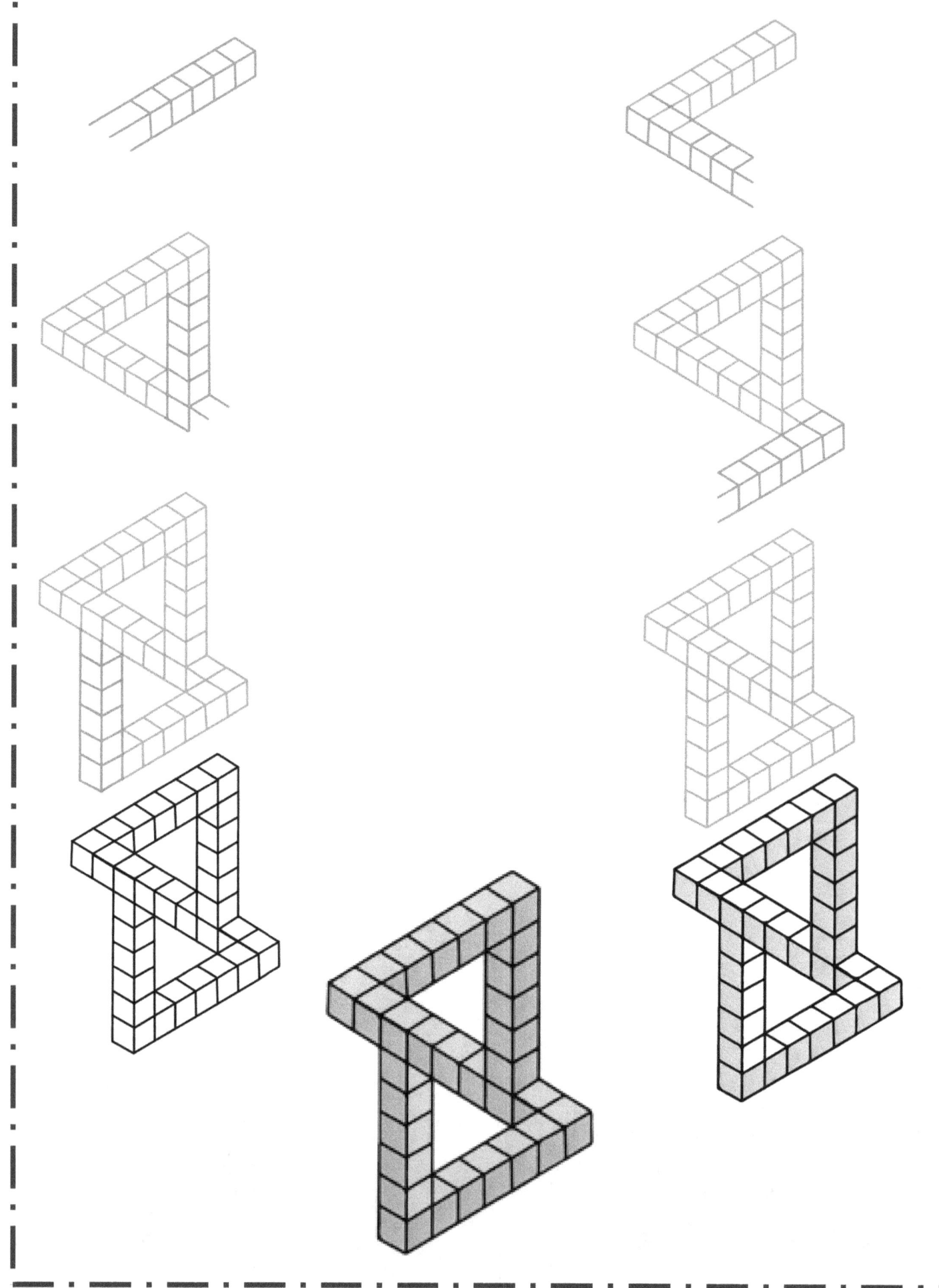

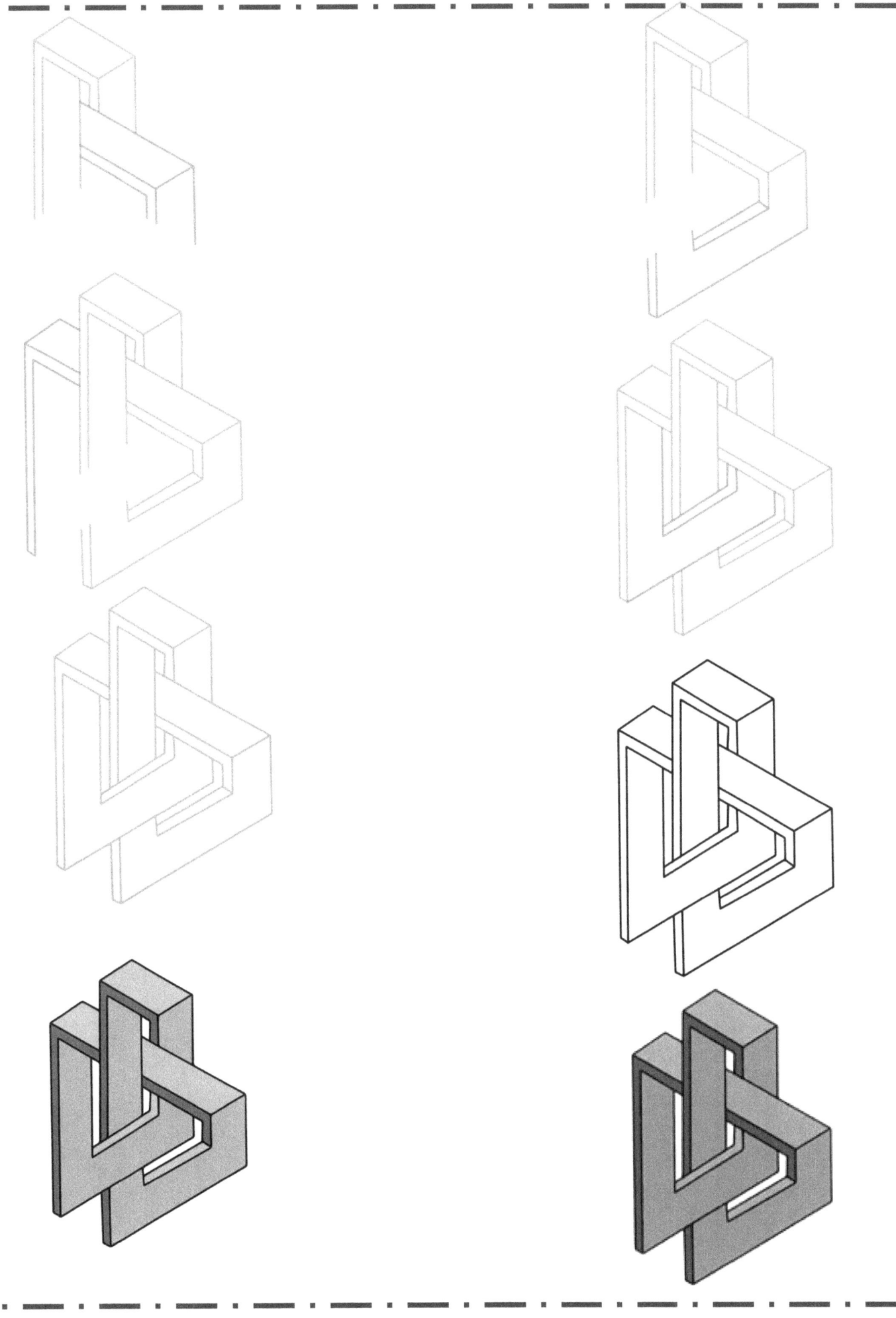

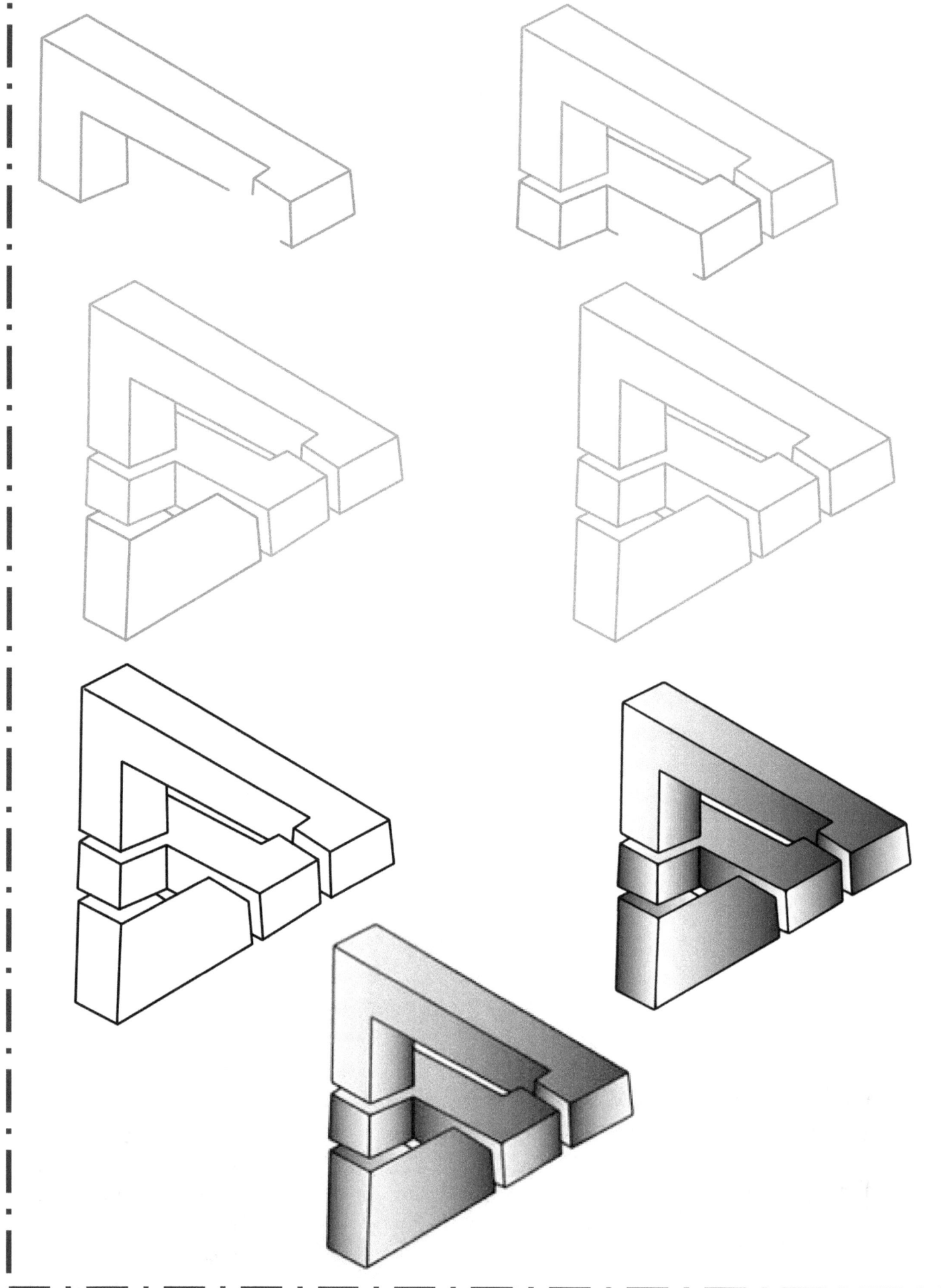

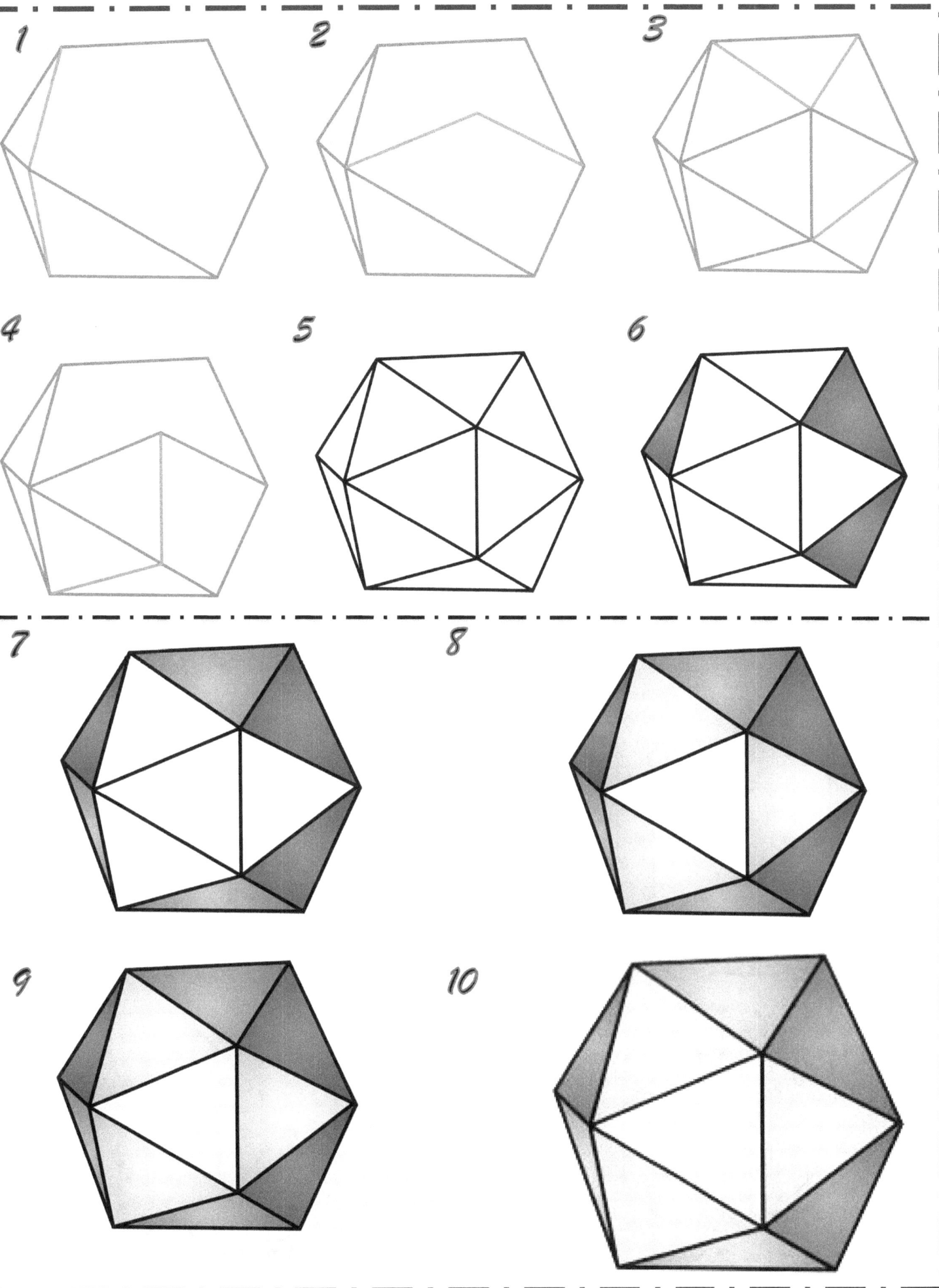

1

2

3

4

5

6

7

8

9

10

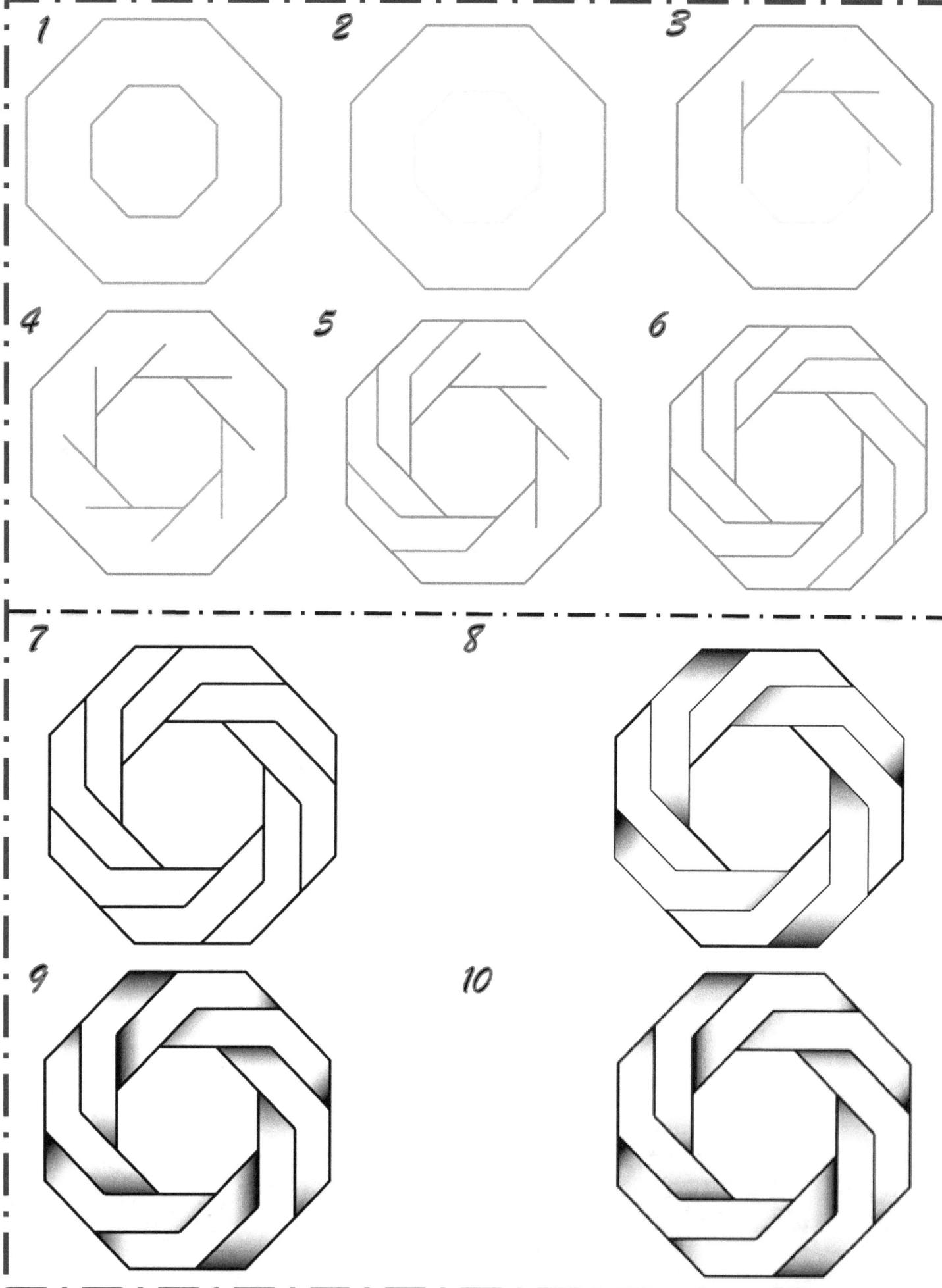

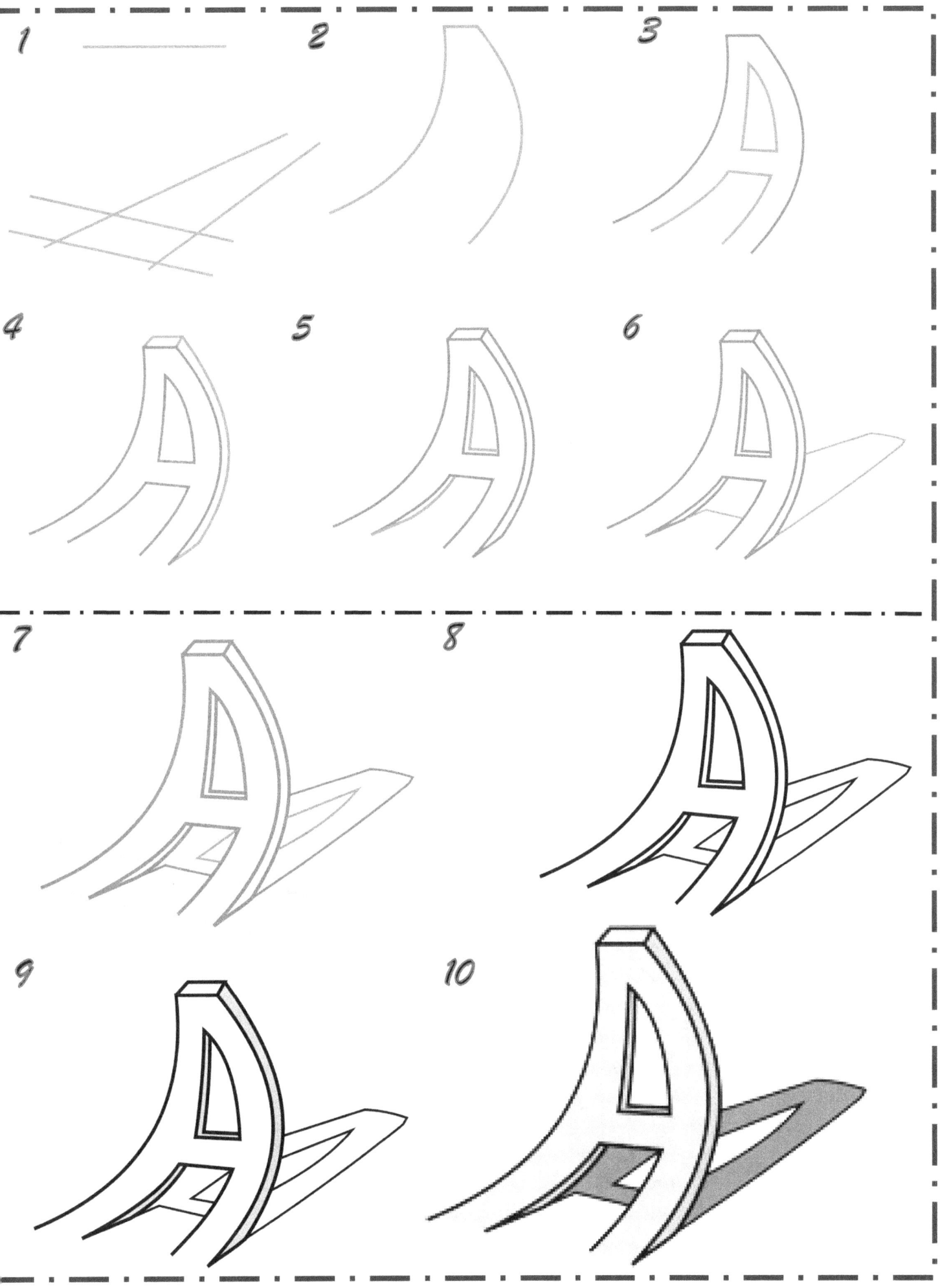

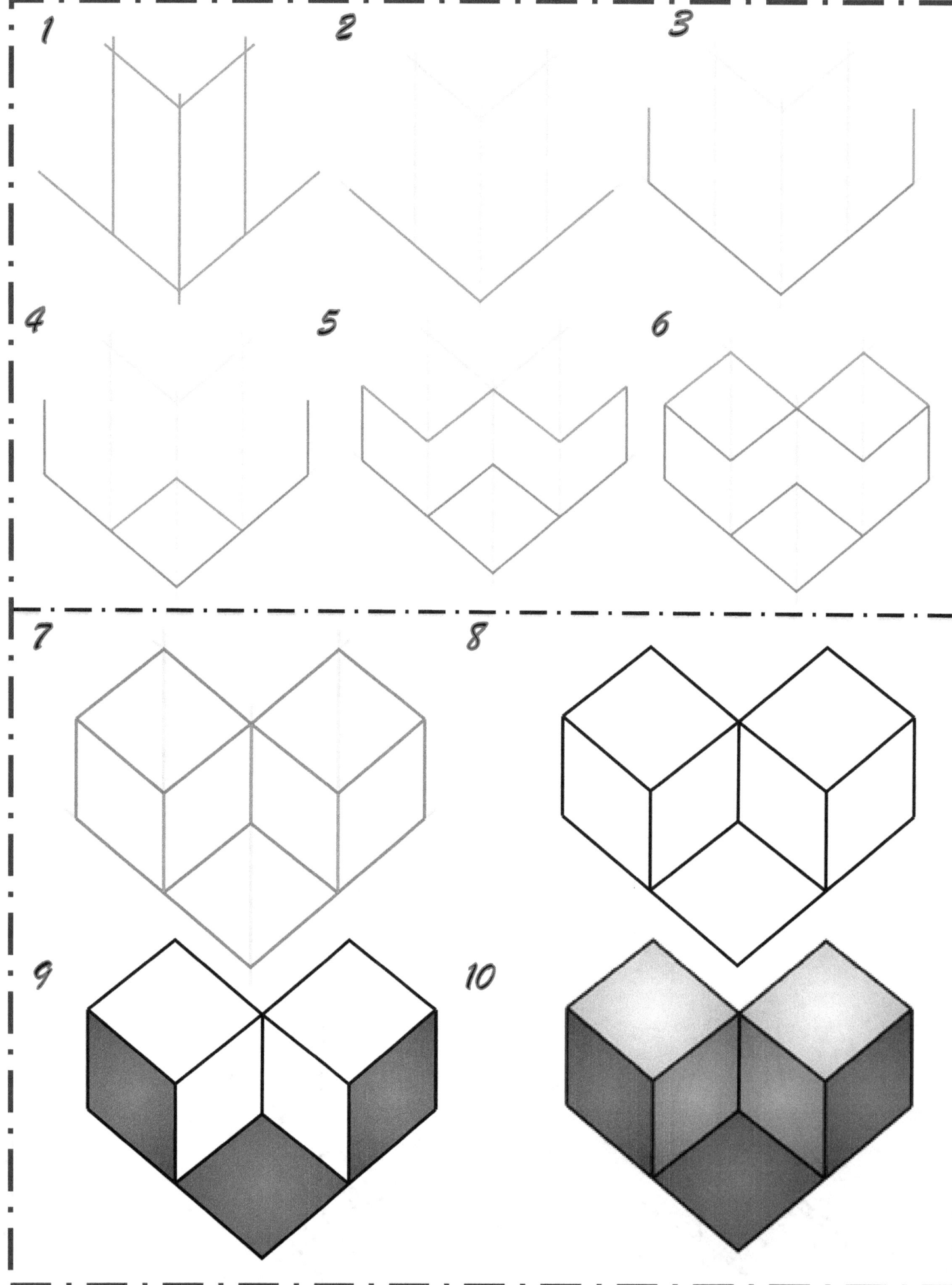

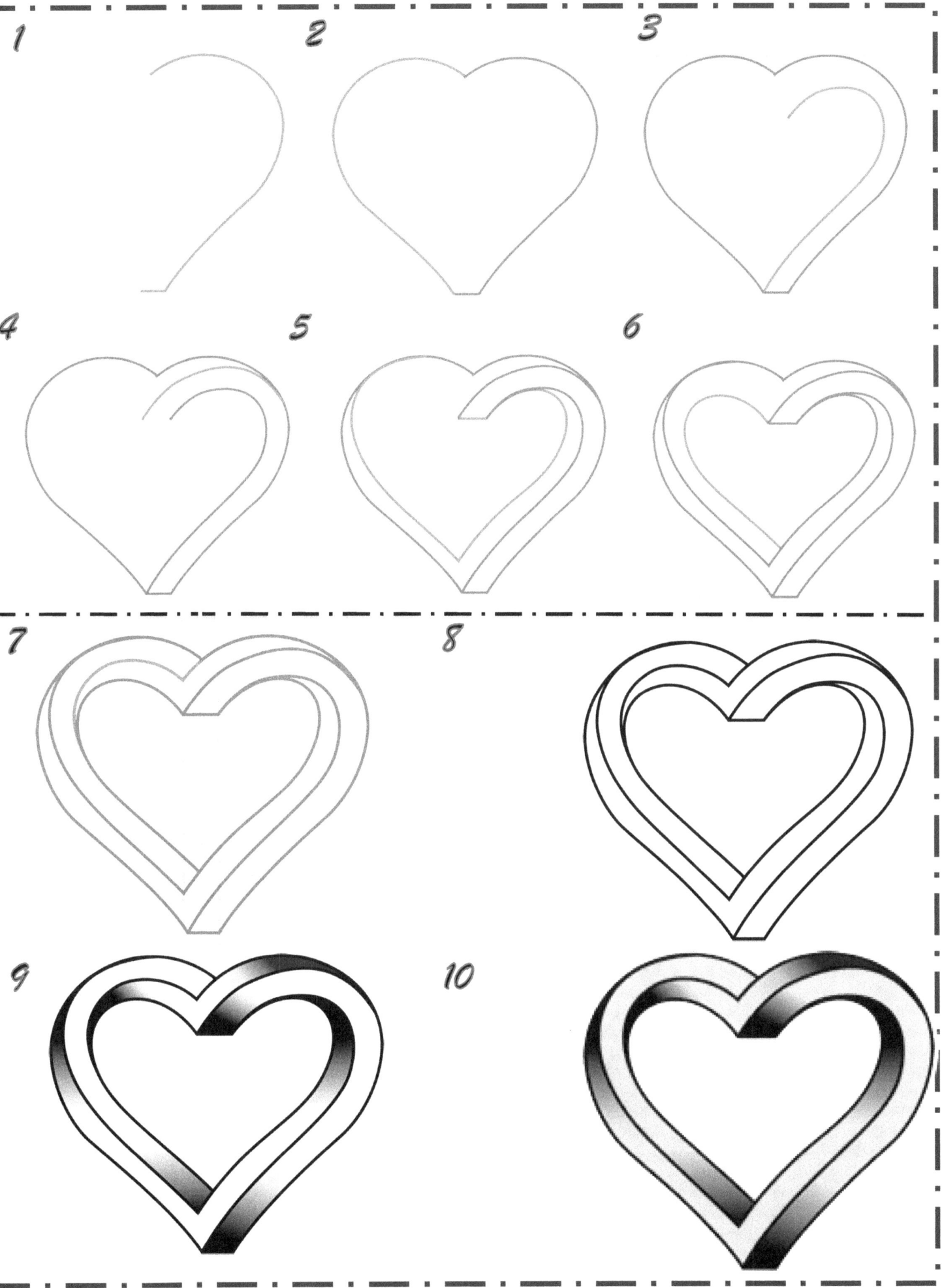

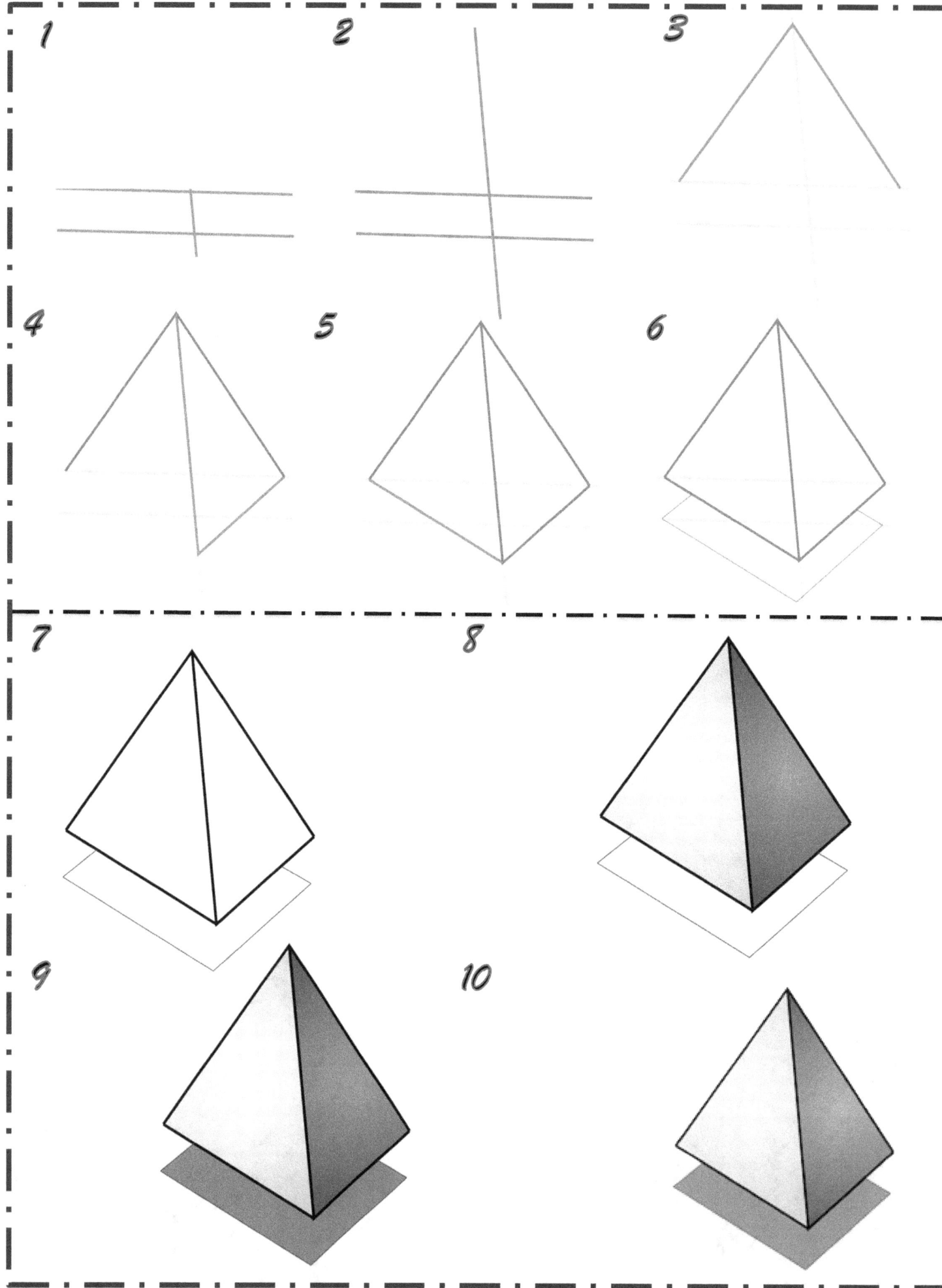

1 2 3

4 5 6

7 8

9 10

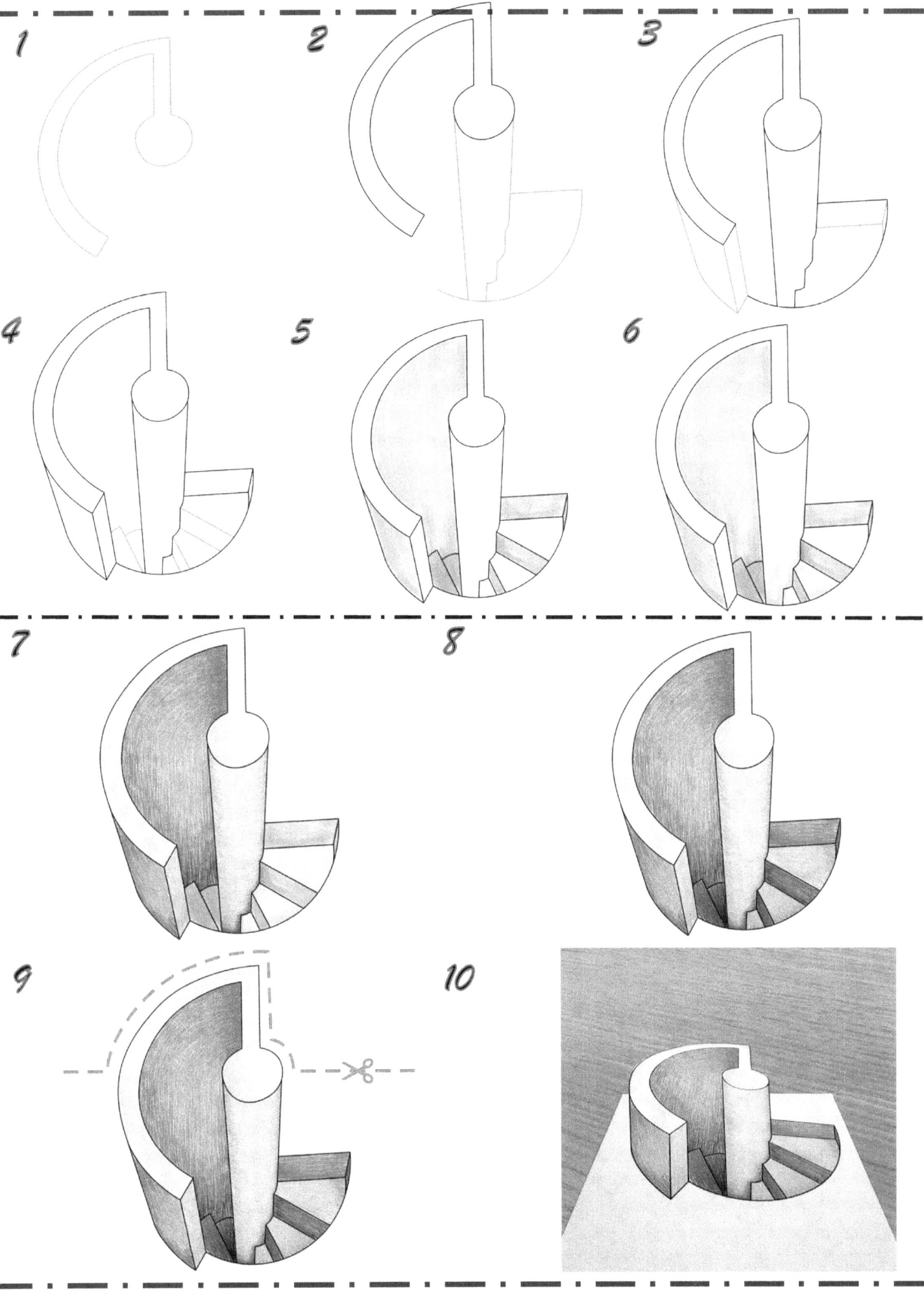

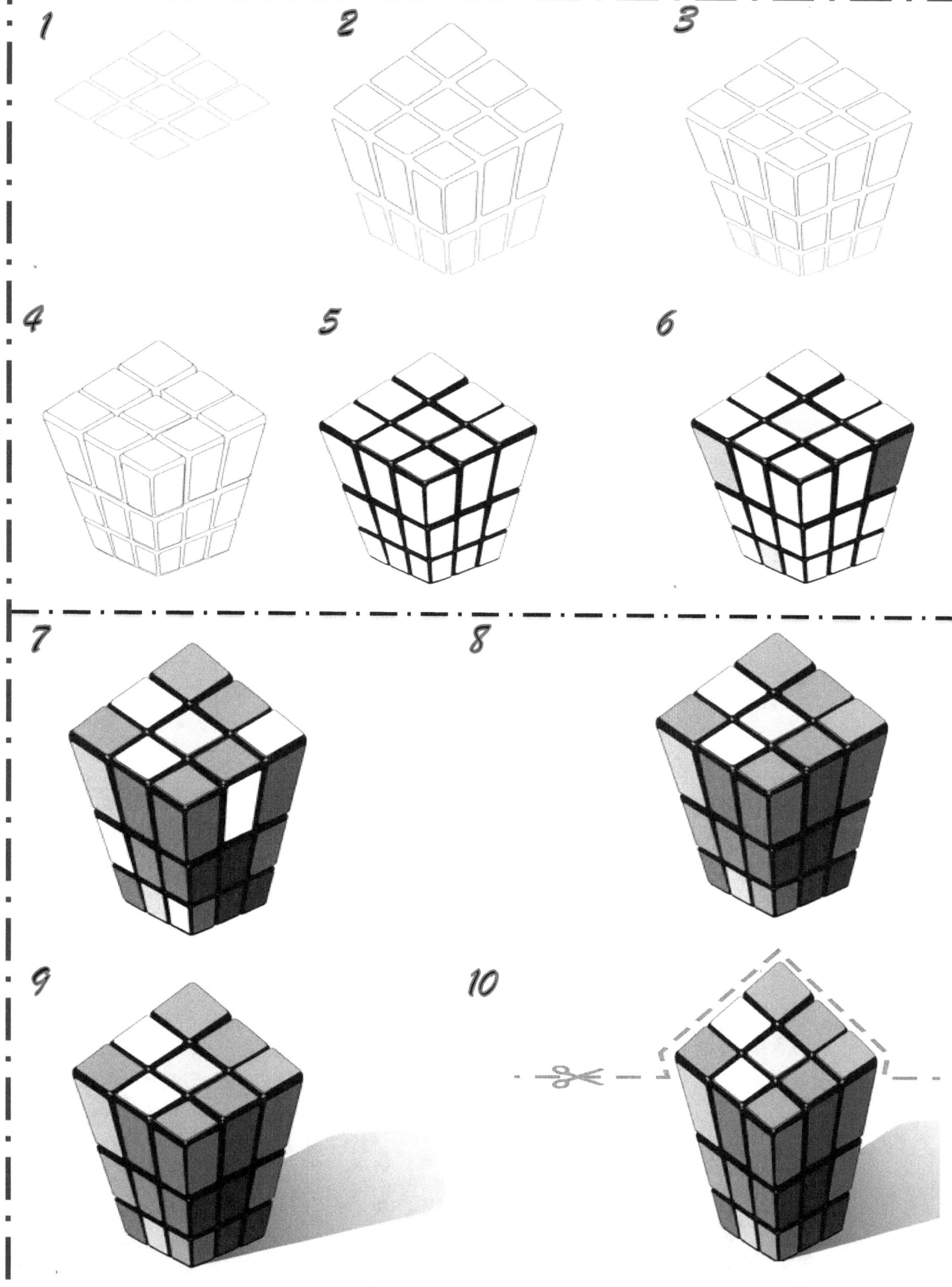

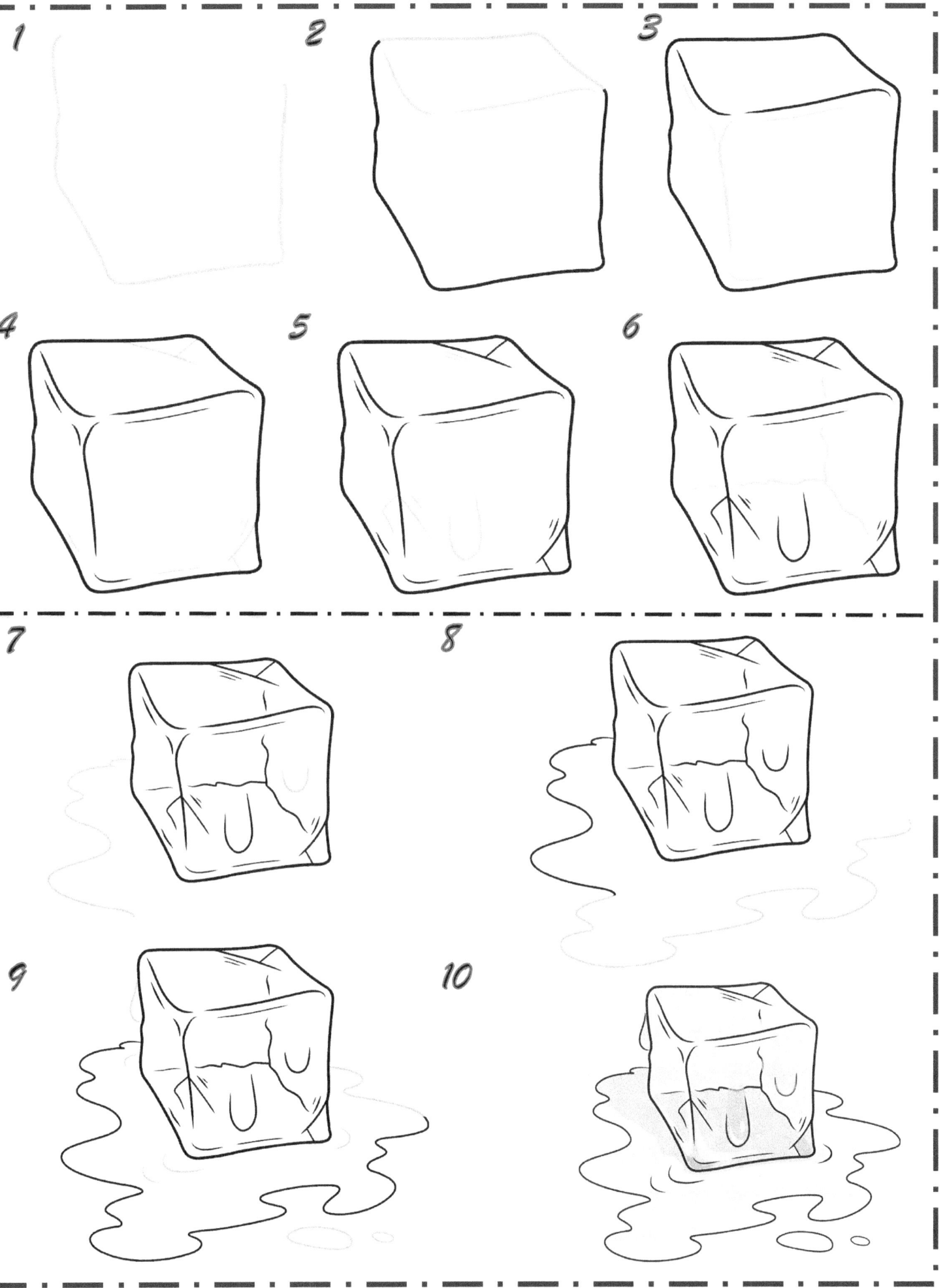

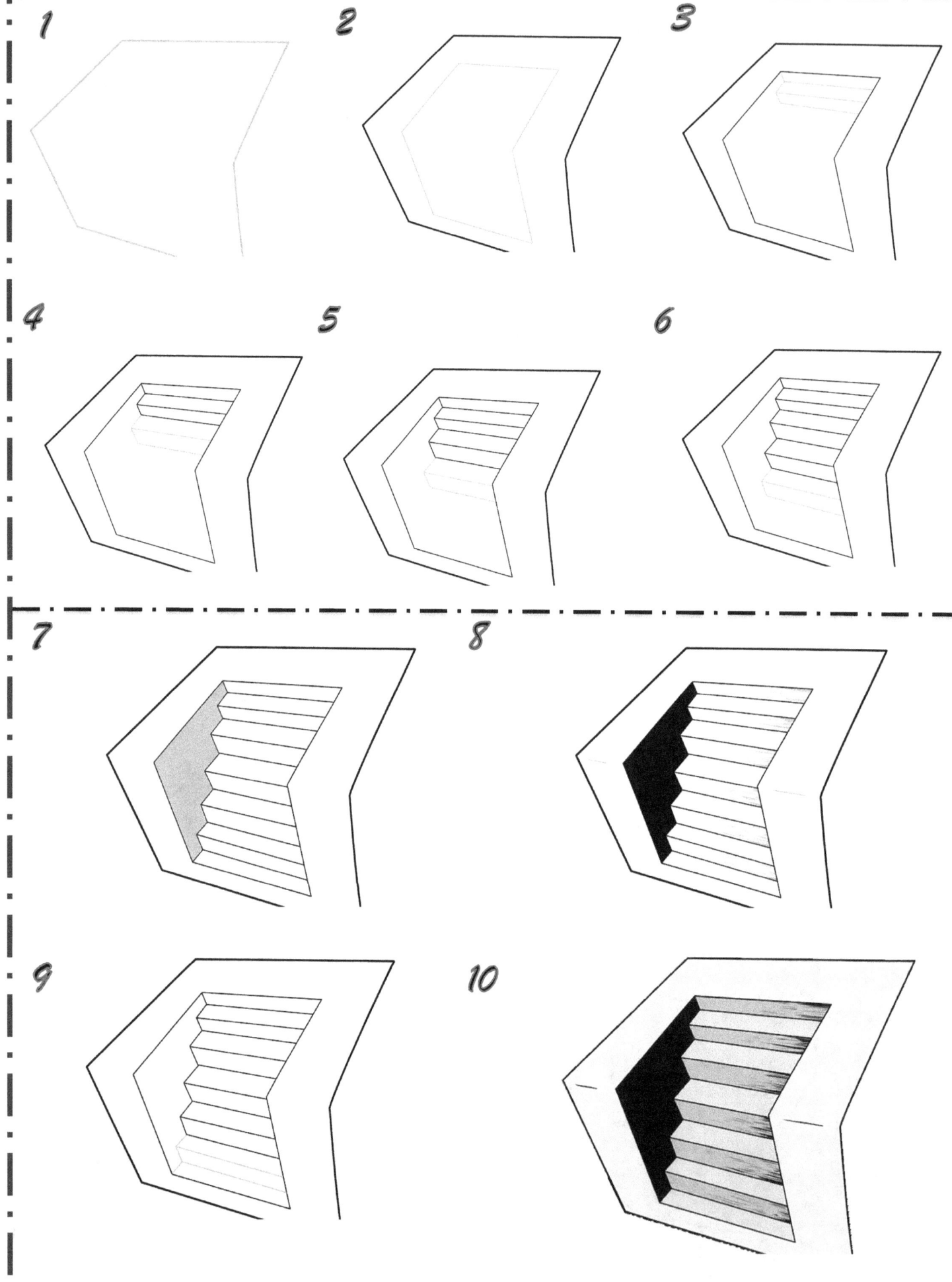

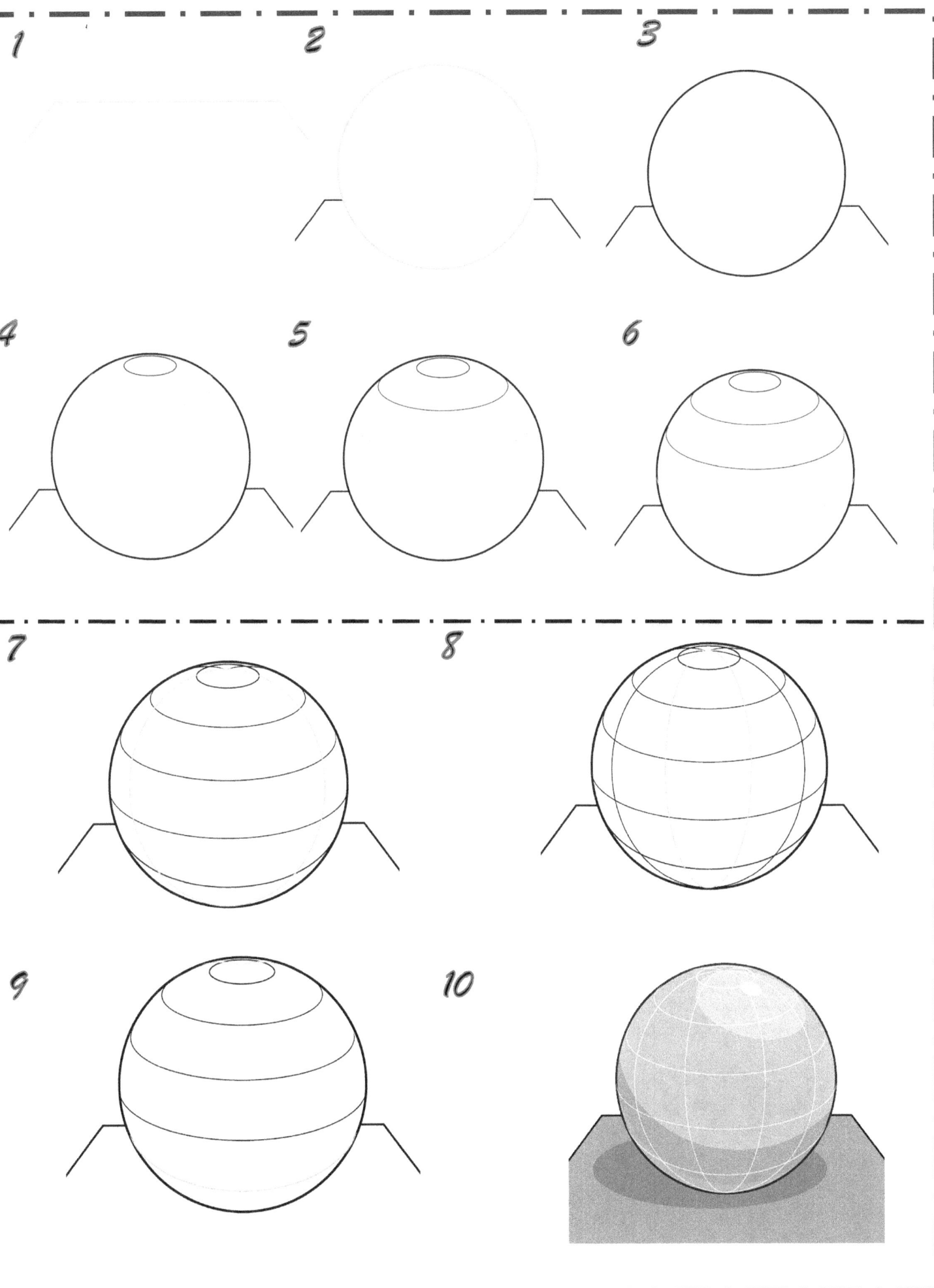

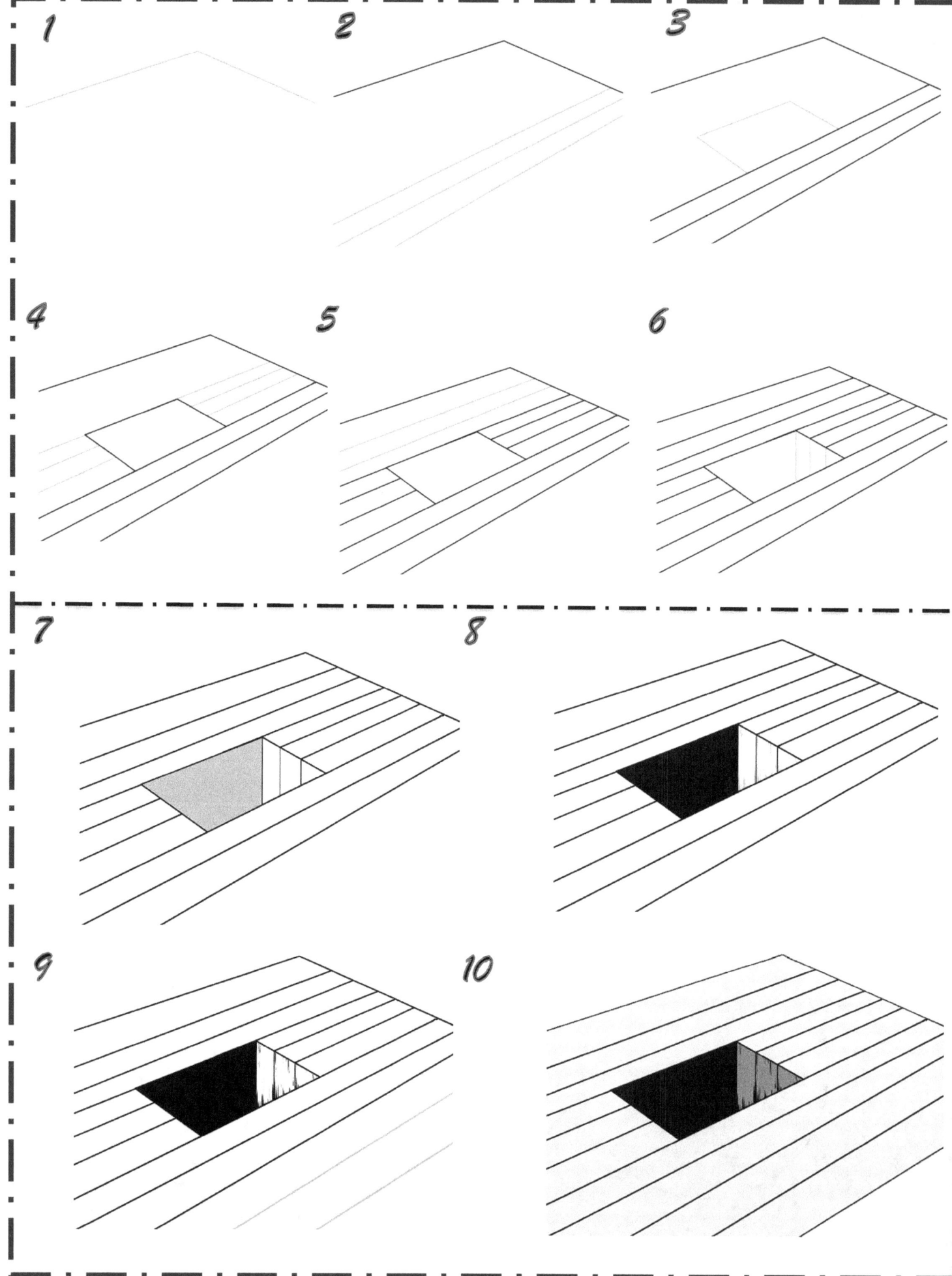

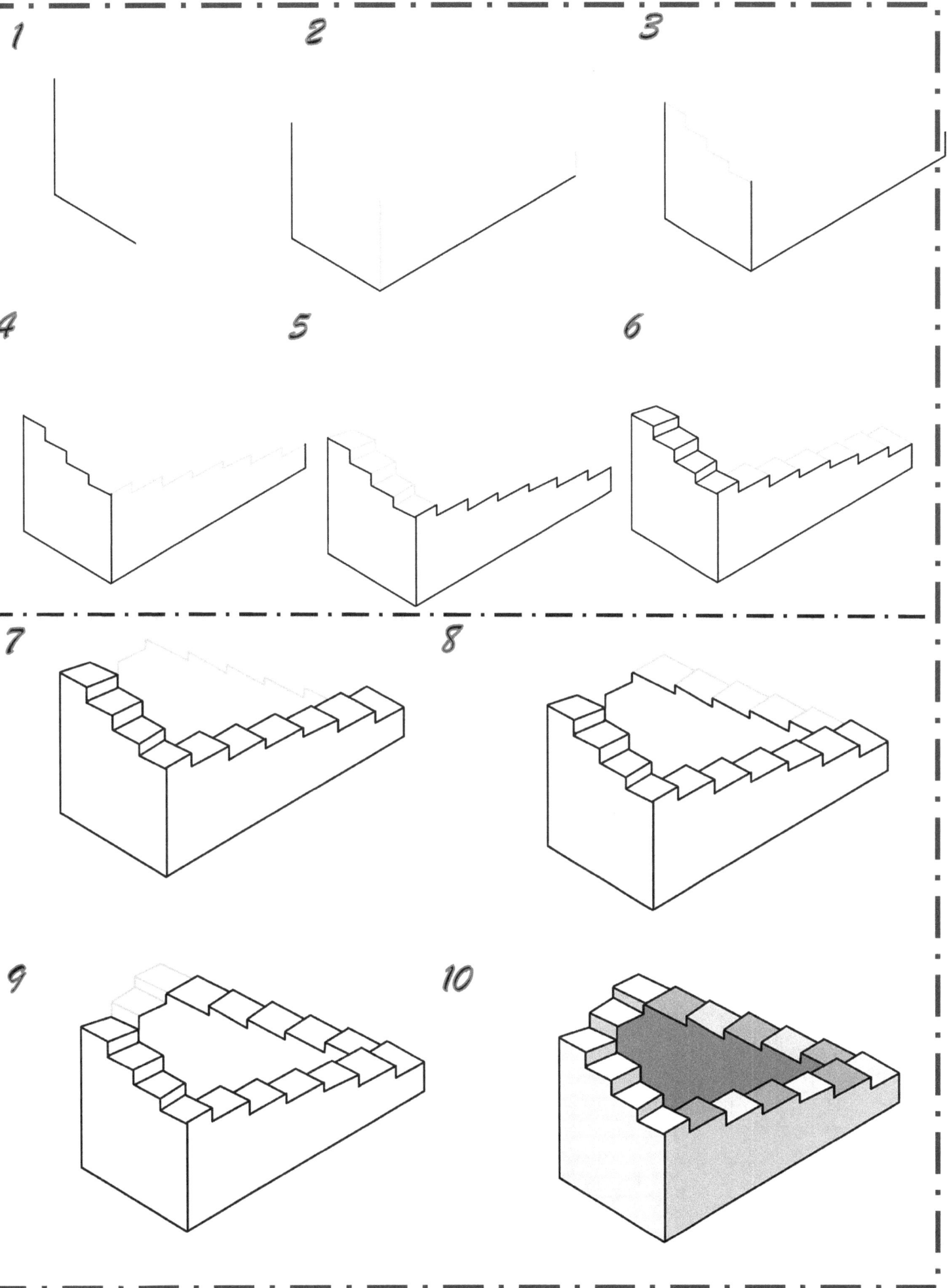

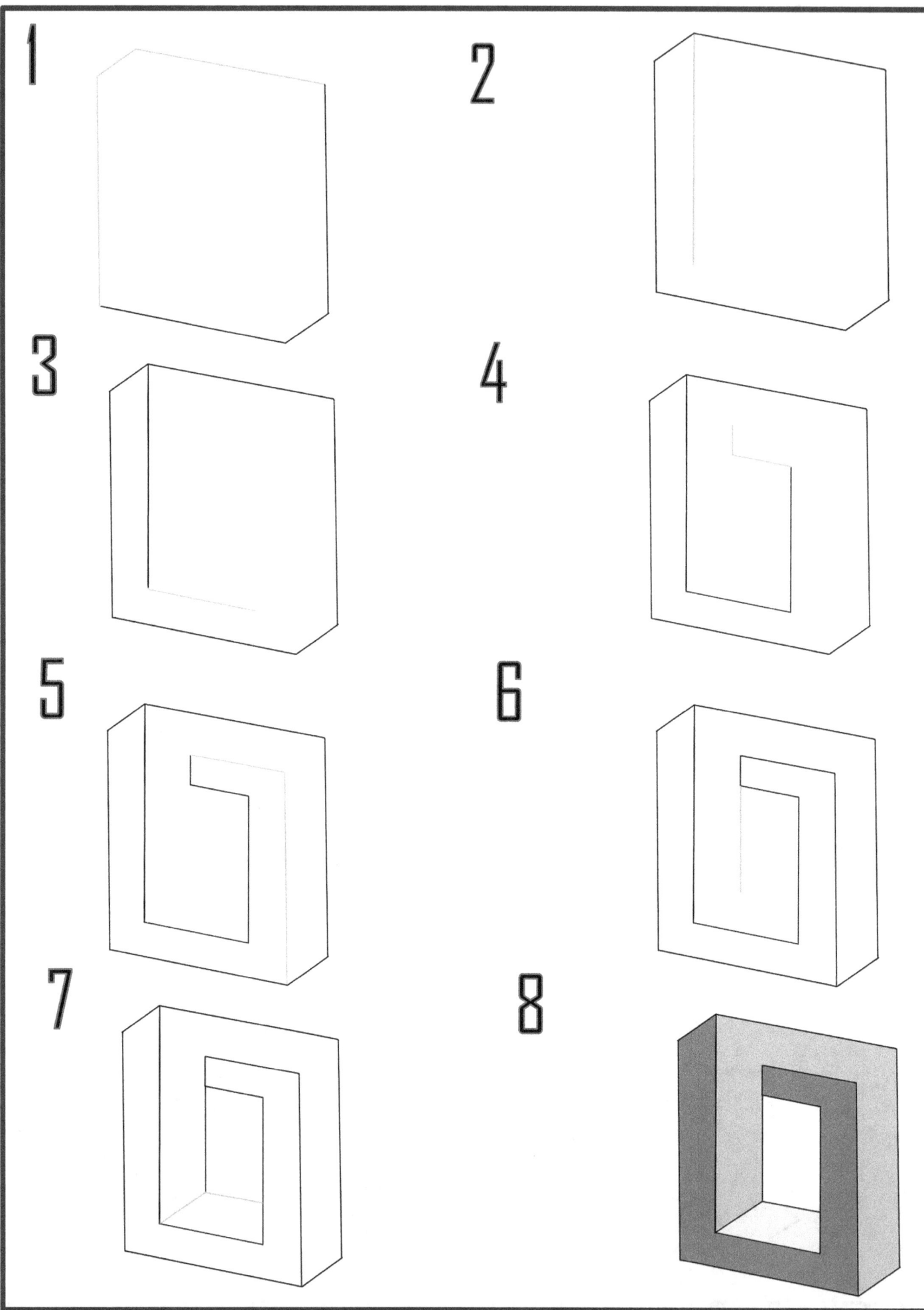

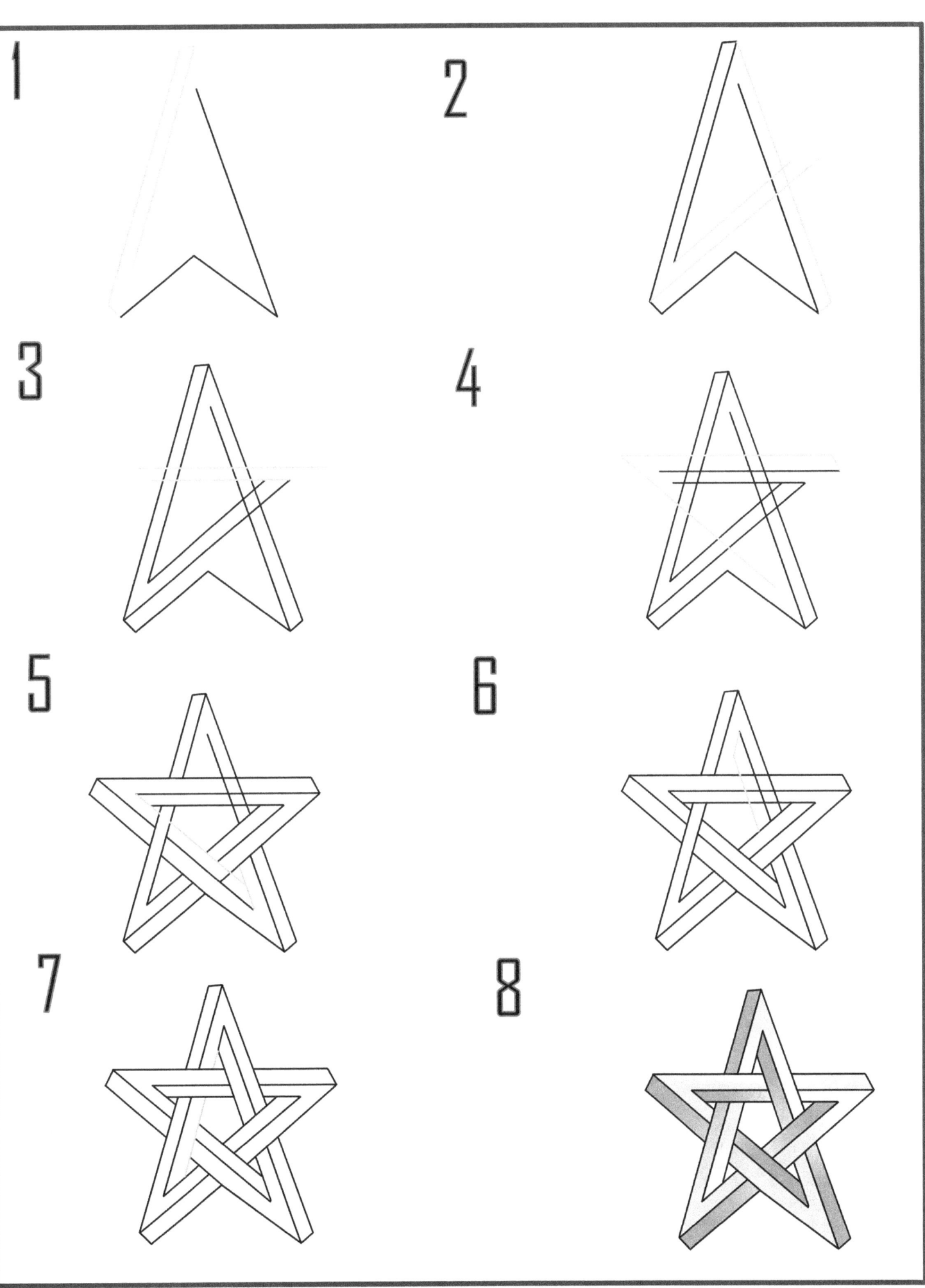

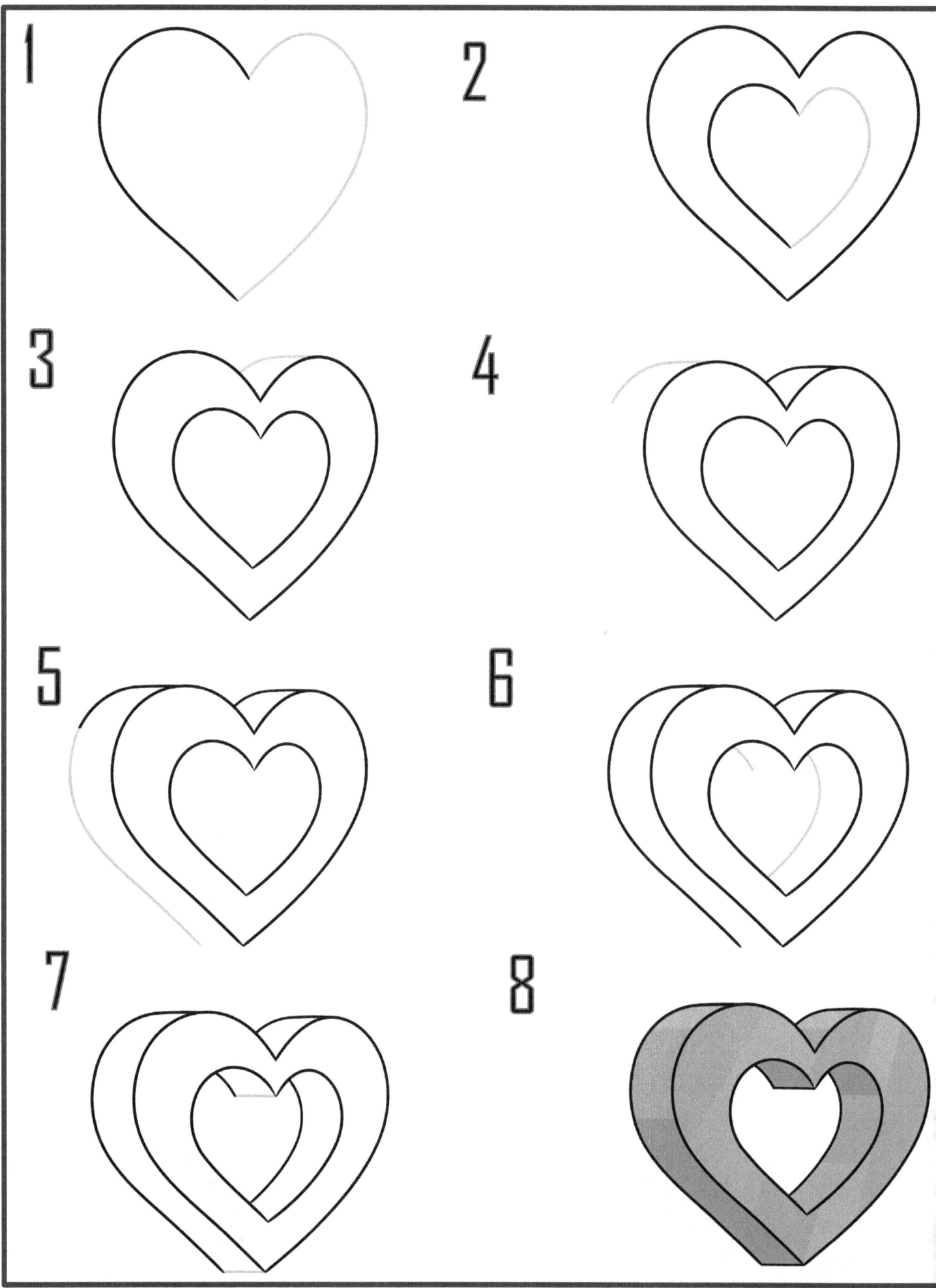

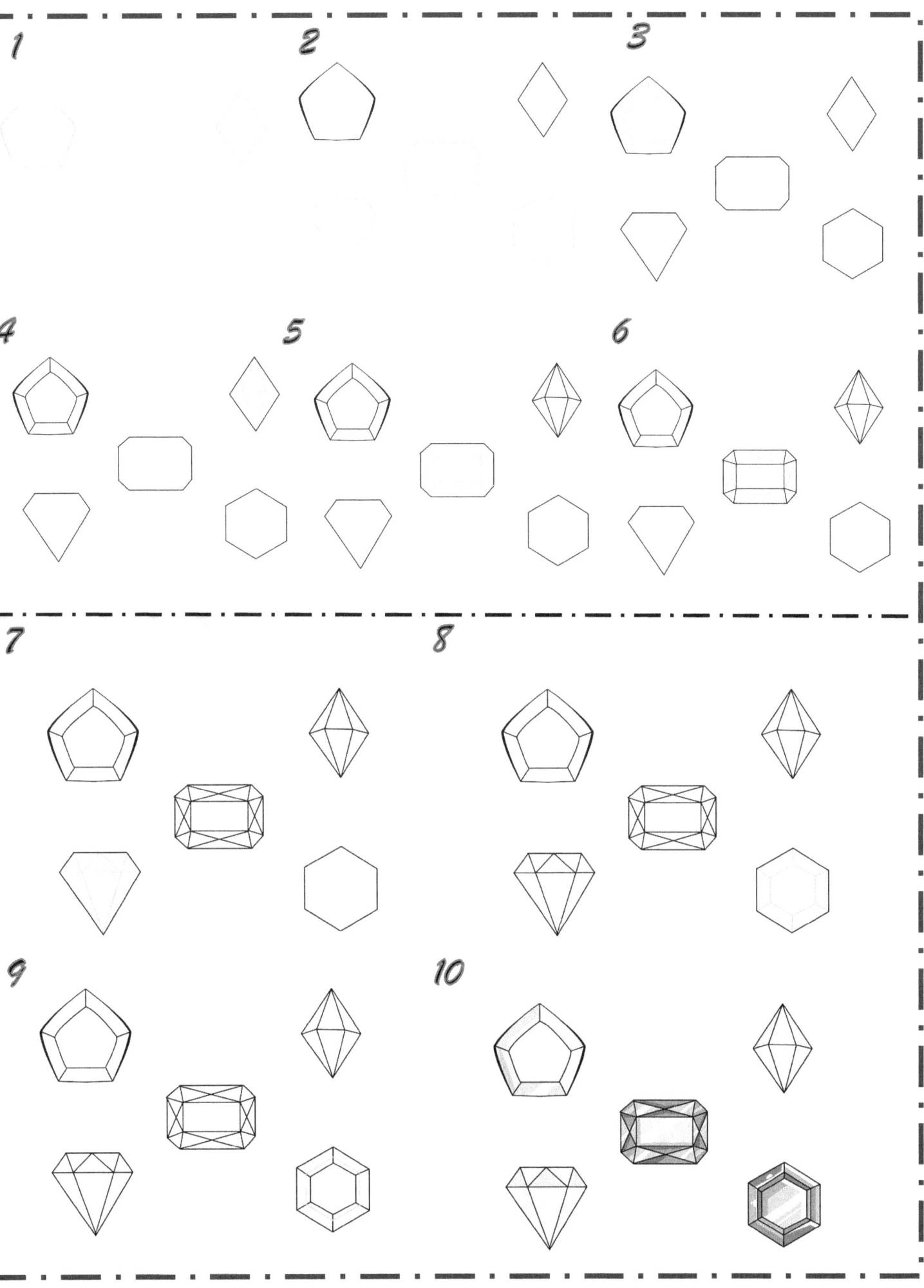

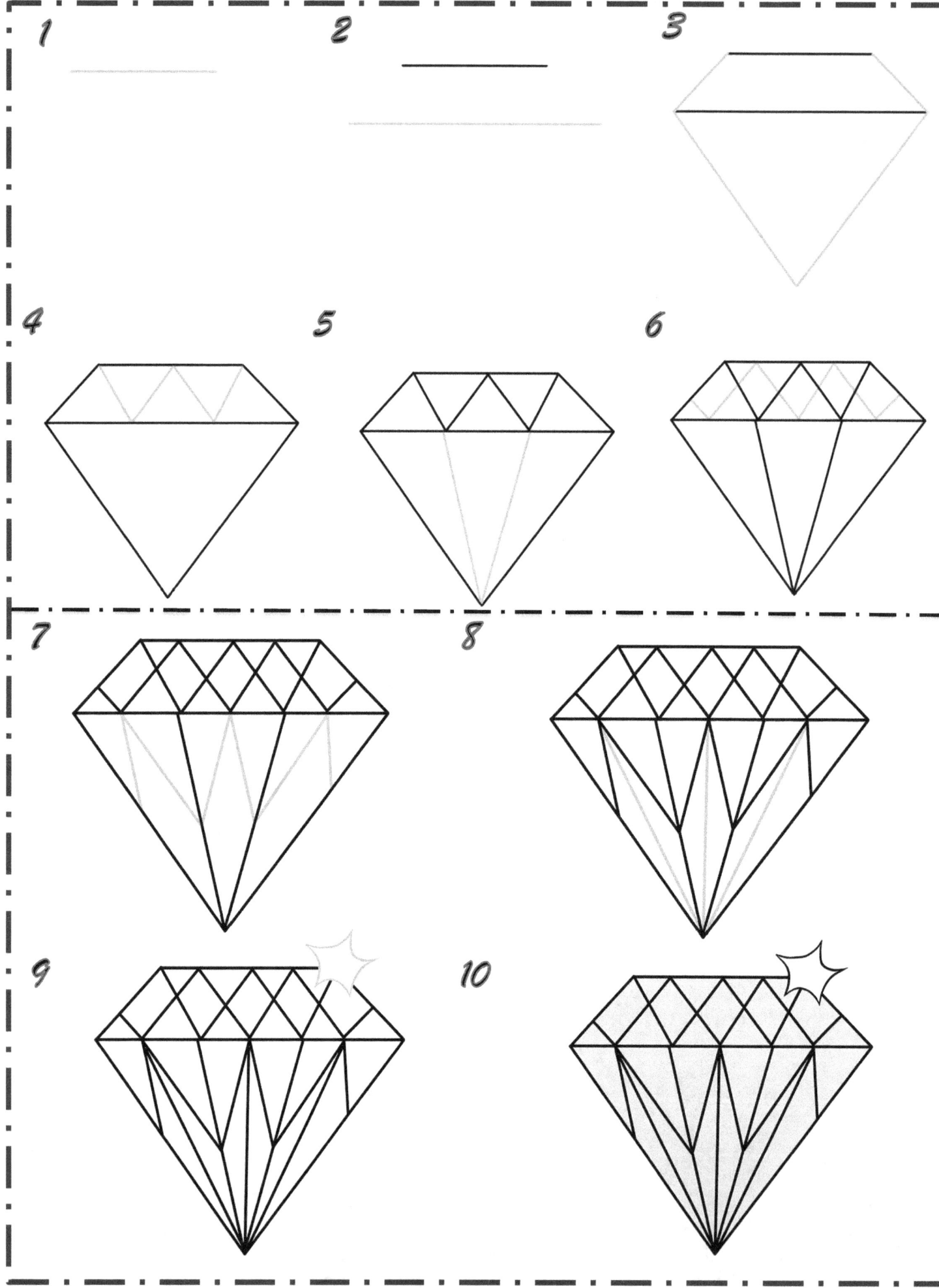

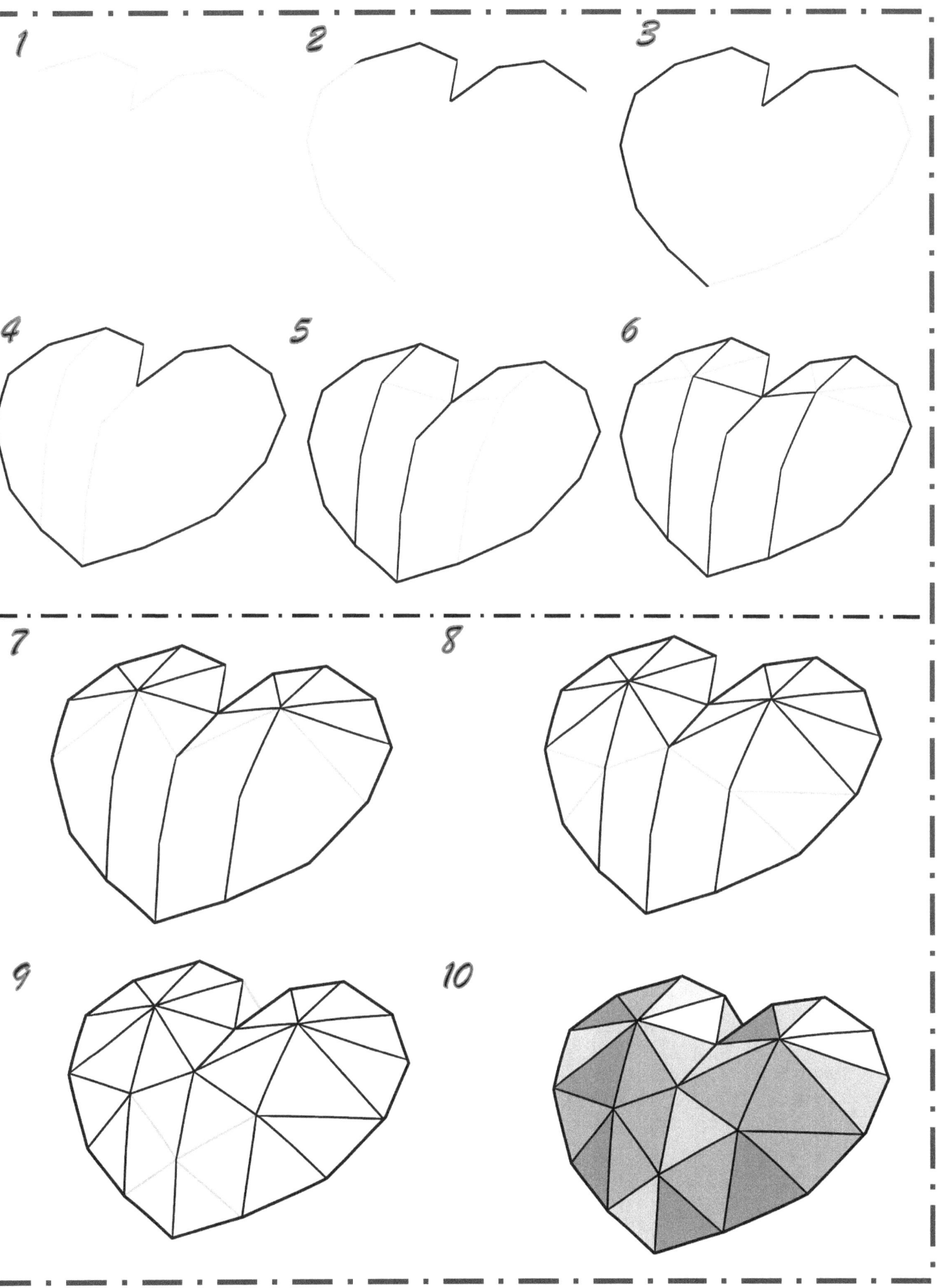

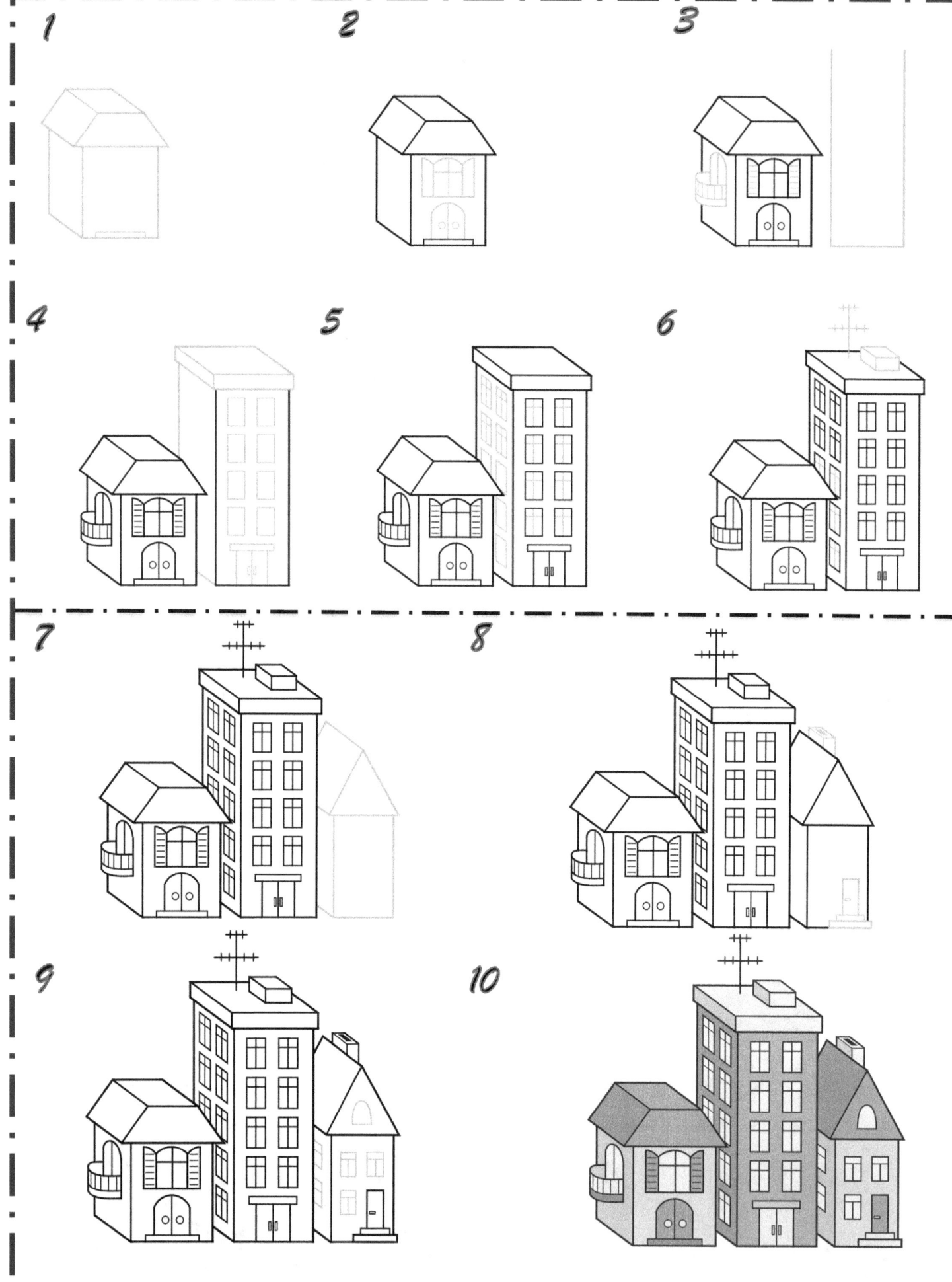

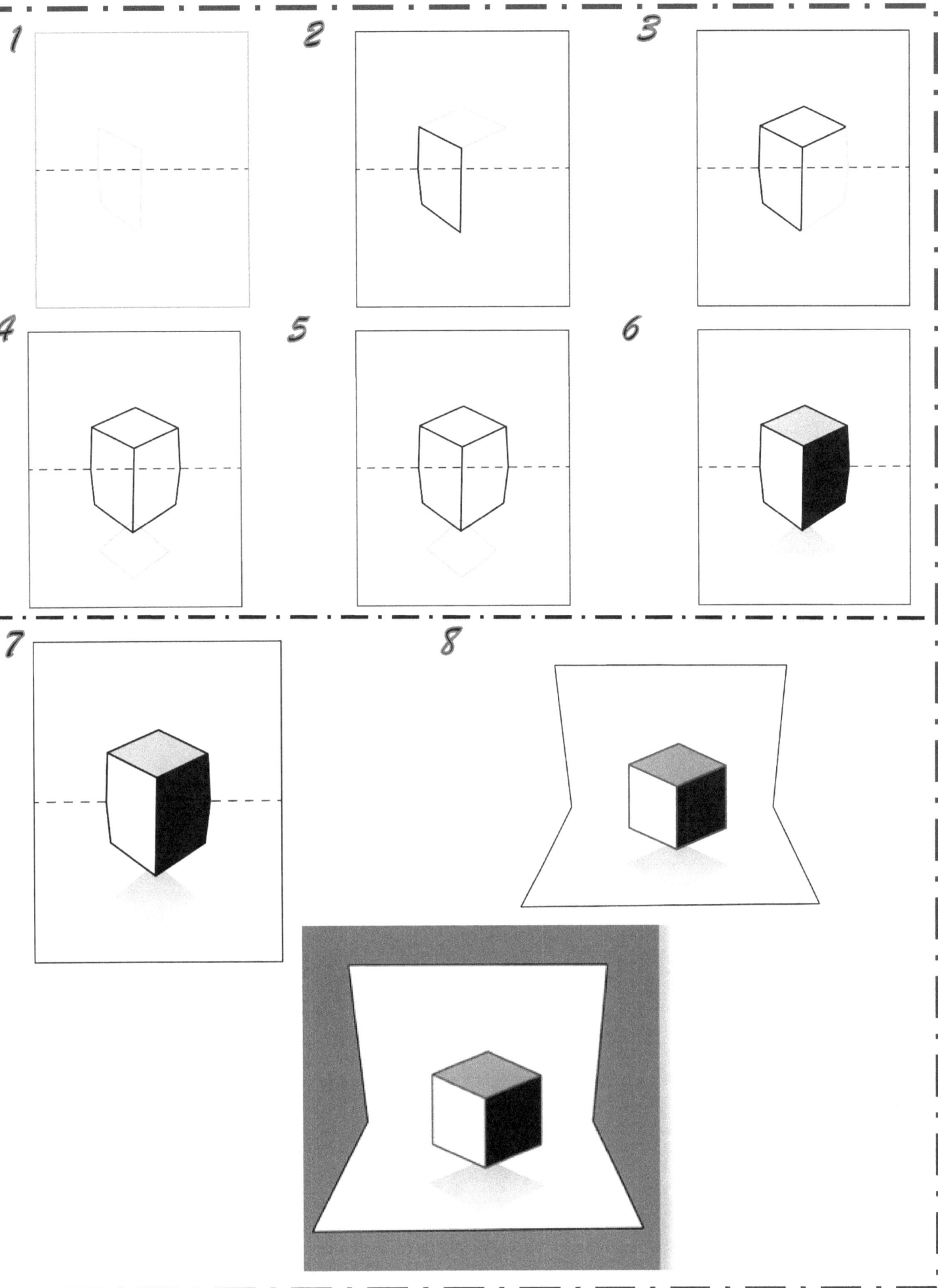

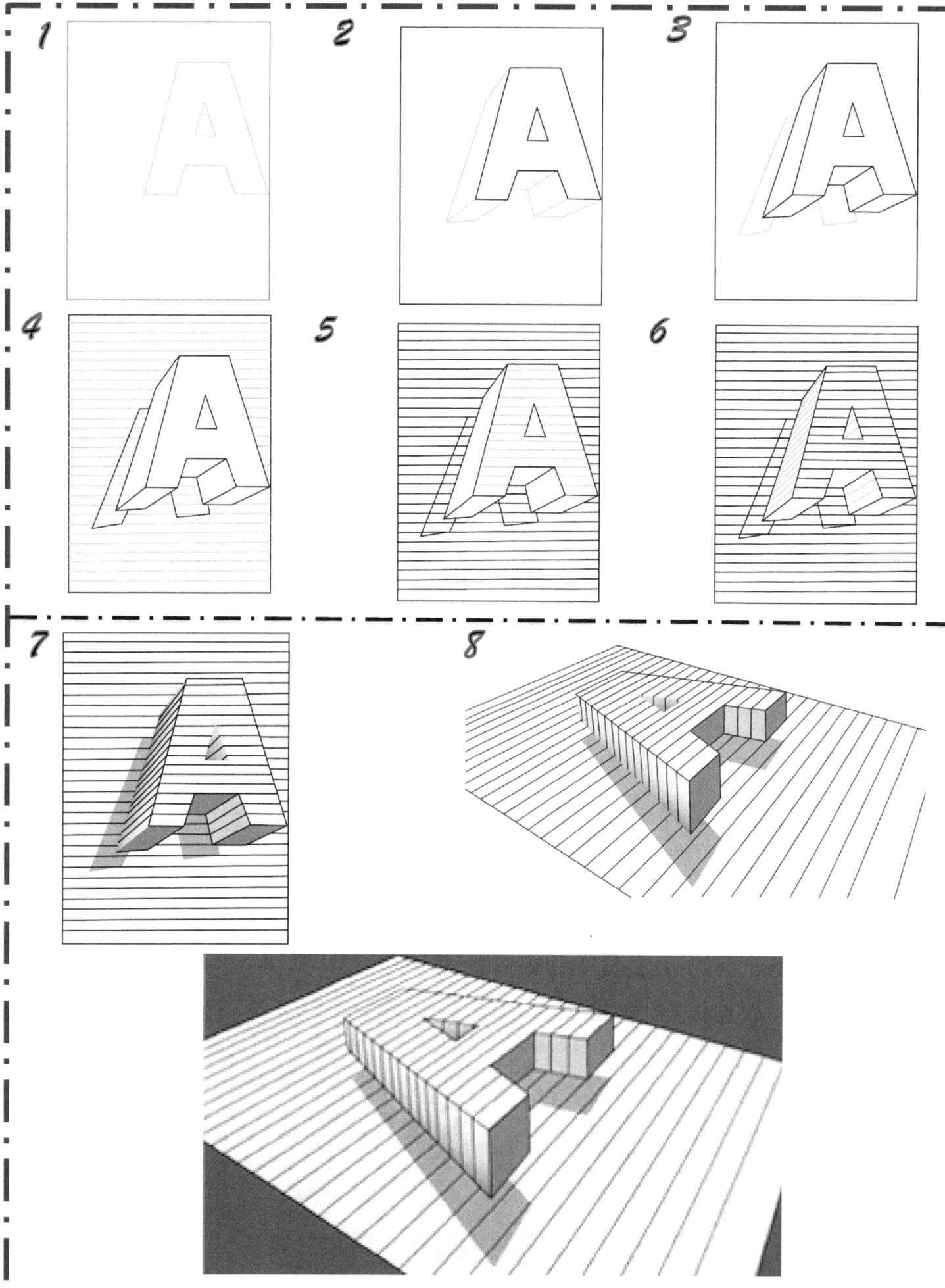

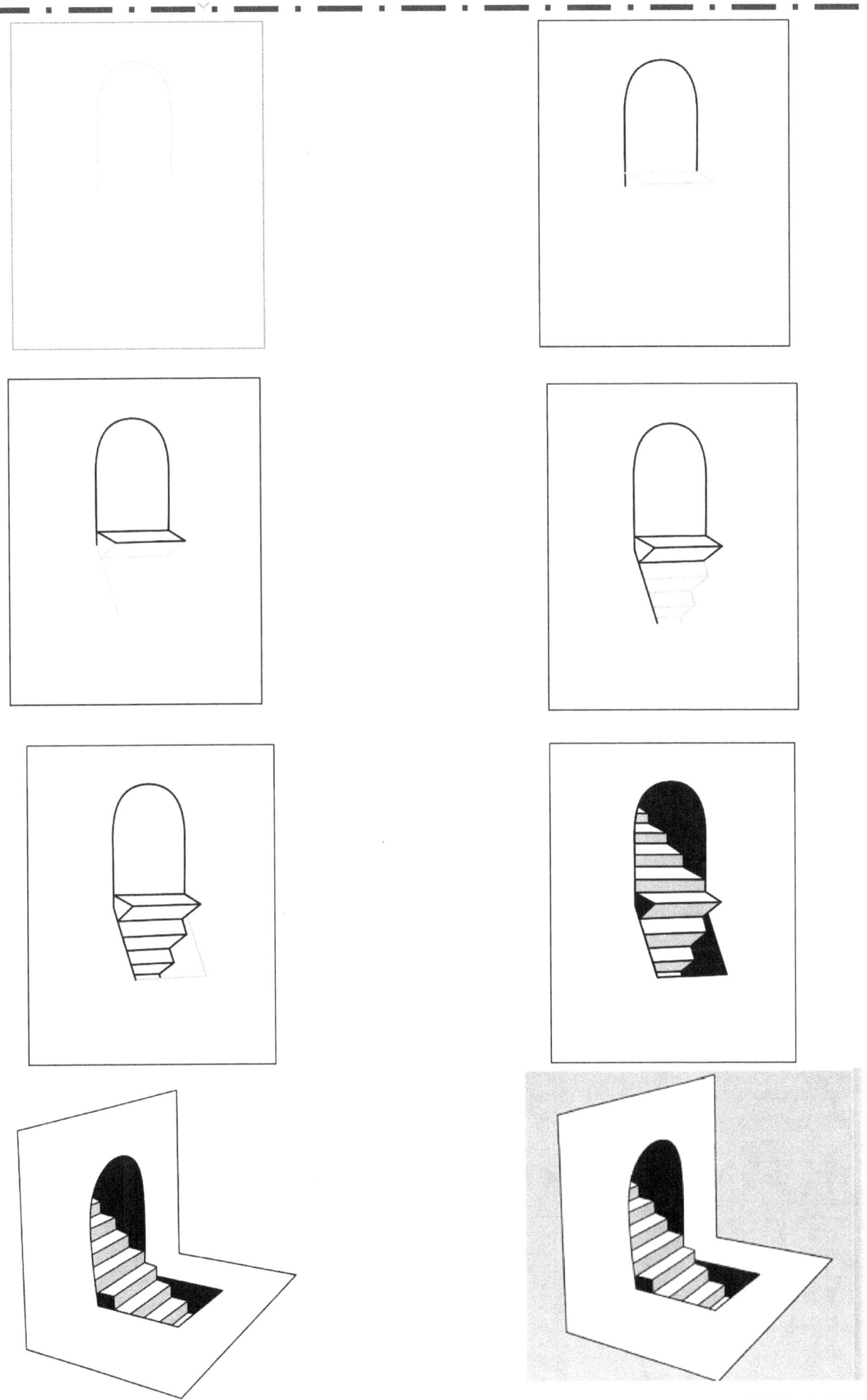

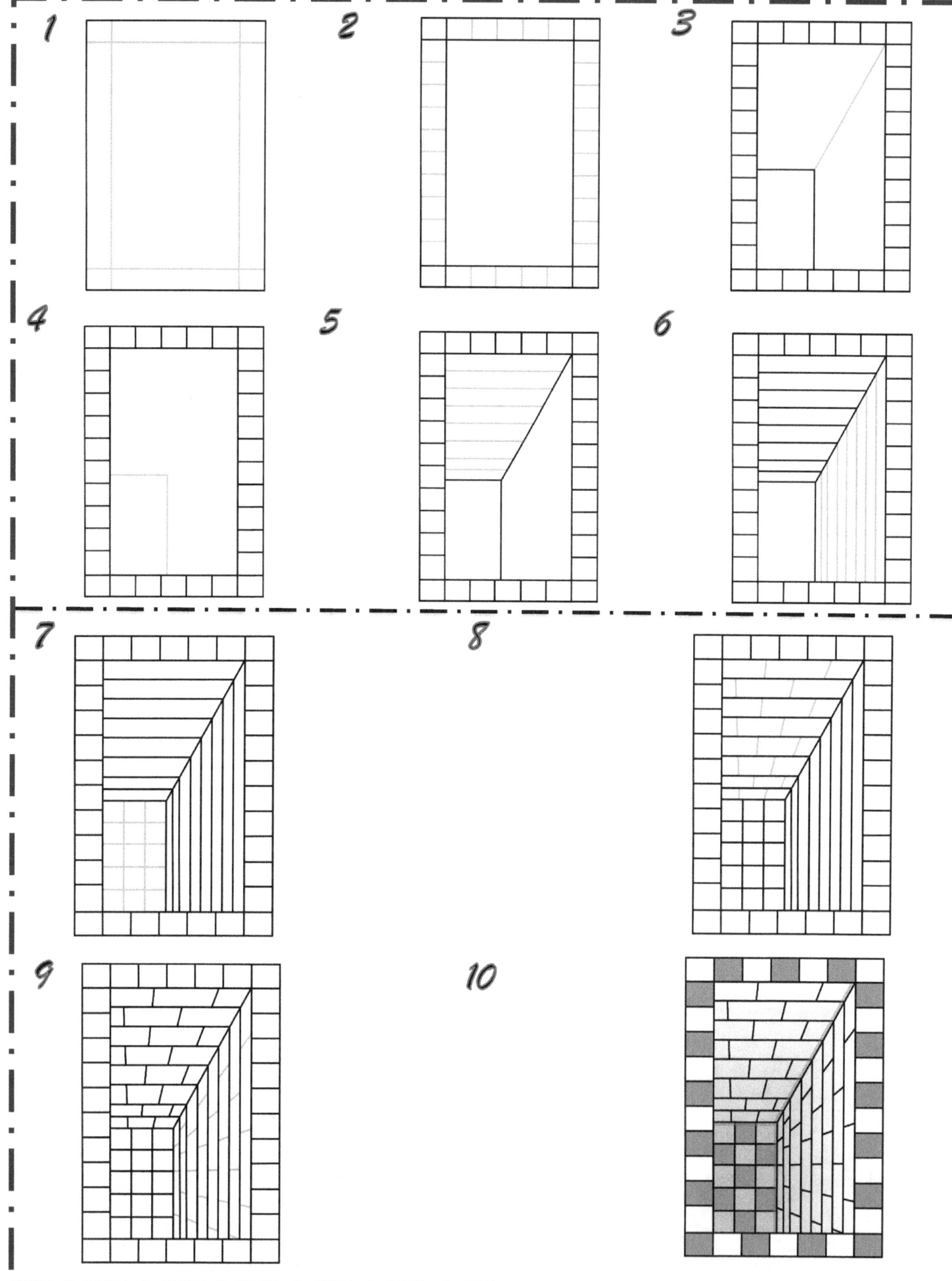

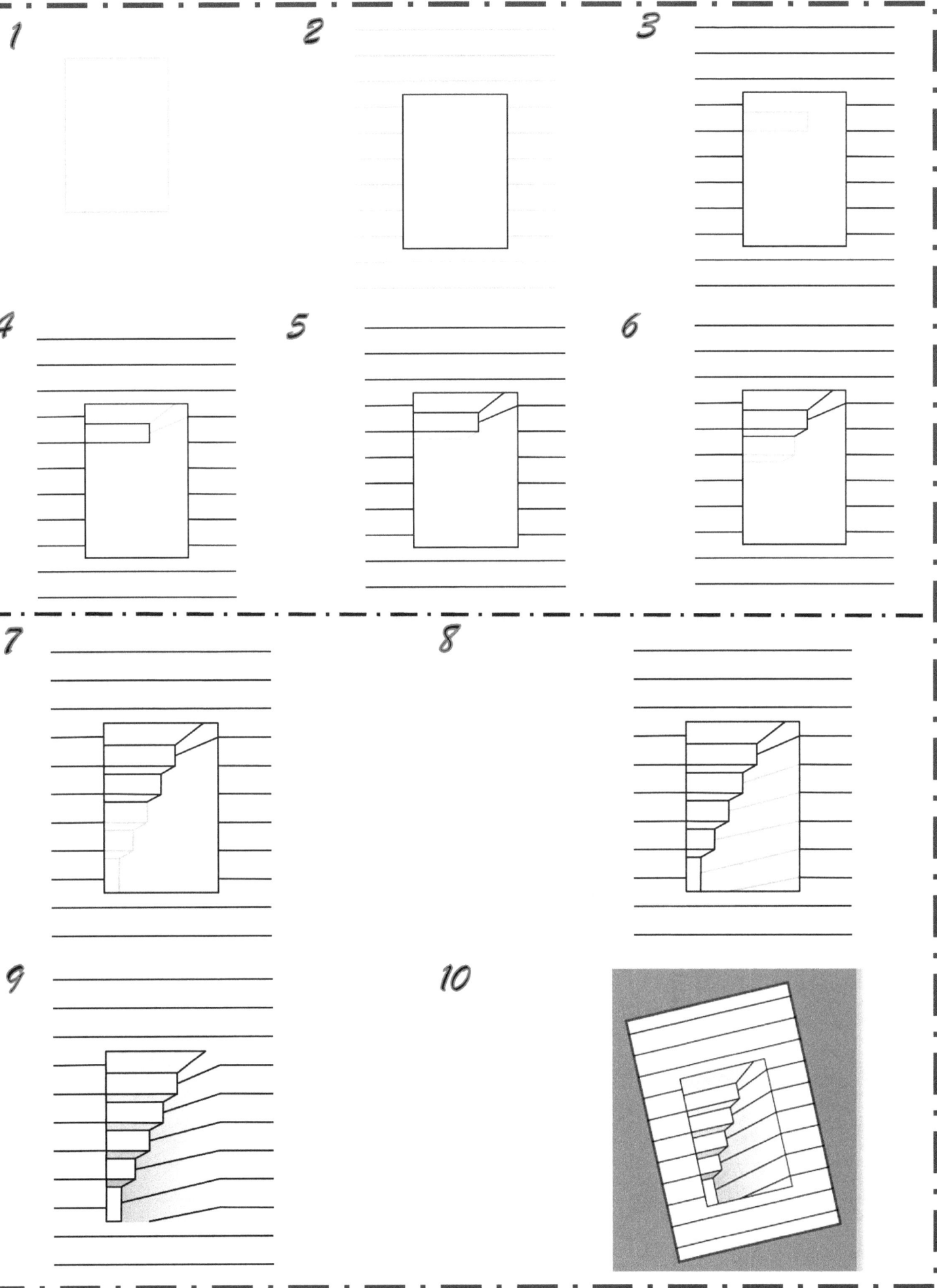

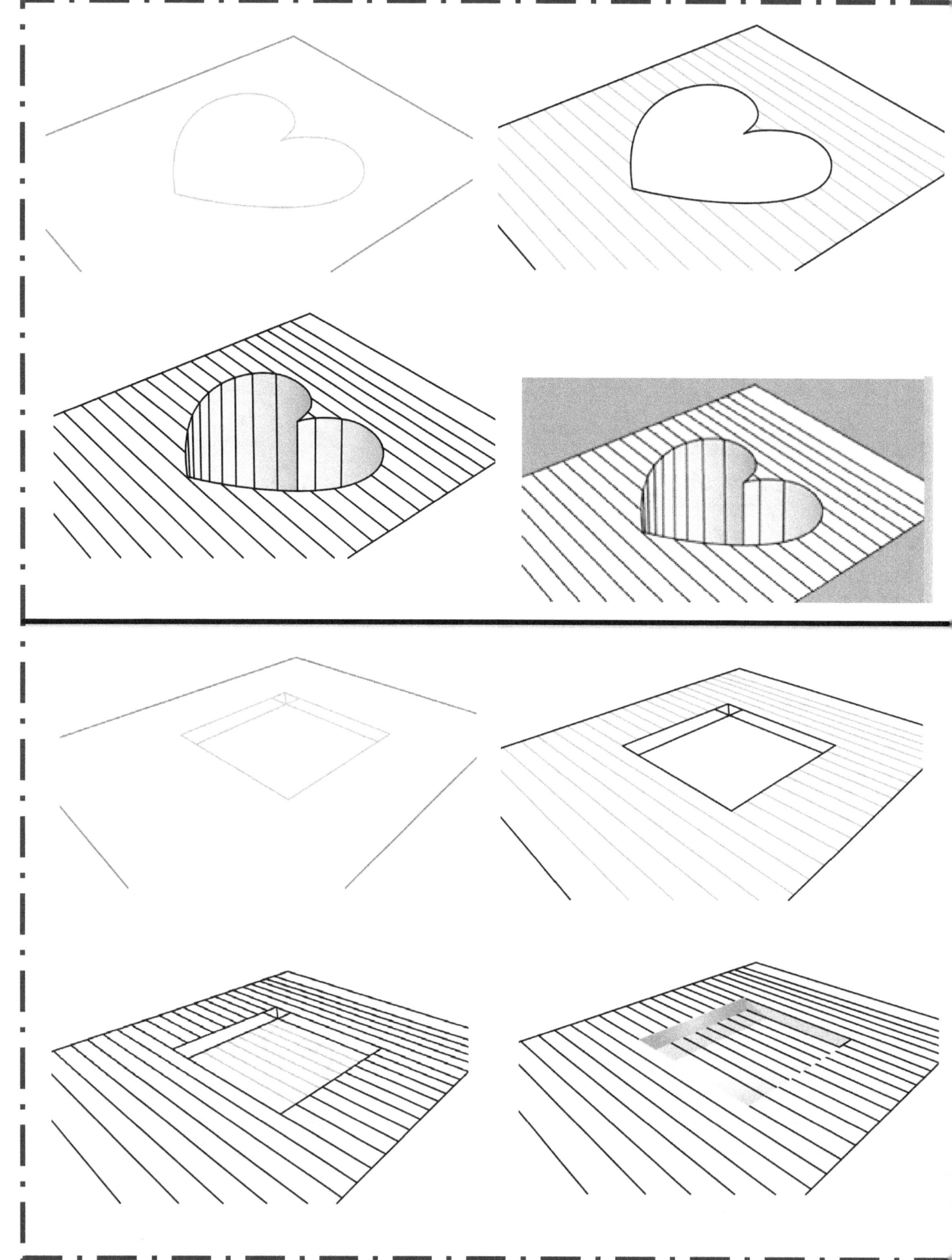

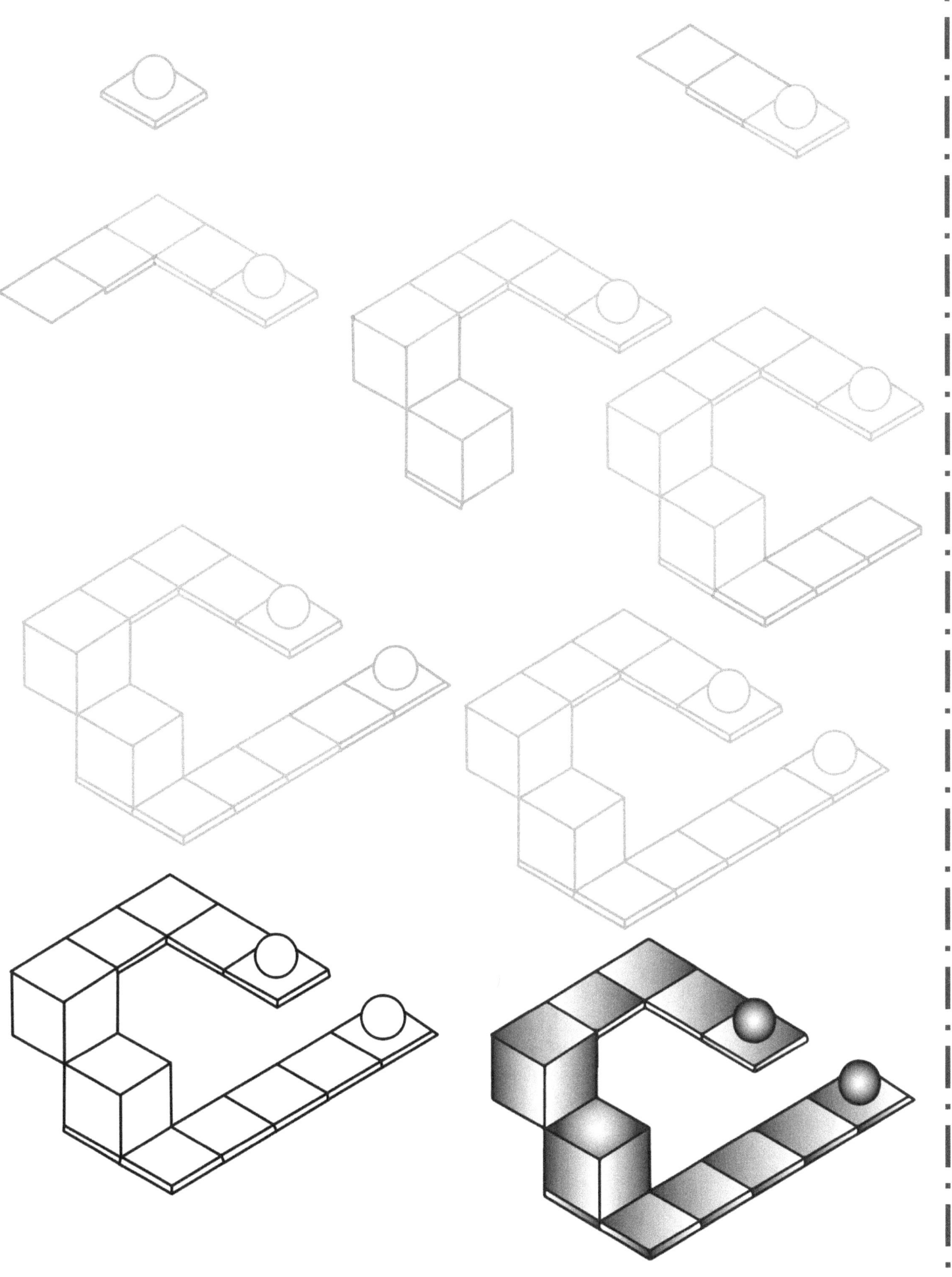

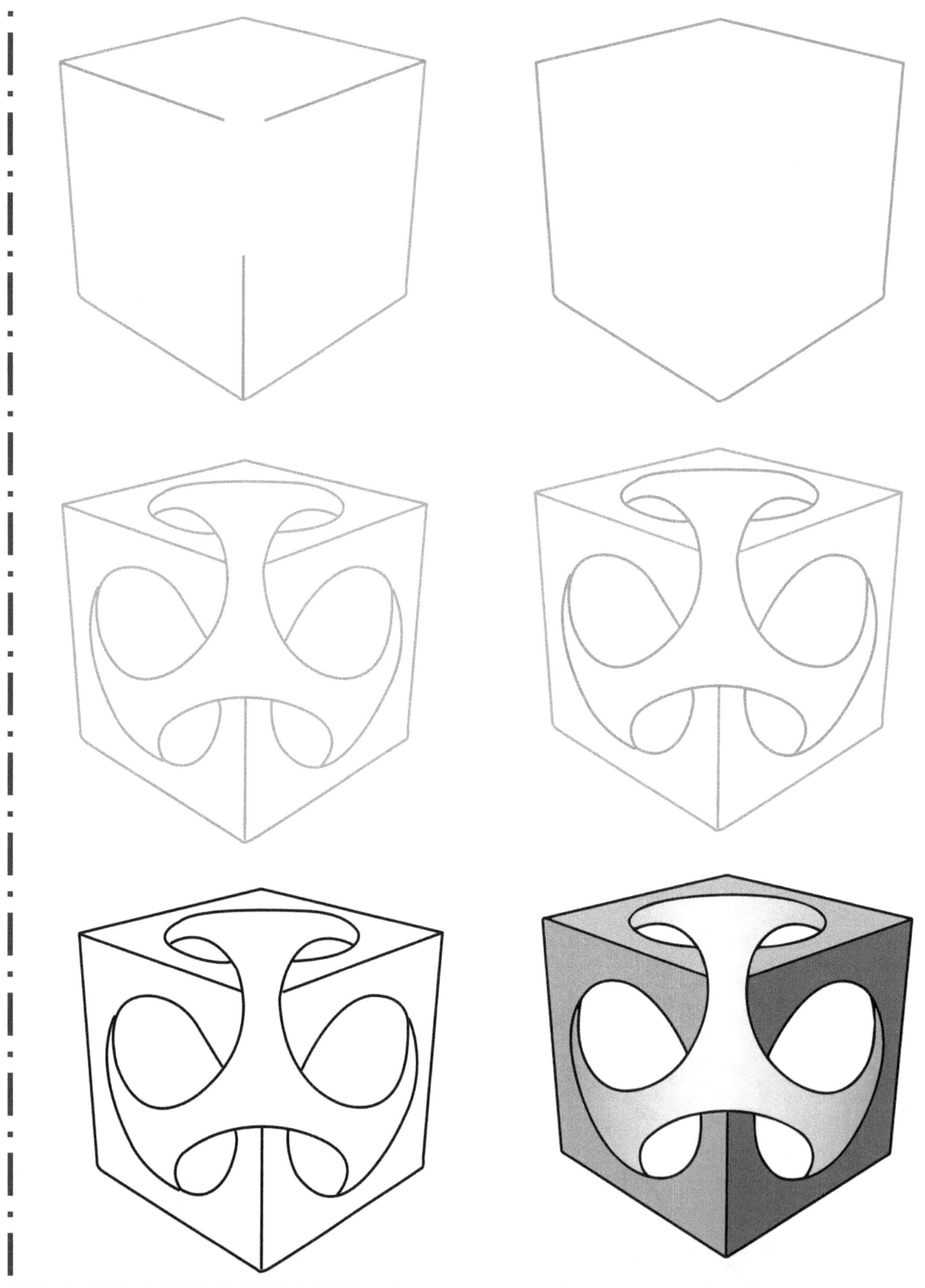

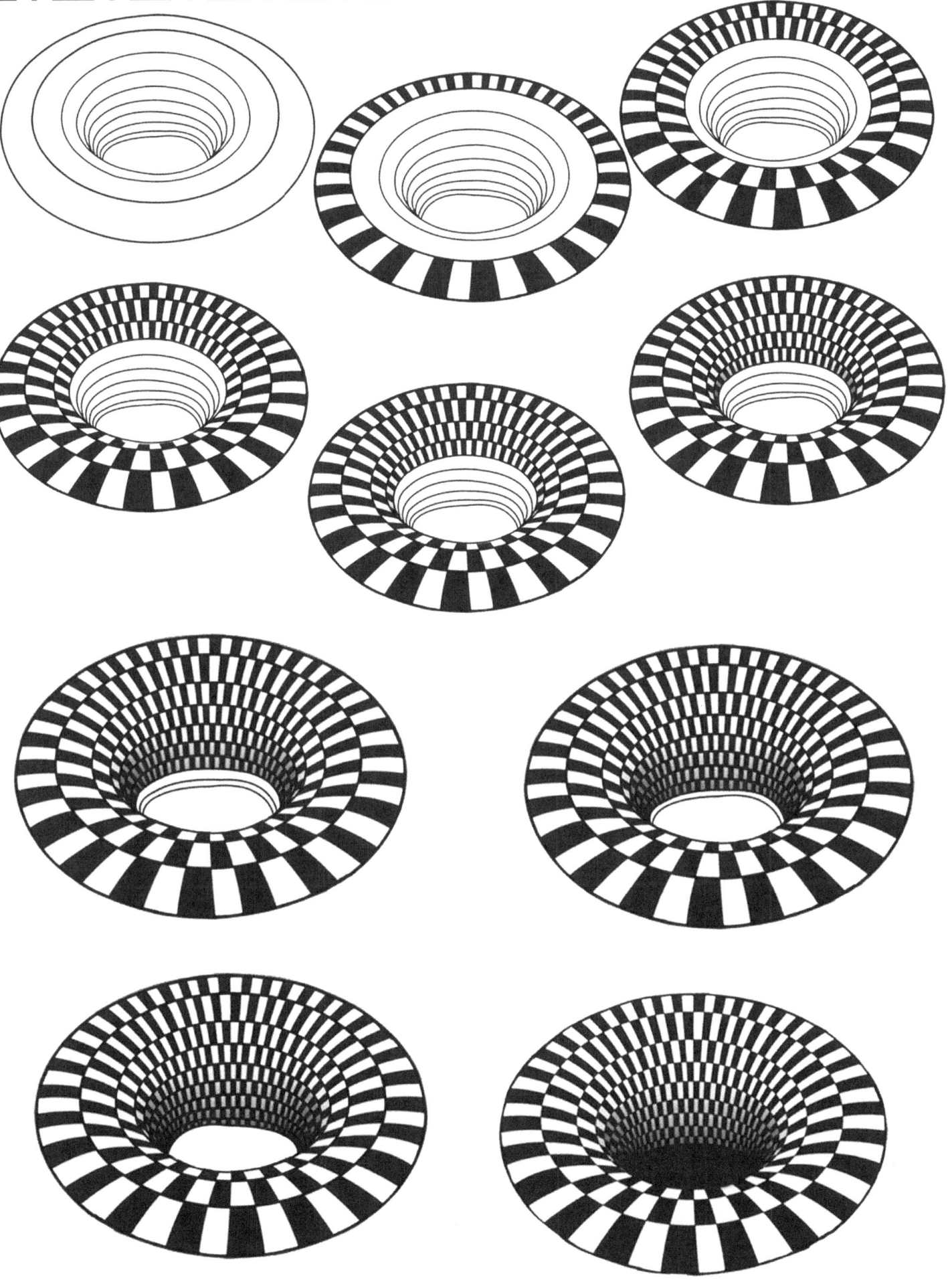

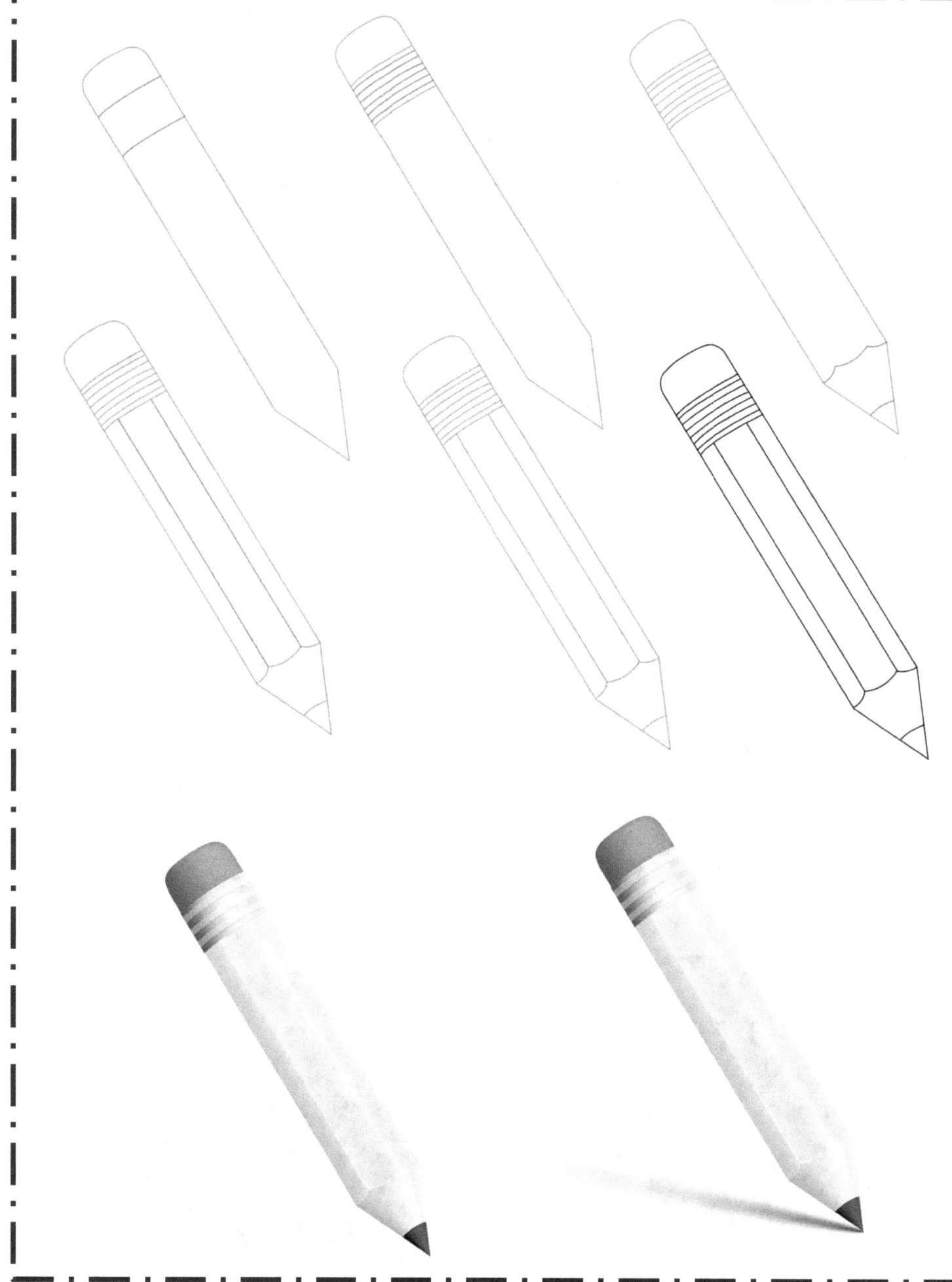

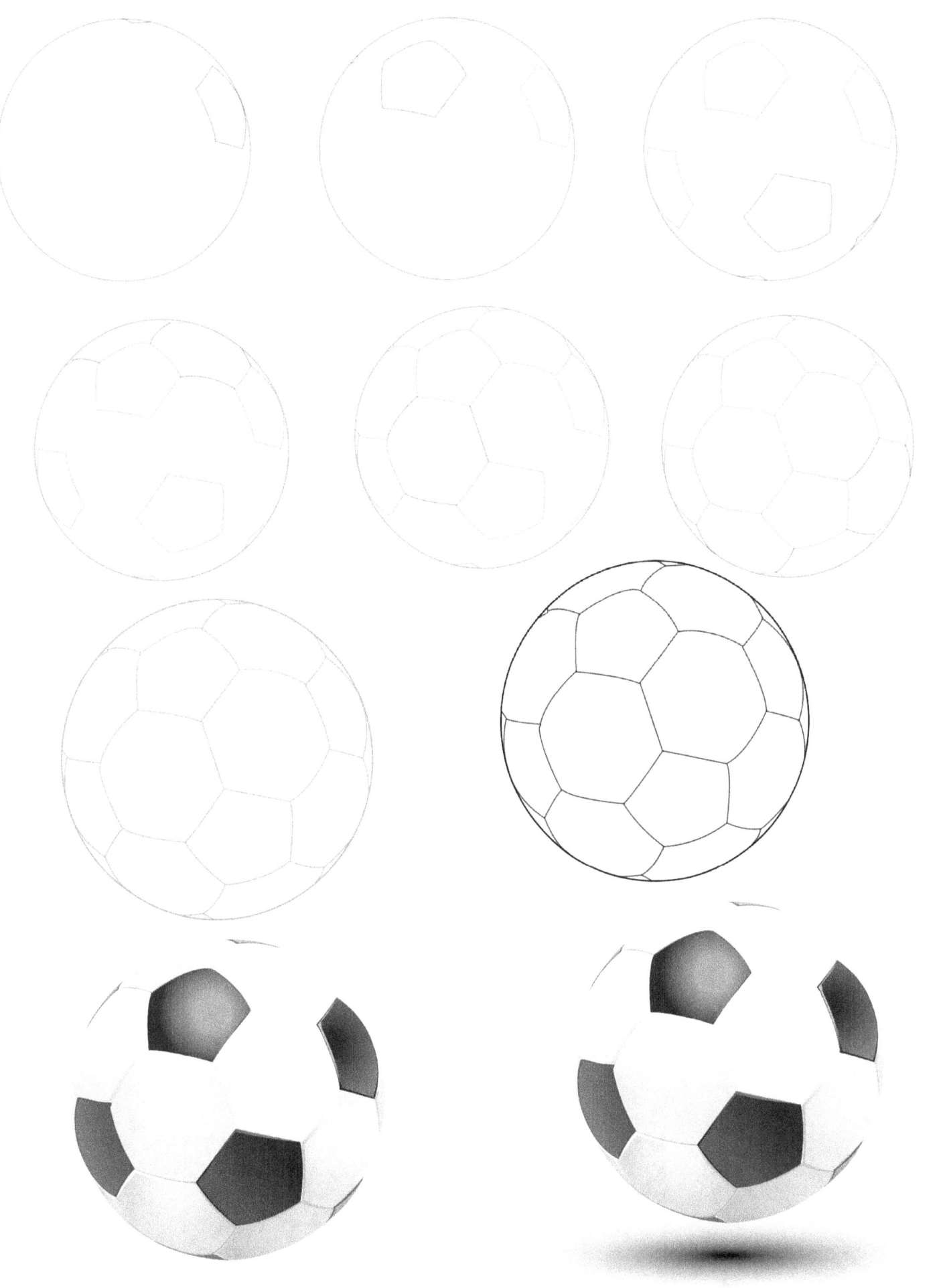

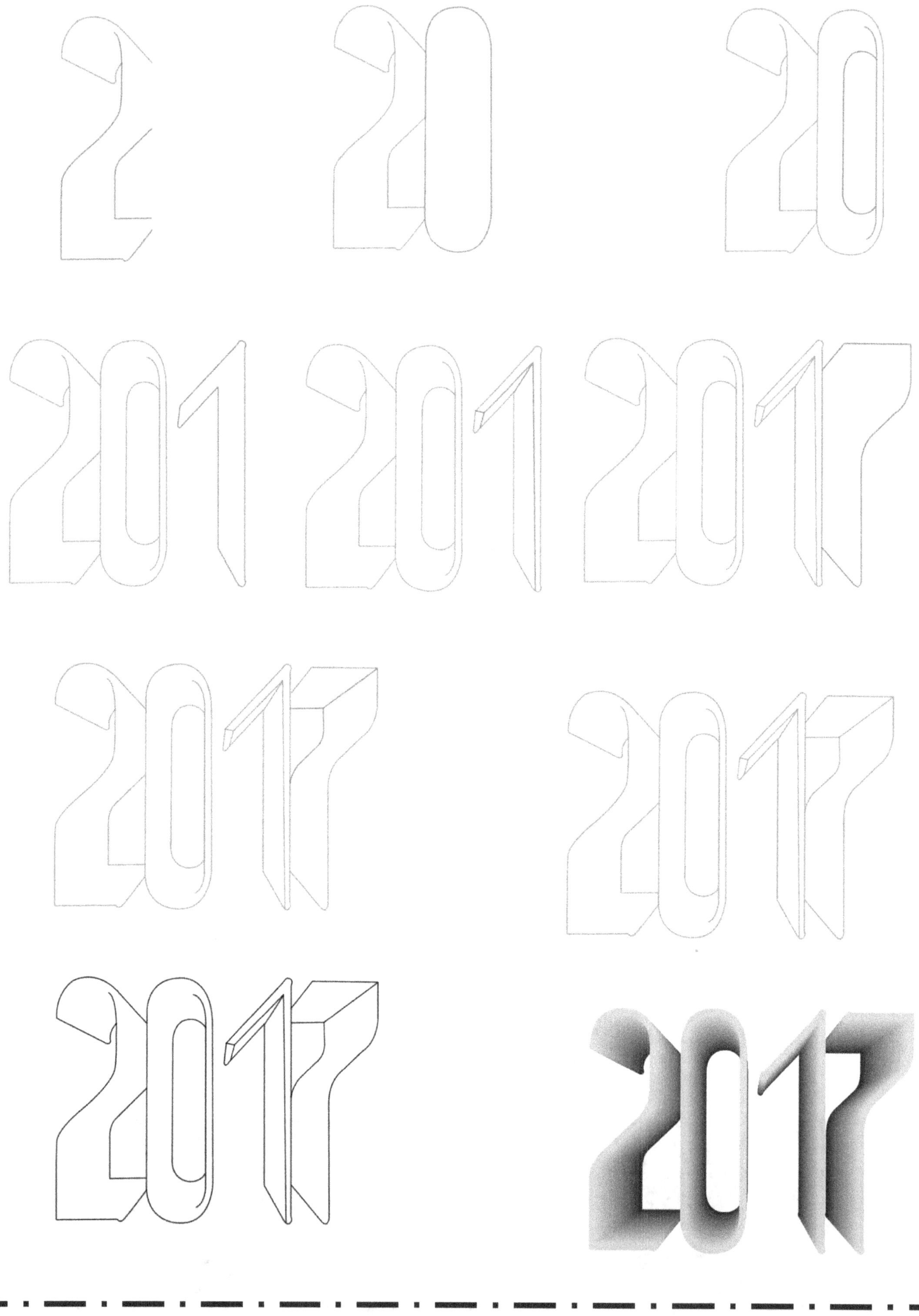

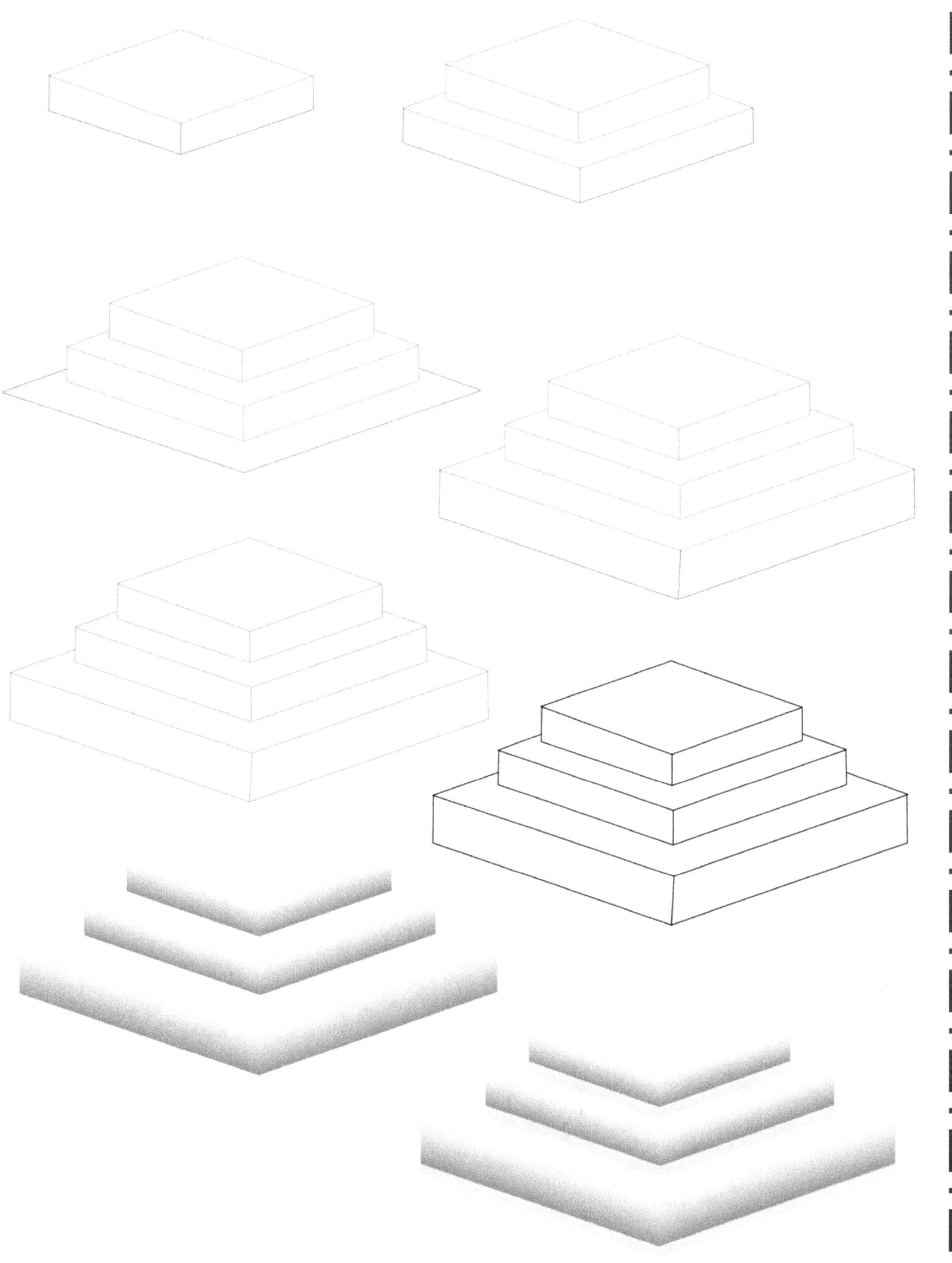

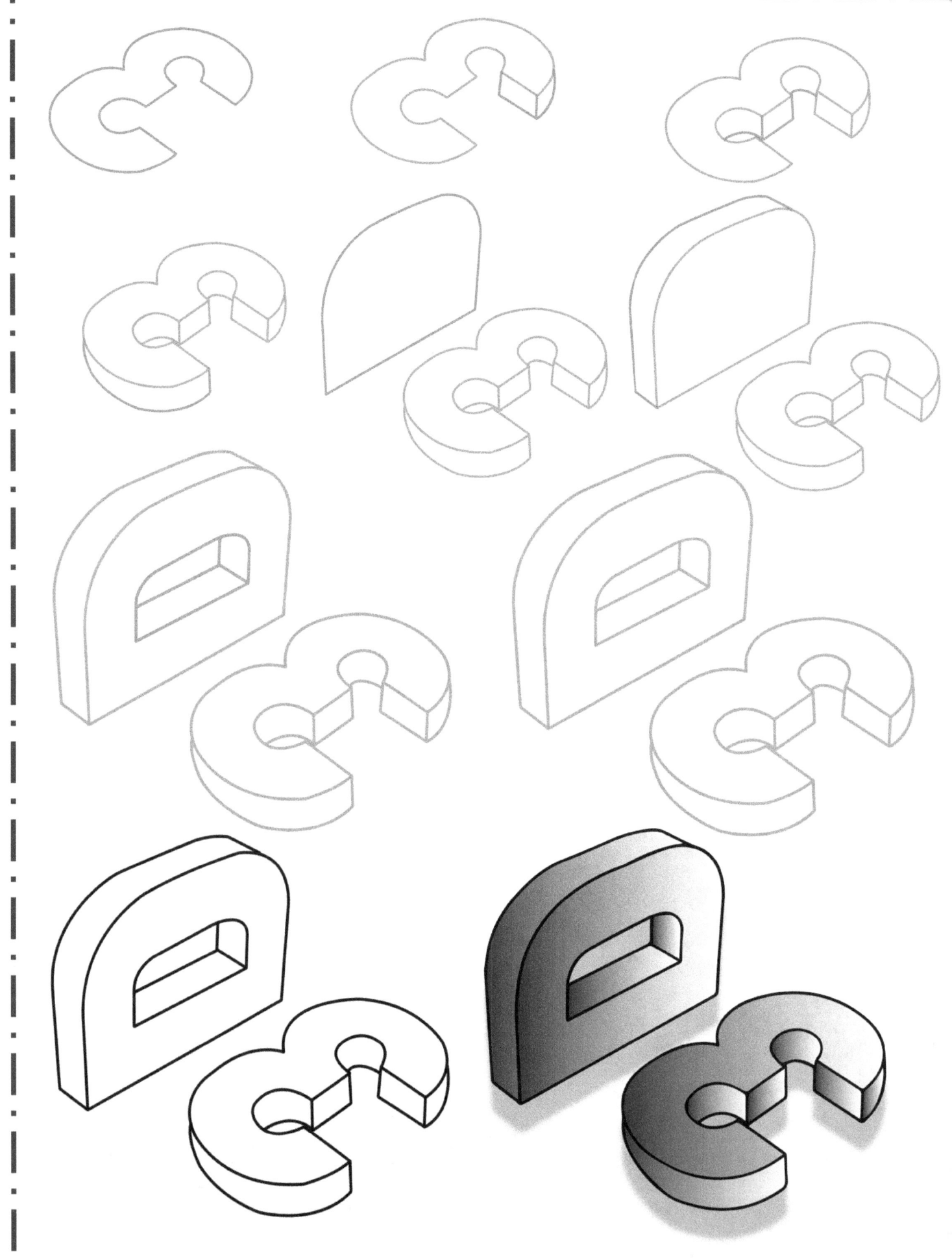

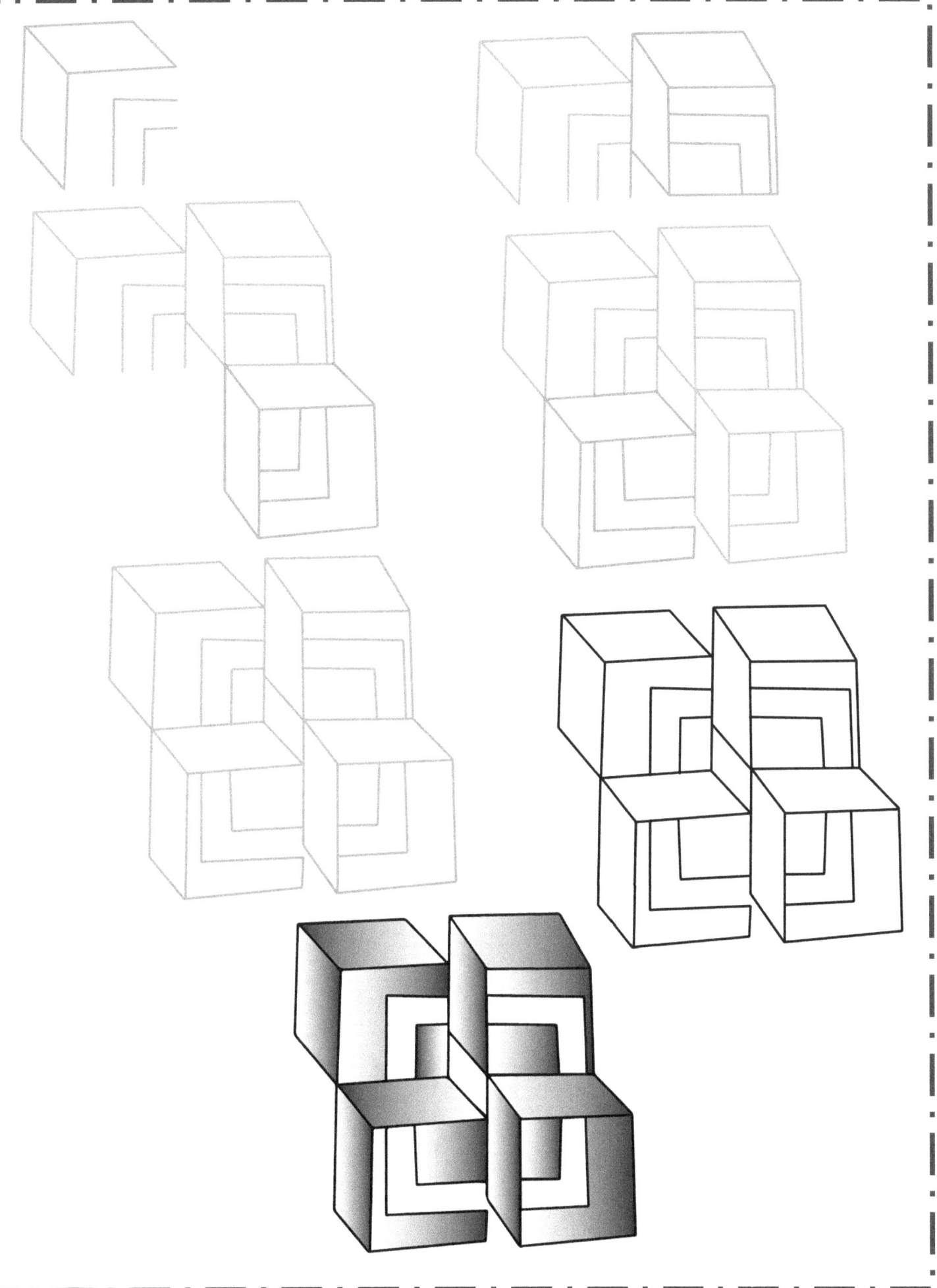

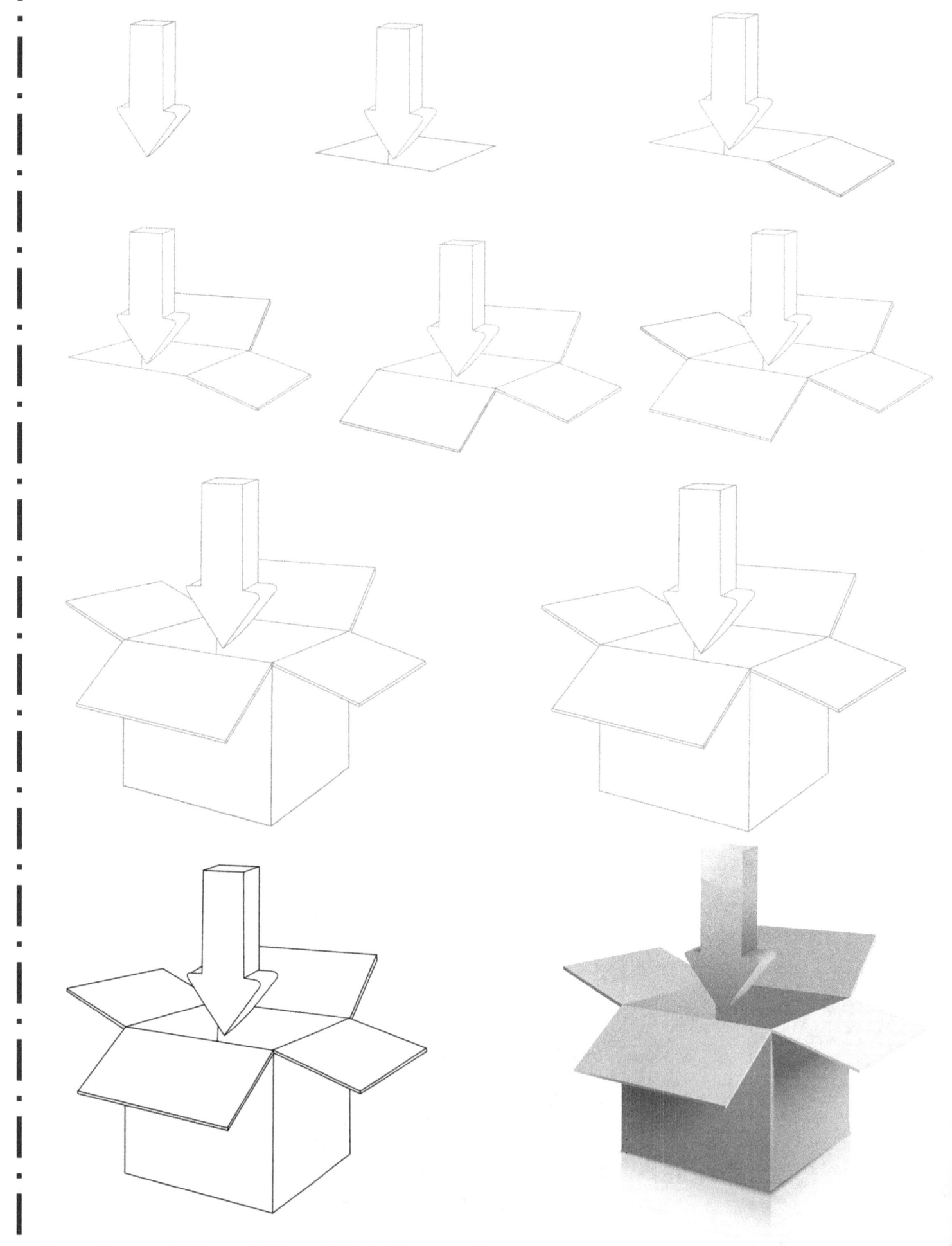

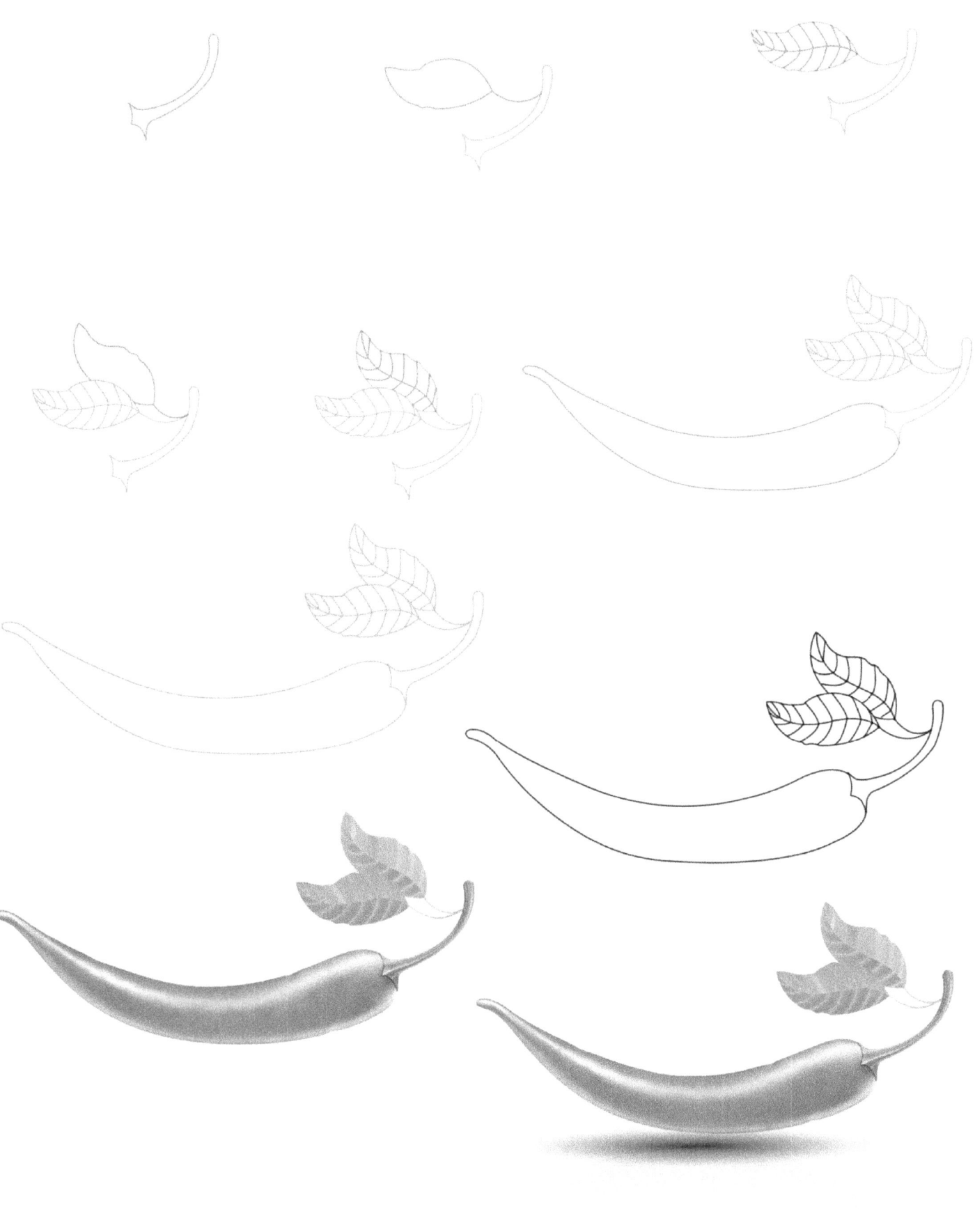

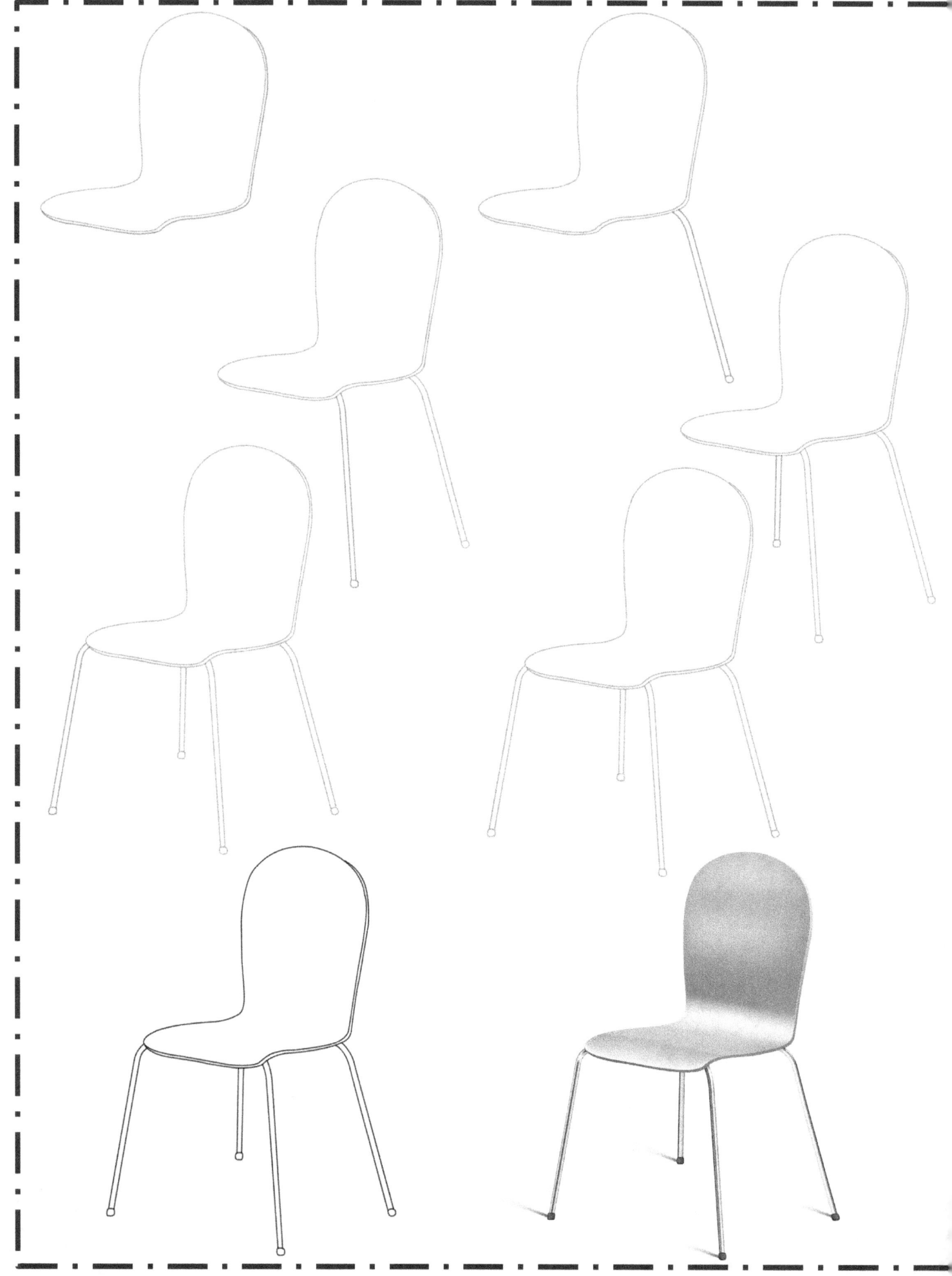

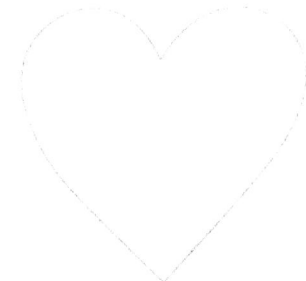

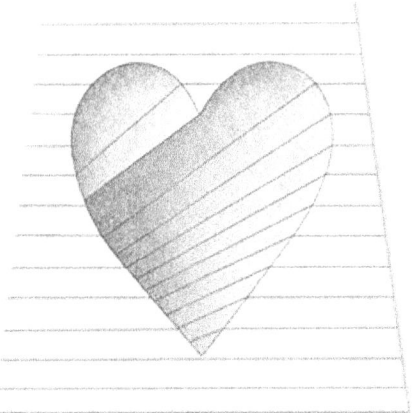

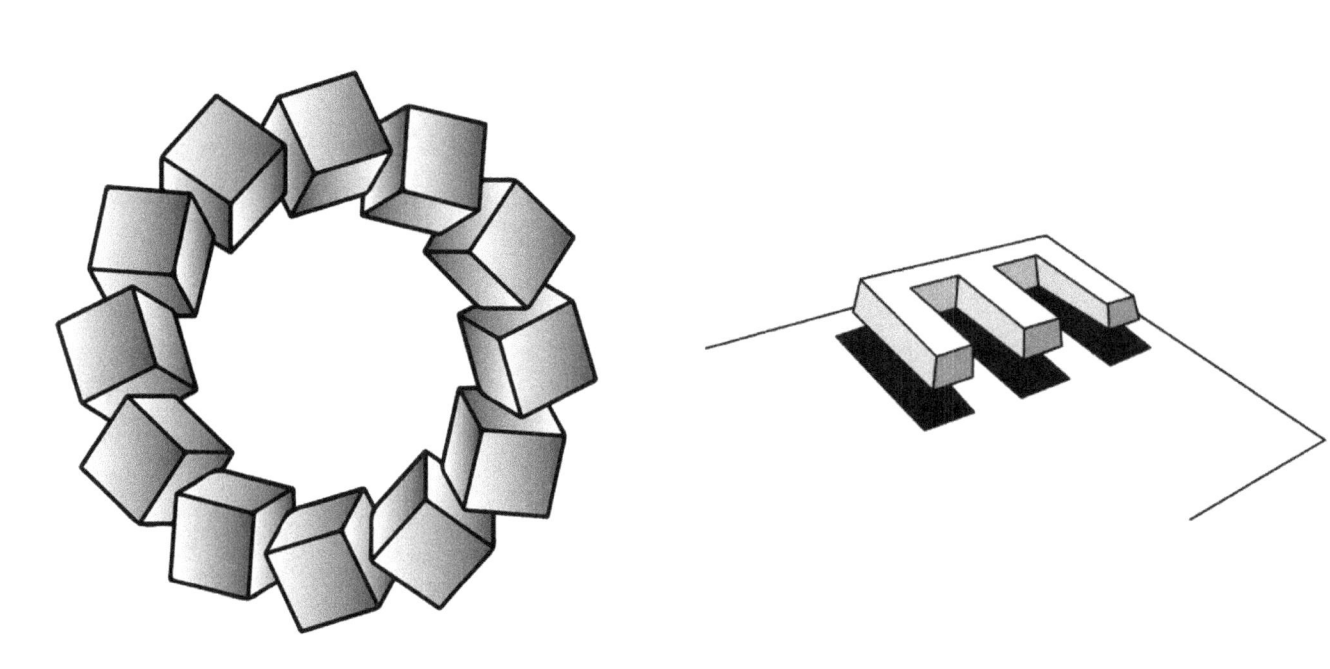

THANK YOU FOR CHOOSING THIS BOOK. WE HOPE YOU ENJOYED EVERY PAGE OF THIS BOOK AND LEARNED HOW TO DRAW STEP BY STEP AND CREATE YOUR OWN ART.

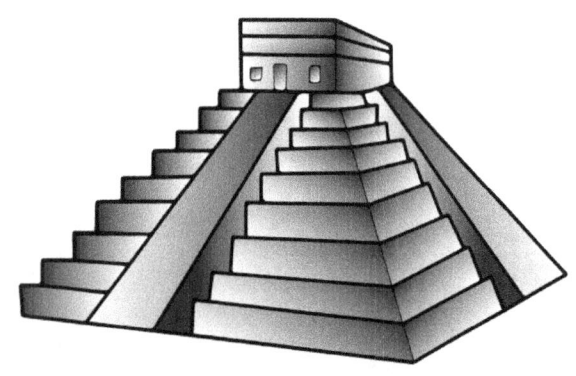

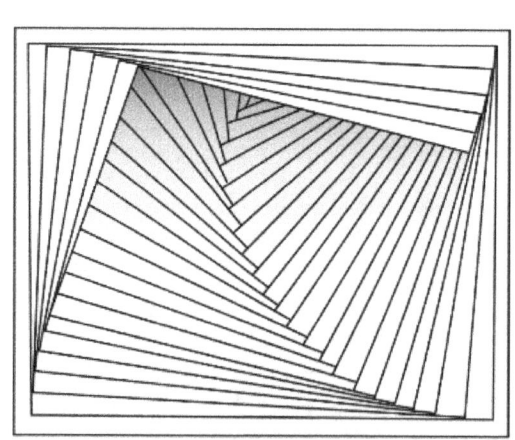